THE MEMORY BOOK

THE
MEMORY BOOK

*One Woman's Self-Discovery
in the Mist of the
Austro-Hungarian Monarchy*

A MEMOIR

LINDA FISCHER

MINTED PROSE

Minted Prose, LLC
New York
www.mintedprose.com

The Memory Book: One Woman's Self-Discovery in the Mist of the Austro-Hungarian Monarchy is a true story. I have changed the names of a few people to protect their privacy.

Minted Prose, LLC

New York

www.mintedprose.com

ISBN: 978-0-9744287-3-4

Library of Congress Control Number: 2014932937

Cover Design: Min Choi
Book Design by Susan Turner
Production Manager: Fausto Bozza

MINTED PROSE® and ® are registered trademarks of Minted Prose, LLC

Printed in the United States of America

2 4 6 8 10 9 7 5 3 1

FOR
PHIL AND DORINA

"Beata Ungheria!
se non si lascia Più malmenare."
—DANTE

*"Oh happy Hungary!
If she once let herself be wronged, let it be stopped."**

* Paget, *Hungary and Transylvania,* vol. 1, title page; Original Latin translation provided by Dr. Kathleen Fischer and Thomas Hart.

"I was forty before I learned anything."
—SÁNDOR MÁRAI, *The Rebels*

AUSTRO-HUNGARIAN MONARCHY

Austria-Hungary was a curious combination of vastly divergent cultures paired by necessity over centuries. Austria-Hungary never existed as a nation or as a people. But these two countries, intertwined by marriage in 1438, finally settled their differences 429 years later by forming the Austro-Hungarian Monarchy.

The Kingdom of Hungary's 125,400 square miles included Transylvania and Croatia-Slavonia. It was bigger than Great Britain and Ireland by 4,000 square miles. In 1900, about twenty million Hungarians, Romanians, Germans, Croats, Serbs, Slovaks, Jews, and Ruthenians (also known as Ukrainians) lived there. At the time, Hungarians were the majority.

The Austro-Hungarian Empire, in the heart of Europe, imposed its cultural, political, and military will on its neighbors as it had for centuries. The Habsburgs, as great as the kings and queens of England, had been sitting on the throne since 1278 after defeating the king of Bohemia at Marchfeld. Strategic and ambitious, the Habsburgs accumulated thrones through marriage and lands through conquest and cunning. Emperor Francis Joseph reigned from 1848 to 1916 and he tried to keep it all together in the face of modernity.

The Habsburg Empire came to a sad conclusion in the years 1918 to 1922, after the end of World War I and the death of Charles I of Austria, grandnephew to Francis Joseph and the last Habsburg emperor. By 1920, the empire had officially dissolved into the myriad of small countries on today's map of Europe.

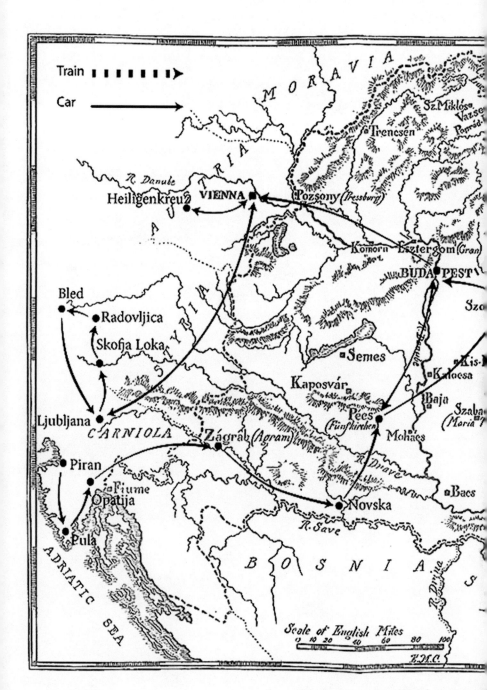

CONTENTS

Contents

PART II

PART III

PART IV

ADDENDUMS

PREFACE

To the Reader,

THIS BOOK RECOUNTS MY TRAVELS IN HUNGARY AND CENTRAL Europe, which began in 2005. I expected the trips with my husband, Phil, would be uncomplicated sojourns: new places, new friends, and more pictures. Yet they lingered and wove themselves into the whole of my life.

I call this story *The Memory Book: One Woman's Self-Discovery in the Mist of the Austro-Hungarian Monarchy* because in the process I became deeply immersed in Hungarian culture and history. This swept me into centuries past. There I saw myself among ruins, enormous castles, and dreams of things that never came.

In 2005, I learned that 1848 stood out as a seminal year. It cast the die for Hungary and Europe over the next 150 years, providing context for my own travels.

John Paget's *Hungary and Transylvania* (1839), published a decade before Hungary's War of Independence, became a favorite guide. It proved so helpful that I purchased a rare first edition.

Paget would be tickled if he knew that I found his travels thoroughly engaging over a century later. He was a noted intellectual and won an esteemed award at the Paris World Exhibition in 1878. Paget died in 1892 and is buried in Kolozsvár, now Cluj, Romania.

I haven't seen Paget's tombstone in Cluj but he deserves recognition through the ages for his passion in producing accurate and fair volumes about Hungary and Transylvania. This struck a nerve with me as I found myself walking down his path, thrashing with the same concerns Paget so eloquently expressed in his preface:

> Before proceeding with the Work, there are one or two matters which I may as well explain to the reader. Such a mark of my confidence will, I trust, incline him not only to treat me more leniently, but enable him to also to judge of me more fairly, and so accuse me only of those faults of which I am really guilty.

> I would not willingly deceive him in anything. . . .

> That I have fallen into many errors I feel certain—not that I have spared either time or trouble to avoid them; but seeing how many other travellers have committed, which I can detect, I cannot hope that I shall be able to escape clear from their scrutiny. . . .

Aspirations always extend beyond the horizon but there does come a time when a book should be set free for people to read and enjoy.

* * *

AT FIRST BROACH THIS HISTORY SEEMS ANCILLARY TO ANYTHING in our century, but it served as central to my understanding of how Europe got to where it is today.

Tales from other travelers long since gone embellished my views of the past, intertwining with my present. Most of these intrepid travelers were socially connected and financially able to choose a lengthy and arduous trip through dangerous territory—for pleasure. The locals thought these travelers were crazy.

The answer for my interest was similar to the reason others gave for going there. Their specific thoughts about the place drove their interest, as they did mine. More than a century ago, each of the travelers had an individual point of view and their stories were not always harmonious. I shuddered reading vehement denunciations of authors, people, and ethnic groups that seemed blatantly libelous to my twenty-first-century sensibilities. I appreciated their courage in going to Central Europe for the sake of adventure. While my travels were far more controlled—on buses, in cabs, or in cars with a guide—the excitement of the early travelers spoke to me in their writings. In time, their words reflected back to me like echoes in a canyon. I have included the truest sounds of the past that resonated with me.

. . .

MY STORY NATURALLY MENTIONS PEOPLE WHO LIVED A LONG time ago. I used the English version of their names. However, the more I worked on the story, the more I wanted to leave their graceful Hungarian names, which I did if they were recognizable. I also used American-style dates for simplicity, rather than the more formal Hungarian style that evokes early twentieth-century elegance. Americans would write May 25, 1919, October 8, 1906, and October 12, 1907, where Hungarians might use:

Szolnok, 1919. V. 25.
(Szolnok, May 25, 1919)

Novska, 1906 X/8
(Novska, October 8, 1906)

Nagy-Várad, 907. október hó 12-én
(Nagyvárad, on the 12th day of the month of October, 1907)

Poetry plays an important role in Hungarian culture and in the lives of the people in my story. I searched for the best English translations of Hungarian poems from the late nineteenth and early twentieth centuries and found them in the works of British linguist Edward Dundas Butler, a librarian at the British Museum; Sir John Bowring, a writer and former governor of Hong Kong; and William N. Loew, a prolific translator of Hungarian poetry. For a few dollars I bought a used copy of Loew's *Modern Magyar Lyrics* (1926).

I tenderly turned the yellowed and frayed pages and in the preface I read that Loew was a transplanted New Yorker. Son of a Hungarian rabbi in Szeged, Loew immigrated to the United States at the age of nineteen, just after our Civil War, ultimately becoming a New York lawyer. He completed *Modern Magyar Lyrics* but died before it was printed. I found my own joy in his translations. A reader can find snippets of Hungarian poetry in the addendum of this book.

JOHN PAGET

John Paget was trained in medicine but preferred writing and agriculture. In the midst of his European travels in the 1830s, Paget met a Hungarian baroness, married, settled in Transylvania, and started farming. But Romanian peasants during Hungary's War of Independence in the late 1840s set fire to his Transylvanian estate. In 1848, many peasants throughout Europe rose up because of miserable conditions. After that, Paget led a peripatetic life, moving across Europe but always bound for Transylvania, where he resumed farming.

PART I

CHAPTER 1

Destination: Central Europe

Hungary is less frequented by foreign visitors than other great countries of Europe; still, it has charms beyond most. In spite of modern development—in many directions—the romantic glamour of bygone times still clings about it, and the fascination of its peoples is peculiar to them.

THIS COULD HAVE BEEN A LINE FROM A TRAVEL AGENT, BUT they are actually the words of British painter and travel writer Adrian Stokes who, with his artist wife, Marianne, ventured to Hungary five times from the mid to the late 1900s and recorded their travels in *Hungary* (1909).

In 2005, Europe beckoned me. Many of my friends had gone there, either during college or just after. I finally had time now, in my forties, to explore the Continent. Austria, Hungary, the Czech Republic, and Poland were peculiar to me and off the beaten path.

· · ·

So that summer, my husband, Phil, and I flew to Vienna and spent a few days there. We didn't know German, the official language. However hard the hotel staff worked, we couldn't find good restaurants in a city full of them. We also missed the pickup for the tour to Mayerling, a former Habsburg hunting lodge, now a small Carmelite convent.

Despite the bumps, we were optimistic and persevered all the way to Budapest on a rather indelicate and loud hydrofoil ride complete with smoking, card playing, and drinking by jovial locals, tourists, and travelers of many nations and languages. At one point, when someone near me had won at cards and a big cheer went up, I remember thinking, these people know how to have a good time. Little did we know, we were joining in a long tradition of a cacophony of cultures traveling the river Danube with merriment.

"No stream, not even old and much admired Father Rhine, can compare with the picturesque beauty of the Danube," wrote travel writer Charles McArmor in his distinguished treatise *The New Handbook of Vienna: Including a Guidebook for the Danube, The Austrian Alps, and Their Watering Holes* (1879), my copy of which was as fragile as it was old. He added:

> Charming landscapes in countless variety, proud cities, old
> fashioned chatty townships, dreamy as well as bustling, opulent
> palaces, frowning old castles, romantic ruins, monasteries,
> cloisters, chapels, innumerable reminisces of past ages, with
> stupendous forests, mysterious valleys, huge rocks and frightful
> gullies, miles upon miles of undulating fields and sloping
> vineyards, crowd upon the banks of the great river.

The same fickle waters of the Danube, pounding at the sides of our tour boat, pressed us forward for five and a half hours, past medieval castles where nobility stood sovereign above the lower classes, past ancient cities anchored by the enduring strength of the river, and past rolling green hills that feed everyone.

Much as I was enjoying the ride, I was glad it wasn't the turn of the twentieth century, when it took twelve to fifteen hours to travel downstream by steamship from Vienna to Budapest, and twenty-two hours to return upstream, according to *Austria including Hungary, Transylvania, Dalmatia and Bosnia* (1900), a handy little red guidebook from Karl Baedeker.

The celebrated Danube has surged along this path for centuries, compelled by itinerants like us to go faster to the dock in Budapest. The river does not rest until it meets its fate in the Black Sea. We wouldn't rest until we got to our hotel in Budapest at the foot of the striking Chain Bridge, spanning the six-hundred-yard-wide river.

The Danube, slapping swirling buckets of water against the side of the boat, pushed us ever closer to Pest, lying on the flat plain on one side of the river. Across the Danube, on the hilly side, is Buda. It grew from Óbuda, which the Romans left behind. Buda, Pest, and Óbuda were united as Budapest, the capital of the country, in 1873.

In 1878, Crown Prince Rudolf of Austria traveled from Vienna on the same route we were taking to Budapest. He was embarking on an ornithological and hunting expedition down the Danube. Accompanying him were naturalists, sportsmen, and a retinue of aides.

Rudolf said of the Danube and the cities of Pest and Ofen, Buda's German name, in *Notes on Sport and Ornithology* (1889):

> The fair Danube, as the Hungarian in his national song so rightly calls it, flowed silent and majestic under the splendid suspension-bridge; and the flourishing, busy, commercial city of Pest formed a striking contrast to all the hoary and historic rocks, walls and buildings of the Ofen side, while the Pest quay, with its lively bustle and many boats, some crossing over and others lying quietly by the bank, gave the whole scene that bright cheerful look which makes it always a pleasure to revisit this beautiful town.

One hundred thirty-seven years later, we maneuvered our way off the boat, taking a wide-eyed look around. But neither the commotion we were making nor the activity from the cars and people could overshadow the towering buildings in Pest or the palace sitting regally on Buda's hilly perch. I had a feeling this was going to be a good stay since we couldn't possibly miss getting to that tourist destination.

It was August 20, 2005.

Antique planes were racing along the Danube, skipping over modern and medieval stone and steel bridges. People beamed and a rock opera was in full swing. A procession of brightly clad people from different regions of the country near the basilica was infectious to us strangers. We had landed in the midst of Hungary's celebration of its most revered king, St. Stephen. He was crowned in 1000 and spread Christianity through the country. King St. Stephen can be rightfully thought of as the George Washington of Hungary.

We hadn't overcome all of our problems though. As in Vienna, we were lost where the language was concerned. But instead of German being the obstacle, it was Hungarian, a tongue completely unintelligible to us.

But somehow language didn't matter. We had lucked out, arriving in Budapest on such a day. As the sun set over the Danube, the night sky opened with fireworks. Phil and I stood, holding hands, alongside thousands of Hungarians. With glittering lights bubbling around us like fine champagne, we were sweetly intoxicated in the moment. The dimples in Phil's cheeks lit up. I squeezed his hand. We embraced like those near us. Other travelers long before us had been overtaken by similar spontaneous reveries exploding from the taproots of Hungarian history.

THE BOAT BRIDGE

B efore the Chain Bridge was constructed in the 1840s, Buda and Pest were connected by interlocking boats. Michael J. Quin, the author of *A Steam Voyage Down the Danube with Sketches of Hungary, Wallachia, Servia, Turkey etc.* (1879), en route to Constantinople—now Istanbul— from "Pesth," described the link created between the two sides of the Danube as "a bridge of forty seven large boats, united by chains and floored with planks."

The boat bridge worked most of the year. But when ice began to form in the Danube, the boat bridge was removed because it was too treacherous to use. The next best thing was employed—a ferryboat. But even the ferryboats had to stop when the ice froze solid, leaving people to hoof it across the river—carefully.

CHAPTER 2

Discovery in Buda

ON OUR SECOND DAY IN BUDAPEST, WE SIGNED UP FOR A HALF-day excursion around the city. We had better luck than in Vienna, largely due to Phil's traveler's sign language and a friendly cab driver who got us to the pickup spot.

The tour: Five minutes at the Citadel. A quick drive through Andrássy Street with a brisk walk through the castle district in Buda. Tourists in one group talked loudly in assorted languages the minute the guide switched to English.

"Thank you for coming," the harried guide shouted over the din.

Applause filled the air. I got up quickly and hustled off the minivan.

Buda. The castle district.

I was determined to go back but Phil said we should return to the hotel and drop off a few things. Once there, he suggested lunch.

"We can eat in the Buda castle district," I said, stomach growling. "They've got restaurants."

"All right. Give me a minute."

I unpacked my bag. Postcards, a sweater, video camera . . .

He was ready.

I turned around and reached for his hand.

The doorman hailed a cab. The driver effortlessly maneuvered his denim blue jalopy of a cab along the busy streets, making his way across the bridge. Within minutes we stood at the spot where the tour had ended an hour earlier. Gray clouds hung low in the sky. A drop or two from an impending storm fell on my arm. We walked up one street, down another, looking at the buildings and memorials, stores, and doors. Phil snapped pictures and I kept looking. My eyes grazed art galleries, souvenir stores, and outdoor stands with local crafts, and then an antique store. I walked briskly toward it.

Once inside I wandered slowly around, perusing the contents of this repository of old treasures from the last century. Family items mainly—spoons, linens, tumblers, and small china, not Fifth Avenue antiques—crowded the shelves. I milled about until, from the corner of my eye, I noticed a pile of books on a small wooden table. I picked up the first book, the second, and the third, turning the pages, and then I was drawn to a book with a dark brown leather cushion cover. The cover's fern motif looked like a simple folk pattern I'd seen on kitchen linens. I counted numerous ferns. They were coming up from the bottom of the cover and growing together in an embrace. The silver lock on the book was broken, but the gilded edging remained.

I opened it. The first line on the first page was one word: AMÁLKÁMNAK followed by an exclamation point. The other pages had different handwriting and watercolors, one of bluebirds and forget-me-nots. Turning the pages, I stopped at a picture of a man in a blue wagon. Hunched over, he held the reins of a horse coming out of a forest. Vines, red buds, and slender green leaves surrounded the watercolor. Other pages had messages written on them, along with maroon chrysanthemums on green vines and a man rowing a boat in a lake surrounded by lily pads.

Yellow spots dotted some of the paintings. In a few places,

some of the watercolors and ink had bled through to the other pages. Someone must have treasured it, otherwise how else would it have survived?

As I looked up, the salesperson was coming to me. "How much is it?"

"Twenty thousand forint."

"How much is that in US dollars?"

"About one hundred thirty dollars."

"I'll take it," I said. The salesperson beamed.

Phil pulled out his credit card before I could get to mine. The store owner wrapped the book in plain tan paper. She handed it back to me and I gently placed the book in my bag.

· · ·

WE WALKED ON, EVENTUALLY STOPPING AT A WINE SHOP. As Phil searched the offerings for the equivalent of a good California chardonnay, I looked at the woman behind the counter. Once I realized that she spoke a little English, I said, "Would you mind if I showed you something? Maybe you can tell me what it says."

She nodded yes. I unwrapped the book and set it on the counter. She turned the first few pages, stopping here and there. After a few minutes she raised her head and said, "Aww, so nice—sweet. How can I say—." She seemed stuck.

In the meantime, Phil had found a good wine. While he paid for it, I thanked the woman and quickly rewrapped the book in the paper.

Leaving the store, I thought she had liked the watercolors— the horse pulling a carriage along a small road spoke of an age when country roads weren't likely to be paved, when horses were the basic mode of transportation, and crudely constructed wooden hand plows worked the soil in the spring—but clearly she had been reacting to the text.

How did this book end up in that antique store surrounded by other, lesser treasures of Hungary's past? Answering this question would occupy the next nine years and bring Phil and me back to Hungary, each time peeling off a layer of history and gaining a better understanding of the text. Finding out what it said was only the first step.

For now, Phil and I walked around the castle district, nearing a tourist attraction we had passed by earlier in the day. Hoards of visitors were standing in front of a labyrinth, part of the caves located several stories beneath Buda Castle. We descended a concrete-lined stairway and paid the entrance fee. In return, a man gave us a map and an oil lantern to find our way through the blackness. Roaming cautiously, we navigated our way around using the light and the map as a guide. Ultimately we found the exit, returned the lantern, and stepped from the cool darkness into the light of the day. We walked down a steep path leading to a folk art festival. Wood carved furniture, woven baskets, and handmade ceramics sat on the lawn. The smell of freshly baked cinnamon bread added to the moment. I teased Phil, saying that I was tempted to buy a wooden throne but it would be his job to get it into our already bulging luggage. He just shook his head and laughed.

. . .

AFTER BUDAPEST, WE LURCHED TO THE AIRPORT. I'D OVER-packed, stretching the bag and the zipper to its limit. When I got to Prague and opened the luggage at the hotel, I broke the zipper for good. A department store around the corner from the hotel offered us options. I convinced Phil, who was starting to feel a little under the weather, that we needed the largest suitcase available. Our new Samsonite was big and lumbering, despite its deceptively banal, light gray color and too-small handle. I was certain that if it fell on my foot, I would end up with a few broken toes. I affectionately began calling it the Killer Kase.

By the middle of our time in Prague, Phil's small sniffles had evolved into a full-blown cold. We had everything in the bag but a good cold medicine.

Being a determined tourist, however, he plowed onward, trekking with me through the old Jewish Quarter, the medieval castle Hradčany, and the nearby gardens displaying a vibrant color palette with flowers pleased to be free. I remember a luminous pink rose preening for me, completely oblivious to the tourists and cameras around it. Phil recorded the moment with his camera and I laminated it later on.

We walked on, winding in and around the castle before heading back over the bridge to town. Phil admired a hand-carved puppet in a small store. He thought it reasonably priced and that it would look good hanging in the apartment somewhere. And so we acquired Mr. Puppet and the three of us returned to the Old Town Square. There, Phil, myself, and Mr. Puppet stood as a tripod of tourists in an ocean of people swarming for a glimpse of the statues of the apostles as they marched on the hour from the city's astronomical clock featured in every guidebook.

It was time to move on from Prague to Krakow. When we finished repacking, the Killer Kase was so heavy that we feared it would exceed the airline's weight limits. On the bus to the plane, I lightly elbowed Phil and pointed out the window. "There's the Killer Kase," I said. His eyes widened in horror as he watched the man fall backward under it. It took two handlers to hoist it into the plane. We couldn't help but laugh.

With tissues in his pockets, Phil forged on with me through Poland. World War II casts a shadow over places like the little museum at a pharmacy under the eagles and the fragments of the city's ghetto wall on the outskirts of Krakow. It took some walking around but we did find Oskar Schindler's old Emalia Factory, which made enameled goods and munitions.

Slipping the guard a few dollars got us inside the dreary 1940s factory complex now holding a variety of artworks in one of the buildings. We wound up the narrow staircase only to be confronted with a 1940-ish black-and-white film on the war—

just pictures and the sound of an old manual typewriter banging the story out on the screen. We sat there alone in the presence of the Holocaust.

Soon we were on our flight to the United States with Mr. Puppet securely wrapped in our clothes in the Killer Kase. I couldn't put the book from Budapest in the luggage. I hand carried that on the plane. Resting in my seat, I found myself reaching for it.

BUDA AND ITS INHABITANTS

Historical accounts differ on the origin of the name Buda. Is it Slavic or did it come from Attila's brother, who lived in Buda's heights? No one knows for sure, but one thing is relatively certain, the Huns arrived first to the Danubian plains, then the Avars and finally the Magyars, or Hungarians, who settled the land around 896.

HOLOCAUST

Memories of the Holocaust, living ghosts of the past, seem ever present in Europe. During our trip, we took a bus tour to Auschwitz. After walking around, the guide asked everyone to join him in walking the length of the rails to the crematorium. I remember the day. No one said a word. The sun was shining too brightly. Each blade of grass swayed lightly underneath a vast blanket of warmth, a blinding, flickering memory. In the distance, to my left, a man, his head dropped, chin almost touching his neck, sat in a wheelchair on the remains of a building. The walk, the silence, the flickering green blades of grass, the old man's chin heavy, anchoring him to the past, the bright sun; anytime I thought of that visit afterward I could barely speak.

CHAPTER 3

Back Home

BACK IN NEW YORK, LUGGAGE OPEN ON THE BED, CLOTHES TO be washed, mail to be sorted, I left everything and walked into the dining room. My carry-on bag sat on the table. I removed the book, secure in its tan paper, and went to the kitchen for a plastic zip bag to put it in. I got a step stool and put the book in the top center drawer of a tall, black chest filled with photographs and mementos.

. . .

ONE NIGHT, AFTER FINISHING FOR THE DAY, I TOOK THE BOOK out. Should it have stayed in Hungary? Did it belong to me?

I heard Phil come in. He sat down next to me on the couch.

"How was your day?" I asked him.

"Busy."

I took that to mean all was okay and it was fine to move on to a new topic.

"I've been thinking about the book and I want to know what it says," I said, not even thinking about how impractical this must have sounded, given my lack of knowledge of the

Hungarian language.

"Look at this," I said. "When I bought the book, I didn't notice it."

A dime-sized brown leaf with frayed edges lay between the pages.

"How hard can it be?" I said, staring at the writing.

"It looks harder than hieroglyphics, but the pictures are pretty," he replied.

"That may be true, but it can't be that hard to read," I said.

"Give it a shot, but don't worry too much about it. Maybe Janet across the hall can translate it," he said. "She has a doctorate in Slavic languages. She might know Hungarian, too, or be able to recommend someone who does."

"Okay, but first I'm going to get some books on the Hungarian language and its history," I said, thinking back to the flowing black habits of nuns scratching timelines with dusty chalk on the blackboards in my youth. Back then I used to wonder if there wasn't anything else to world history other than the long-gone Roman Empire and the role of Christianity.

"Do you know Hungarian history?" I asked Phil.

"Some. I'd certainly like to know more."

After a while, I had accumulated over a dozen new and used books, some of which smelled of mold. Phil suggested that I put them in the freezer. I did and the smell went away.

"I guess I'll have to make some room," Phil said, looking at the bookcases.

CHAPTER 4

Living with a Mystery

MY GROWING LIBRARY OF HUNGARIAN TOMES LAID OUT THE culture: vivid, glorious, and tragic in relentless detail. I was aware of some of the country's history. It suffered two world wars and harsh penalty for involvement in them—heavily redrawn borders. I did not know the open wound the wars had left on the nation in the twentieth century. Those wounds—losing almost two-thirds of its population and around three-quarters of its territory—were inflicted in the last century of Hungary's eleven hundred years of existence.

While I was reading about Hungary, I connected with Janet. She couldn't help though because as it turns out, Hungarian is not a Slavic language.

"A dead end," I said to Phil. "She doesn't speak Hungarian."

"Why don't you try the Hungarian Institute of New York City?" he suggested over coffee.

"Wow, I didn't know there was one."

"I don't know either, but there must be one. New York has everything," he said, with a grin.

Instead of Phil's suggestion, I called a translation service and sent some pages by messenger to them. After they said that I would have no interaction with the translator, I changed my mind and cancelled the service.

When Phil came home I said, "So what do we do now?"

He looked back at me.

"You liked Hungarian food, didn't you?" he asked, with a glint in his eyes.

"Yes."

"We should go to a Hungarian restaurant and see if anyone can help us."

"We can't order goulash and then ask the waiter to sit down and translate a page," I said, shaking my head.

"Let's just try to pick off a small piece for now," he said.

"Okay," I said, not fully convinced but willing to take a leap of faith, just for his dimples.

I looked at the bookcases in our apartment. Phil owned hundreds of books before I added to the collection when we got married. I figured we must have some New York City guidebooks. After looking around, I found five.

Turning to the back of three of them, I thought, you've got to be kidding me. None had the letter H in their indexes. The fourth book had a listing for a Hungarian Pastry Shop near the Cathedral of Saint John the Divine.

Later I said to Phil, "Let's go to the Hungarian Pastry Shop on Saturday."

"Sure, it will be fun," he replied.

*   *   *

WHILE I HAD COMMITTED TO THE PASTRY SHOP IDEA, I DECIDED to get some backup in case it didn't work out. I e-mailed a girlfriend to see if her daughter, who was studying at Columbia, knew anyone at the university who spoke Hungarian.

I got an immediate reply.

"Sorry, my daughter doesn't know anyone who speaks

Hungarian. I'd give Craigslist a shot, and if that doesn't work, call the language departments at Columbia and New York University."

Upon hearing these suggestions, Phil said, "All good ideas, but first let's try the pastry shop."

. . .

ON SATURDAY MORNING, THE ALARM CLOCK SOUNDED LIKE THE bell of an old fire truck. Soon we bolted out the door and into a cab on our way to the shop.

Halfway there, I asked, "Won't they think we're crazy?"

"I'm sure they get Hungarian questions regularly—something or other. It's New York."

"That's right."

He closed his eyes, his right hand on his forehead.

I continued on.

"Budapest. What a mysterious city. The shadows ran deep. Krakow struck me as raw with its distressed buildings in the ghetto. But Budapest was intricate, secrets, unspoken messages oozed from the old walls."

"Budapest is an old city. Lots hidden, lots of sins," he said.

"I bought a book in Budapest, *Kaddish for a Child Not Born*," I said. "On the back they referenced Northwestern University Press. We could have called them about getting a translation."

"Let's see what we can find here first. There's everything in New York," he said.

We got out of the cab, facing a red-and-white awning announcing THE HUNGARIAN PASTRY SHOP. Students and their paraphernalia overflowed the tables and the chairs. We ordered at the counter and grabbed a free table at the back. When the waitress arrived with the coffee, tea and pastries, I figured it was high time to ask her about what we really came for.

"Are you from Hungary?" I asked.

"No, no I'm not," she replied.

"We went there this past summer. It's an interesting place

and we got the sense that things are growing, with new restaurants and shops," I said.

"Yes, I hear that from some of the Hungarian girls here," she answered.

"While I was there I acquired a Hungarian book in an antique store. I was hoping maybe someone who speaks the language might just give me an idea of what's on a page or two. Are the owners Hungarian?"

"No. They're Greek."

Phil leaned back.

"The girls, are any here today that speak Hungarian?" I asked.

"No, I don't think so. But the baker speaks Hungarian. I'll see if he can come over."

She left. I sat searching for words.

Phil put his coffee cup down and said, "This is New York. You just can't make this stuff up."

The baker arrived in a minute, pressing his hands hard against his apron to wipe off the last of the dough stuck to his fingers.

"Hi, hi," he said, sticking out his hand to shake mine.

"I know this may sound strange, but I was hoping you could help me understand what's on one of these pages," I said, pulling a copy of the first page from our bag.

He looked it over. Then, someone called for him, stopping him in midstream.

Startled, he turned toward the kitchen. "I'm so busy right now. Can you come back on Monday, Tuesday, or Friday?"

"Sure," I said. "How about Tuesday at ten a.m.?"

He nodded.

"Great," I replied.

A baker to translate?

"We're on the right track," Phil said, with a wink.

"I hope so," I said, slowly sipping my tea.

· · ·

On Tuesday, I rode the subway back to the pastry shop. This time, the place was almost empty. I ordered and within minutes a waitress was at my table with the food.

"Hi, I hope you don't mind a quick thing. I was in the other day and the baker said he'd tell me what's on this page," I said. "It's in Hungarian."

She didn't say anything but tilted her head and looked at me quizzically.

"The baker suggested that I come by this morning," I said cautiously, so that I didn't blow my chance at getting a translation. "Would you mind asking him if he has a moment to come out?"

She paused and finally said, "Ok, let me go in the back and see."

Five minutes passed. Suddenly a different waitress, blond and svelte, came to my table.

"I hear you can use my services," she said. "I know you were looking for someone who can speak Hungarian. The baker, he can't come out. But let's see if I can help you."

The waitress, Brigitta, sat down next to me and I handed her my papers. She examined them closely.

"It's hard to translate. It's like, how would you say, Shakespeare? It's old Hungarian. Some of it is poetry."

A crowd was gathering at the counter, the line extending out the door. Brigitta stood up and said, "We're getting busy, let me come back to you."

On a postcard I wrote my name, e-mail address, and phone number, handing it to her on the way out.

"I'm off on Friday," she said. "Why don't we meet at the Time Warner building at Columbus Circle? There is a nice Whole Foods inside. We can get lunch and sit down."

· · ·

On Friday, I dashed to the Time Warner Center where a happy Brigitta was waiting for me.

We shook hands and sat down.

"So tell me, how did you end up working at the pastry shop?" I asked.

"Well, I came to the United States and to him. I met my husband on the Internet. He called me. He kept calling me. Six months after that, he came to Hungary to visit. Then he came back a few more times. He met my family on the second visit—we went to Nyíregyháza, that's where I'm from—and he came again, in July 2003. Then, I came to the United States and we got married in September 2004. He is tall, so smart, so cute. We're very happy."

"Did your parents like him?" I asked.

"My mother passed away when I was young so I'm close to my aunt. She liked him."

"Is he Hungarian?"

"Yes, he is," she said.

"That's a plus."

"I know," said my newfound friend. "So tell me what you need translated."

"I made copies of the pages of the book because the original is fragile," I said, pulling out a small stack of papers.

"It's hard to read. Do you have the original with you?" she asked.

"Yes."

I hesitated, then took the small book wrapped in tan paper out of the plastic bag.

Opening the book to the first page, she leaned in close to read it.

"Yes, now I can see it much clearer."

"On the first page, there is a poem written by her mother, from Novska, in 1906. We know her name is Amálka. 'Amálkámnak!'—For my little Amálka," she said.

Brigitta took a piece of paper and began to write. "Take my name as an example. 'For my Brigitta' would be Brigittámnak. It's different because of spelling and pronunciation but the meaning is the same: Amálkámnak—for my dearest or little Amálka." She explained that *ka* is the diminutive for Amália and the *mnak* meant for my.

Turning each page, Brigitta then gave me a rough description of what was in the book but not an exact translation. She said it was written in a style that's not often spoken in Hungary today and it also had poetic writings, making a literal translation especially difficult in all but a few places.

Brigitta said that she thought that Amálka was the owner of the book and that she was an artist, but had never heard of her. She also said that people who signed the book used their husbands' last names and abbreviations. I looked at Brigitta awkwardly as she picked up a pen.

"In Hungary, we have three name styles. The first one is when we use our husband's name, exactly as it is, and then add an 'n' and an 'é,' " she said.

"Kiss Lajos. That's a man's name. His wife can use this: Kiss Lajosné. Or there's another way: She could use her husband's family name and then her first name, Kiss Amália. There's a third possibility—if she used her husband's family name with the 'né' like Kissné and her full name Nagy Amália. So that would be Kissné Nagy Amália. So who knows what she used."

"Okay," I said, exhaling.

Brigitta, undeterred, continued. "Her grandmother lived in Nagyvárad—that we can tell from the book. In that time, it belonged to Hungary. But now it belongs to Romania."

"Amálka must have lived around Szolnok," she said, pointing to a page in the book and then another and another, all mentioning Szolnok, a city southeast of Budapest.

"Novszka: Her mother lived there," Brigitta wrote, using the Hungarian spelling for the city. Then she added,

"Now it is part of Croatia."

Croatia was south of Vienna, just above Bosnia and Herze-govina. I had never been to either and I suddenly developed a passion to go.

"Amálka's mother signed a page in the book and added Novska as the location and the date November 1, 1906," Brigitta wrote. "We know for sure that it was her mother, that she lived in Novska because she signed that and we know the year, because she wrote that. I remember that someone else made an entry from Novska too. We have to check. It was a different date but same place."

Brigitta said she would call her best friend's husband, who grew up in Szolnok and subsequently moved to Las Vegas, to see if he knew of anyone who could help. Asking a Hungarian now from Las Vegas seemed as long a shot as asking the baker. But the baker had led to this sweet young woman in front of me. So I said, "Sure, why not?"

She took down the names from the book and promised to do an Internet search. We hugged good-bye.

· · ·

BRIGITTA E-MAILED HER SEARCH RESULTS BUT THEY DIDN'T help identify Amálka. We couldn't identify the person known as the "student" or the "fiddler of the house," though the latter shared the same name as a twentieth-century Olympic medalist. The identity of others in the book remained just as elusive.

She had her best friend's husband to call, the one who was born in Szolnok, but by this point, my optimism was dimming. I suggested a better alternative. Why not call the store where I bought the book?

I told Brigitta that I purchased the book on August 21, 2005, the day Phil and I toured the castle district. I sent Brigitta an e-mail and attached images of the front and back of the store's flyer.

Dead end again. The employee didn't remember the sale but suggested that Brigitta contact the owner. She did. The owner remembered the little heirloom, which she got on the "free market" in Budapest.

I e-mailed Brigitta: "Let's get together and look at the book again. Maybe we can identify the people who got married and see if we can find them."

Brigitta sent me some more details—some helpful, others simply intriguing, but none conclusive.

We connected again in person. The conversation quickly turned from the details of the book to how much Europe had changed since the turn of the twentieth century, especially Hungary.

I talked to Phil about my conversation with Brigitta. He suggested that we put the New York Public Library on Fifth Avenue on our schedule. If any place had detailed maps of Central Europe from 1906 to 1919, it had to be there, he said.

In the meantime, Brigitta continued to look online and found some names. She thought that maybe they were related to someone who had signed the book.

We scheduled another meeting. We planned to examine each page of the book, hoping to glean something substantive. Finally getting together, Brigitta reviewed the pages.

She showed me two entries from August 1909: "They're poems. You know, what you might see on a postcard—really nice wishes."

Pointing to other entries, Brigitta said that the people were either quoting a line from a poem or had penned something special to Amálka.

On May 11, 1907, about twenty-two people—husbands, wives, and daughters—attended a wedding.

"How many more people were there? Exactly who? We don't know," Brigitta said.

Looking at another page, Brigitta thought it was signed by a classmate and that Amálka was about age ten or eleven. But it seemed unlikely to me that a middle grader, either Amálka or her classmate, could paint pictures like the ones in the book.

We proceeded to turn the pages. My favorite entry was a throwback to simpler times: an apple-picking outing on October 8, 1907, when about two dozen people signed the page, including her grandmother. A note says that they had been in Nagyvárad.

"Nagyvárad, or Oradea, as it is called now, is one of the largest cities in Transylvania and right across the eastern border of Hungary," Brigitta said.

"The home of Dracula?" I asked.

She just looked at me.

Brigitta went on struggling with the translation. She said other poems alluded to tears, enticements, emotions, dreams, and even trains.

Finally she said, "Everything what you do your heart will be the leader. The life will only be . . ."

She raised her hands, looked up, and stopped. Locking her eyes on mine, she said, a little too loudly, "We need someone to translate this!"

DRACULA

When Brigitta first mentioned Transylvania, a devilish Gary Oldman as Dracula popped into my thoughts. I didn't think that's what Brigitta had in mind, so I looked into Dracula and how he came to be tied to Transylvania, since now, of all things, I had questions about that. I started my research with the movies. How many Dracula films have been made? About two hundred, dating back to the days of silent films. Evil is a big box-office draw.

Irish writer Bram Stoker obviously spawned an ever-expanding industry based on a historical figure in Romania, Vlad Țepeș (1431–1476), known as the model for his 1897 Gothic novel *Dracula*. Stoker's book drew from centuries of fascination of occult legends of Romania and Transylvania.

Just for the record, there are no vampires in Romania or anywhere else for that matter. But don't tell that to the believers—and there have been many through the ages. Vampires sprung from folklore, that powerful fountain of imagination. A vampire craves blood as his salvation and our abomination. He attains immortality through the blood of others. Blood is the life source. Belief in these mythological creatures runs broad and deep across multiple cultures.

Amálka had traveled to Transylvania so she had to have known about the bloody legend of Vlad Țepeș. In short, Vlad's father, Vlad Dracul, belonged to the Order of the Dragon, which was created to fight against the Turks. Along the way, Dracul double-crossed the Holy Roman Empire and the Turks. Ultimately, he was forced to leave two of his sons, Vlad and Radu, with the Turkish sultan. In the course of time, Vlad's father and brother Mircea were both killed and Vlad escaped from the Turks. The Turks then decided that having Vlad on the throne of Wallachia, a part of southern Romania, was an improvement over their enemies, the Dănești princes, who were aligned with the Hungarians around 1448.

Five years later, Constantinople fell to the Turks, a terrifying event for Europeans. The Turks kept advancing and Vlad kept fighting, regaining his throne for a second time in 1456 and hanging onto it until 1462.

During this time, the malevolent Vlad imposed his will on his countrymen, pillaging cities in Transylvania, including his former home, and becoming the blood enemy of the Saxons. The Saxons got their revenge when Vlad was arrested as an anathema to the human race and all things civilized. Germans launched a literary campaign against him, forever destroying his reputation.

Yet Vlad, an authentic prince, lived a complicated life, even building churches and monasteries to honor the Eastern Orthodox religion.

In the latter half of his life, Vlad lost his throne in Wallachia to his brother Radu and was tricked into capture by Hungarian King Matthias, who held him for several years at the castle in the city of Visegrád. In between, Vlad married a relative of Matthias and converted to the Roman Catholic Church. With the help of his cousin Stephen the Great, Vlad reclaimed his throne in 1476. He died in battle that year.

His death is shrouded in mystery, but according to a contemporary account in *Vlad the Impaler (Dracula)* (1999) by Romanian historian Ştefan Andreescu, he is remembered as "the mortal and awe-inspiring enemy of the Turks" and "one of the bravest princes in Central and Eastern Europe during the Middle Ages."

CHAPTER 5

Hunting and Pecking

BETWEEN WORK AND HOME PROJECTS, AMÁLKA'S BOOK quietly lay on my desk, a continuing mystery to me. Periodically I picked it up and looked inside, romanticizing its contents. Amálka was ordinary yet extraordinary, like a watercolor rose engrossing one hundred years on.

Then suddenly I would turn hardboiled, staring in the distance, buried in questions with no answers. How could we be certain that Amálka's friend, "the fiddler of the house," was related to a twentieth-century Olympic medalist with the same surname?

This was the case with the surname Kiss. Brigitta turned up a person with that name living near Szolnok from 1861 to 1932, whose family had lost a relative during World War I. She found the right time period, but was he the same Kiss who spent time in Pécs in 1907 with Amálka, her family, and friends? Kiss is a very common last name in Hungary.

Brigitta had also pulled some information on various people with the last name Szathmáry. She was exhaustive and came across someone from the 1500s. Don't even ask how I could ever prove he was related to the person by that name who signed Amálka's book. This seemed as impossible a task as winning an Olympic medal.

When Brigitta sent me a biography of the nineteenth-century Hungarian poet, translator, philosopher, and playwright Mihály Vörösmarty (1800–1855), we suddenly seemed to be on better ground.

A friend of Amálka's had quoted a line from one of Vörösmarty's works, "To the Day-Dreamer." The entry was made on April 12, 1914, shaded with a cluster of white and bluish purple pansies on their lazy green stems. The line quoted by Amálka's friend talks about daydreaming creating false hopes.

Brigitta said this is one of the most memorable lines in all of Hungarian poetry. Hungarian students often have to write reports on it. Now Brigitta was introducing me to works by Vörösmarty. His efforts laid a corner for a golden age in Hungarian literature. Vörösmarty wasn't on my New Jersey high school reading list, but it would have been valuable to have learned about the fine literature of Central Europe. No time like the present so I dived into it.

•   •   •

TOWARD THE END OF 2005, I RECEIVED ANOTHER E-MAIL FROM Brigitta. She had finally reached someone at the museum in Szolnok but she couldn't help.

I was having little success but becoming ever more curious about the book.

CHAPTER 6

Translating

ONE DAY IN THE WINTER OF 2006, I BRUSHED PAST KERTÉSZ'S *Kaddish for a Child Not Born* in one of the bookcases in my apartment. How could I have forgotten to contact Northwestern University for help in finding a translator?

I immediately called. A series of discussions led to a reference. They suggested I speak to Columbia University professor Ivan Sanders, who they identified as being among the best Hungarian translators in the United States.

I e-mailed Dr. Sanders, providing him some minutia about the project, word count, and page length. In his reply, he addressed me as "Ms. Linda Fischer" and signed "Yours Sincerely." I imagined him to be like one of those astute, erudite, discerning, and respectful Hungarian gentlemen from the turn of the twentieth century. Before accepting, however, he asked to see a sample. After reviewing the material, the professor agreed to do the translation. The text, he said, consisted of "short poems, rhymed aphorisms and adages" from the turn of the twentieth century, material very different from straightforward prose. Of that I was already aware, given how much trouble Brigitta had with it.

As spring edged out winter, the translation of the text in Amálka's book was finally underway. Several weeks later I got an e-mail with an attachment from the translator.

"Some of these reflections and pearls of wisdom are deceptively simple," the professor wrote.

I immediately clicked open the file. Now I understood the reaction of the woman at the wine shop. I printed the pages and went to the dining room table. I looked at the translation and the copied pages from the book, going through them one by one, from beginning to end.

Her mother gave the first entry. She wrote between twigs, freshly sprouting.

To My Dear Amálka,
Search through your heart,
And pull out the weeds you may find there,
Even if it pains you.
It's not blind fate that steers
Your life without and within
We merely get back what we once lent out.
Let sadness come, or pleasure.
Everything is a warning, a redress, an enticement.
Our strength is still great: what penetrates all like a
      mighty voice
Is the belief that
God in heaven is in charge of our fate.
Your Mother
Novska, November 1, 1906

On the next page, the artist drew a cascade of flowers, leaves, and ferns.

To Amálka!
Do not give up on love!

Only your heart can really make you happy.

D. Vajnai

Novszka, October 8, 1906

Three years later, a husband and his wife made mirror entries on the next two pages. The husband began each sentence with the first letter of Amálka's name while the wife wrote delicate, even hesitant, script to her with a tiny date. Alas the acrostic structure is lost in the translation to English.

As a bee in search of honey
Visits every flower cup,
So memory revisits the past.
Thus, when in thought you come near us,
Do not, like a stranger, take off again –
Linger awhile at your pleasure.
Respectfully,
Dr. Ferenc Szöllösi
Szolnok, August 14, 1909

Don't be taken in by the world's empty enticements,
Nor by people who set aflame too many hearts,
And then leave them burning in forsaken torment.
Give your love to one; share your life with only one:
One who knows your heart's desire, your soul's wish.
Look for the one, love that one,
And you'll see how happy you will be.
Affectionately,
Ferencné Szöllösi
Szolnok, August 14, 1909

On another page, pansies splash against the green leaves of a vine. The artwork is unsigned.

"Daydreaming ruins life with a lying view."
(Vörösmarty)
Pál Temesi
Szolnok, April 12, 1914

Here, pencil signatures twist like ribbons on a birthday present, joyous and amorphous. There, Amálka's name waltzing among the guests at Valéria and Józsi's wedding on May 11, 1907. Each page has its own motif.

Tightly woven, jagged script in brown ink looks like a seismograph recording of an earthquake. 1918—the worst of the war over. The signature is illegible but the quote from sixth century BC poet Theognis is clear.

"Curb your emotions, make sure
your words are always amiable.
For only the weak expose
their aching heart."
                                    THEOGNIS

To Amálka with fond greetings,
(name illegible)
Szolnok, April 9, 1918

I turned the page.

An oversized red poppy bursts out from the flowers and wheat. Amálka's name is bold with an exclamation point. Amálka herself embedded her tiny signature under the poppy's broad, red petal, as if for protection. Katinka quoted Hungarian statesman József Eötvös.

To My Amálka,
"The human heart is a sea of emotion; and if the danger
    that

whips up its waves is past, it swells in a storm of its own
making."
(Eötvös)
Fondly,
Katinka
Szolnok, June 1908

László Elek signed his name above a sketch, almost a doo-
dle, of Art Nouveau flowers, an artistic afterthought also known
as Secession.

May fortune scatter rose petals
in your path, young maiden;
Where others find mere shells
cast out by the sea,
There may you find precious pearls.
László Elek
July 1919

Text framed by two vases with Art Nouveau flowers, vines
twisting as a background to the message, squarely laid out in
front like a shadow box.

To My Amálka,
May your heart be like a cloister,
Locked to stranger
If a friend approaches
Look at him, though only through the grating.
But when the real one comes along,
Get going and catch him!
Fondly, as always,
Vicuska
Szolnok, May 25, 1919

The next image, a pencil drawing of flowers, just sprigs this time, frames a simple sermon.

To my Amálka,
Only with innocent tears in your eyes,
Can you say Dear God, I am happy.
Affectionately,
Your Katinka
Pécs, July 10, 1907

Amálka signed her name in thin blue ink, weaving along the stem of a rose overpowered by one flower in full bloom and humbled by a passionate soft pink bud, against a pale blue horizon. Close by someone wrote, "Think of us, too, sometimes, dearest Amálka." Multiple signatures crowd the lower part of the page, including a wife and her "faithful husband." The last person to sign penned: "Think of your sad Anna." The occasion was Kucika's wedding, October 4, 1916, Szolnok.

I continued.

Clusters of forget-me-nots frame two plump bluebirds perching on a branch, contented, relaxing. Amálka signed her name underneath. The text, supported by a base of purple flowers, sparse but essential, completes the thought.

To live is to act
To be patient is to possess genius.
UNKNOWN AUTHOR

A thousand pleasures are not worth a single torment.
PETRARCH
Noskovci, September 12, 1914

On the next page, pencil signatures in riotous fun, remembering the time spent in Pécs in 1907. The student, the fiddler of the house, and Amálka's aunt commemorated the event.

Hung like a yellow moon between the boughs of a tree, I passed a silent medallion of a man in a wagon being pulled by a horse, trekking across the sky.

The ensuing page seems more boastful—two boats and a villa facing a shore. On the first level of the villa, two archways welcome visitors and above it, green vines and shrubbery creeping down the walls. Bluish gray mountains loom in the distance. A small bird flies overhead. An outstretched flag, tall, slender trees, and sharp cliffs surround the villa. Hungary? Italy? Austria? The flag bears no insignia.

> May all the days of your life
> be happy ones.
> *Márton Fekete*
> *Szolnok, March 6, 1914*

Signatures with exuberant twists. Amálka remembers being in Nagyvárad with her grandmother, her friend Anna, and a lady named Lenke Kárász. Kárász signed her name.

Clusters of grapes hang on the vine, fruitful and promising. Signatures sprawl under the phrase, remembering the harvest in Várad [Nagyvárad], 1908. Grandma came, so did Aunt Mária and Aunt Klári.

I passed a page, blank except for the sketch of a vine with red flowers in full bloom. It is an empty process waiting for a happy event, pregnant in its potential, sad in its barrenness.

Another holds irises and a bold signature from Amálka.

> *Amálka!*
> If you find someone
> Fancying you,
> And Your Heart's in Hiding,
> You are "FREE TO GO!"

Like the train leaving the station.
l.b.s.
Miklós Lindner

A page later, signatures with the accents like lines from blades twirling in the ice recall skating in the winter of 1908–09. A few blank pages and then Erzsike's consolation.

Don't ask to be happy
too soon.
After being pricked by thorns, it's better
to rest on a bed of roses.
To Amálka, with love,
Erzsike
Szolnok, April 19, 1918

Ink smudges darken E. Bolatinácz's signature on another page but do not obscure its truth.

There isn't a man who is too wise
to be made a fool of by love.
Your admirer,
E. Bolatinácz
Szolnok, April 20, 1918

Green leaves with pink cyclamen-like flower and buds fall from winding vines. This time Amálka signed along the curve of a bough. Ink from Imre Havasi's signature seeps into the paper. The page, set up like some others, holds a bit of true text in the tender palm of a loving Nature.

"May you experience such immeasurable happiness as
   only you are capable of giving."
Imre Havasi
Nagyvárad, October 12, 1907

The next page is stark. Ink this time, well-lettered, but harsh.

To Amálka
In your actions let your heart
be the guide, and your head the inspector.
Fondly,
Judit H.
Szolnok, April 21, 1914

Amálka's signature sits as if a ghost, visible to the caring eye
on the edge of nothingness, nestled in calla lilies and vines. An
apparition, less present than viewing.

"Memory is but the sediment
Left behind by rushing time,
To forget past evil and past bliss
Is - oh so hard. -"
(Gy. Varsányi)
[Name indecipherable]
Nagyvárad, October 12, 1907

Then, a rose and a rosebud, patiently waiting for a message
to Amálka.
   Next, Tibor Berényi underlined his name and Amálka's with
a broken semi-circle, a thin line, shallow in text and deep in
meaning.

To Amálka:
Love, dream, then wake up.

Know disappointment, for that too you must learn.
I only wish that your dream will be long,
your awakening late, and your disappointment brief.
Affectionately,
Tibor Berényi
Szolnok, April 20, 1918

I came again upon diminutive, refined script. It was moving
even without being translated.

For Amálka!
May your life's dream shimmer like a star.
And your soul be shielded by the angel wing of peace.
Never know sorrow; joy should follow your every step
And the rose of your hope should never be torn by
      disappointment!
Fondly, your
Jolán Barabás
Szolnok May 12, 1914

Seismographic lines once more and a message for men and
women of our time.

My Darling Amálka,
Thrift is the mother of wealth. Hence the saying:
Look at the mother, marry the daughter.
F. Szikszay
Szolnok, March 18, 1918

At Gizuska's engagement party, November 28, 1909, several
guests signed Amálka's book—the father of the bride and a
schoolmaster, a merchant, and a doctor.

Moving through the book and the pages of her life I found
an entry with Amálka's name and two exclamation points. Its

scolding nature is less a rebuke than a loving lesson.

Remember:
If ever you should suffer, look at the innocent rose
    glistening in the light of a rising sun.
You will see it too is moist with tears.
To Amálka, with love,
Lenke
Szolnok July 23

The book continued and I was face-to-face with a lonely man in a boat. He looks like he's fishing for Amálka. But nothing was written, so I went on. The sun is sitting low on the horizon, forcing its yellow warmth past the clouds. The green trees exalt, reaching high. The water lilies lay in the shadow of the small boat. Is it sunrise or sunset? I may never know.

Another exhortation from Lenke Kárász again to a young Amálka.

"The sun will appear in all its fullness
and purity only in a calm body of water,
with nary a ripple. So the wonders of nature
can gladden only those hearts
that are pure and calm."
(Gedeon Mindszenty)
Fondly,
Lenke Kárász
Szolnok, August 23, 1907

On the last page, in the upper right-hand corner, the final message:

Love compensates for everything;

But there is no recompense for love.—
P.—

This truth emanates from the suffering of the human heart. Later I was able to identify P. Whoever wrote the letter "P" in Amálka's book knew that these were lines from the poem "The Starry Sky" by Sándor Petőfi (1823–1849), the lyric poet thought of as the "Sir Robert Burns" of Hungary. A veritable comet hurtling onto the poetry scene at age twenty-one, Petőfi often penned poems about love and rural life on the Hungarian plains, the Alföld. Prolific, the bulk of his poetry was born in five short years.

In August 1847 at Szatmár, Hungary, Petőfi wrote "The Starry Sky." This was one month before his wedding, which was exactly one year after he first met his betrothed.

A year later, Petőfi put off his translation of Shakespeare into Hungarian and joined the army in 1849. He died for his country at the tender age of twenty-six. At the time of his death, he was the most noted poet in the country. Petőfi—a firework, a flash for beauty, a spark for memory and then gone. He could have been a cannon shot.

British traveler and writer Charles Boner said in *Transylvania: Its Products and Its People* (1865), Petőfi's "grand imagery, his fire and boldness, make him the favourite of his countrymen; and in many a room I found his portrait on the walls, and his works among the last-read books lying upon the table."

Petőfi often noted where he wrote his works and I appreciated his sense of geography. Amálka left me with the location of her memories, too.

· · ·

THE ENTRIES READ LIKE GOOD WISHES ONE MIGHT FIND ON A greeting card. Later I learned that the messages were typical of the period and, for the most part, evergreen truisms. Even so, intent was behind them. Someone chose to share these words and they are often very high literature. They spoke to me of the time and place where they were written, not the advancement of scholarship but only the hopes of a young girl. They represent the best understanding of the human condition that people had at that time and have been repeated frequently, though are less in vogue today. They were valued in the context in which they were created, just like the letters my mother wrote me.

• • •

IN SEARCH OF MAPS, PHIL AND I HASTENED OFF TO THE NEW York Public Library. The librarian began with a quick primer on using latitude and longitude markings on maps of Central Europe. We knew about meridians and generally how to find any place by using them. However, the maps we wanted of Central Europe in the late nineteenth and early twentieth century didn't always use Greenwich Meridian as the reference point, even though it had become the international standard after 1884. Instead, these maps marked the Ferro/Hierro Island in the Canary Islands as the start of Europe.

The librarian stood patiently as Phil and I provided her with the names of the four places most commonly cited by Amálka's circle—Novska, Szolnok, Pécs, and Nagyvárad—along with the coordinates under the Greenwich Meridian system. She converted those into the coordinates we needed, then proceeded to give us two-by-three-foot copies of maps drawn by the Austrian military in the late nineteenth century. I also got a patchwork of smaller maps showing Central Europe from 1683 to 1923. We rolled them up and put them in a long, narrow plastic bag.

• • •

WHEN WE GOT HOME FROM THE LIBRARY, PHIL AND I STUDIED the detailed work done by the K.u.K. Militärgeographisches Institut, the military cartographers of the Austrian army's map institute. The Austrians seem to have pinpointed every significant mountain, village, group of houses, and road. Does Google list soil types? The Austrians did.

After all, these military maps were intended to guide commanders on how to move their troops and where to feed and hide them. A quick Internet search and a comprehensive history book explained that the acronym *K.u.K.* is an abbreviation for *kaiserlich und königlich* in German (imperial and royal).

Using the map's key page and Google Translate for German to English, we identified Szolnok as it looked in 1883: a developing city with a crosshatch of roads populated by ten to fifty thousand people. It sat on the banks of the winding Tisza River, surrounded by farmland. A railroad passed through Szolnok. Didn't one of the people who wrote to Amálka use railroad jargon? Maybe he lived in Szolnok, or even Novska?

I traced the railroad track markings northwest from Novska, a city of fewer than two thousand people surrounded by farms, into other parts of the country. The landscape was mostly farmland, hills and valleys, ripe for apple picking. Mountains hovered to the north of the tightly twisting Sebes-Körös River.

One of the challenges posed by these maps was identifying names that had changed over time. Grosswardein was the German word for what Amálka might have called Nagy Warad, or Nagyvárad.

Fünfkirchen, the German name for the city of Pécs, peeked through in small letters near where I thought Pécs should be on the map. Again, it showed a city surrounded by small towns separated by farmlands and connected by local roads. A railway running through the area could have transported coal to the Danube to fire the boilers of steamer ships in the late 1900s. Professor David Thomas Ansted, a geologist and the author of *A Short Trip in Hungary and Transylvania in the Spring of 1862* (1862), wrote that the coal from the region was prized because it "burns slowly, giving out great heat, and with little or no waste."

I continued my investigation. A quick comparison of maps before and after World War I illustrates the winners and losers in that war. Gone was the Austro-Hungarian Monarchy in the center of the European Continent. Hungary, so large before the war, was just one small country among numerous newly created nations, among them Czechoslovakia and Yugoslavia. In an instant, the remains of the Ottoman Empire had become Turkey. Germany, Poland, Romania, and the Soviet Union dominated the post-war map of Central Europe.

Another map provided a clue to Amálka's religion. I believed she was Christian, probably Catholic, because of the tone of the entries. An ethnographic map from around 1900 showed relatively few Jewish people in Hungary generally. Certainly that was true compared to Poland and Russia, which had far larger Jewish populations. Nevertheless, Hungary did have established Jewish communities in Budapest and Nagyvárad as well as in and near the Carpathian Mountains in the 1900s. In the 1890s, about two thousand Jewish people lived in Szolnok, making up about 9 percent of the population.

JUDAISM IN HUNGARY

Jewish names appear in Amálka's book and these people were her close friends. They had a long Hungarian heritage. Hungarian King Béla IV reigned from 1235 to 1270. He allowed the Jews to inhabit what is today Castle Hill in Buda, to build synagogues, and to practice Jewish traditions in the wake of a Mongolian Tatar massacre of the local population. They prospered over the generations, even underwriting one of the days of reverie marking the wedding of King Matthias and Beatrice of Aragon in 1476. By the seventeenth century, however, the Jewish population came under siege by the Turks and the Austrians, and most were killed or captured by the Austrian-led Christian armies in 1686.

The Jewish community reemerged in the last part of the eighteenth and early nineteenth centuries when Jews and Christians lived together. In the terrible Danube flood of 1838, the Lutheran Church sheltered Jewish families; when the waters receded, the Jewish community thanked the pastor with a silver chalice.

About this time, Pest was home to the country's most powerful Jewish community. It supported the Hungarians in their fight against the Habsburgs in 1848–1849. Even so, problems inspired Sándor Petőfi to lash out in his diary against those who persecuted the Jews. Thousands of European Jews began emigrating to the United States. Those who stayed behind fought heroically for Austria-Hungary during World War I.

CHAPTER 7

Magyar Beauty

BENT OVER, ONE HAND PROPPING UP MY HEAD, I KEPT thinking about the translation.

Phil got up from the couch and walked to another area of the apartment. He returned carrying a framed picture and put it down on top of my papers.

"You're reading Amálka's poems just the way I used to read Alfred Tennyson's 'Ulysses'," he said.

Phil had resurrected a very old memory from his college days, telling me that when he was in his twenties, he read the British poet's verses a hundred times and finally committed a good portion of them to memory.

"Reading that poem enough times makes it come to life," he said.

> *I cannot rest from travel: I will drink*
> *Life to the lees: all times I have enjoy'd*
> *Greatly, have suffer'd greatly, both with those*
> *That loved me, and alone . . .*

I did not want to rest from travel. It brought me to Hungary and its women.

. . .

THE WORDS FROM AMÁLKA'S MOTHER AND HER FRIENDS RAINED down on me. The way I pictured Amálka and her mother—because the book left me filling in many of its empty spaces—they must have been similar to each other and in the tradition of Magyar women.

Travel stories penned in the 1890s by British writers Margaret Fletcher and H. Ellen Browning describe Hungarian women as graceful, devoted to their families, but also frank in expressing their views without hurting their social status or femininity. In her travel memoir *A Girl's Wanderings in Hungary* (1897), Browning quotes nineteenth century Hungarian novelist Mór Jókai (1825–1904) as saying, Magyar women are capable of "leading an army to soothing a baby; from ruling a county to ruling a hospital; from managing an estate to managing a household."

Heroism and patriotism are renowned qualities of Hungarian women. One of Hungary's immortal writers, Géza Gárdonyi (1863–1922), in his historic fiction *Egri Csillagok*, recounted the brave women among the two thousand people who defended the castle at Eger, northeast of Budapest, against forty thousand Turks in 1552. This story, widely read today, is available in English under the title *Eclipse of the Crescent Moon*.

Victor Tissot, author of *Unknown Hungary* (1881), quoted Petőfi as saying, "If my country has ever need of my arm, my wife herself would buckle on my saber."

A woman at arms is as sexy as a woman *in* arms. Mrs. Nina Mazuchelli, a chaplain's wife in the British army and nineteenth-century fellow of the Carpathian Society, found the Magyar women very unpretentious. She described one of "these Magyar sirens" with her face having "a tint like the damask rose just showing through the delicately transparent skin . . . I am sketching her, but looking up smiles sweetly . . . the expression of her face imbued in its every line with that unconscious grace and charm of indifference to admiration." This she gives us in her volume *Magyarland: Being the Narrative of Our Travels Through the Highlands and Lowlands of Hungary* (1881).

Perceptions about Magyar beauty continued into the twentieth century. Hollywood actress Eva Gabor played the sophisticated but misplaced wife of Oliver Douglas in the television show *Green Acres*. Convinced that they needed fresh air, he buys a farm and devotes himself to running it, however unably. As a child, it was among my favorite shows.

At the time, I had no idea that I was looking at the embodiment of Hungarian beauty. "Hungarian girls are the most beautiful girls in the world," wrote Bess Rattray in "Belles of Budapest," *Vogue* (1999), calling them "as intriguingly diverse as the seraglio of a Persian prince."

These images, old and new, of Magyar women blended into a picture of Amálka, a young woman with warm and kind eyes. Amálka's entries lived in the spirit of her mother's entry. Like mother, like daughter. How could it not be?

CHAPTER 8

Eötvös

AMÁLKA'S CAREFUL HANDWRITING AND DELICATE PAINTINGS attracted urbane well-wishers quoting intellectuals of their time. Baron József Eötvös (1813–1871) was a Hungarian statesman, a visionary and liberal thinker, a novelist, a poet, and a philosopher. Any of those could have been reason enough to quote him, but it didn't explain to my satisfaction why Amálka's friends chose to quote Eötvös instead of other notable Hungarians. Why not István Széchenyi (1791–1860)? This nineteenth-century Hungarian patriot selflessly cultivated the country by personally funding a scientific academy, spearheading the development of the Chain Bridge, and introducing steam navigation down the Danube. Surely Széchenyi had also said many things worth repeating. I dug further into Eötvös's political and literary career for an answer.

The British author and intrepid traveler Julie Pardoe, author of *City of the Magyar, or Hungary and Her Institutions in 1839-40* (1840), provided crucial insights, helping me understand why Eötvös was quoted in Amálka's memory book. Pardoe offers a firsthand account of a young, handsome Eötvös, full of hope at the Hungarian National Assembly in 1839 in Pressburg (Pozsony to Hungarians), now Bratislava to the Slovaks. Bratislava sits between Vienna and Budapest.

Of Eötvös's dreams for "universal freedom and happiness" Pardoe wrote, "his hand was as open as his heart," but that the times had made him "more temperate and more practical in his views. He is still a liberal, however, openly and fearlessly advocating the principles that he has adopted."

By the turn of the twentieth century, the statesman's ideals lived on. Eötvös, "though dead yet speaketh," declared British journalist and businessman W. B. Forster Bovill in *Hungary and the Hungarians* (1908).

Eötvös wanted to be remembered for his egalitarian ideals and not his political accomplishments. Least of all did he want some successor government to memorialize him in a bronze statue, as he wrote in the poem "My Last Will."

> *When I shall once have trod*
> *My rugged path of life,*
> *And in the tomb am laid,*
> *Where is an end to strife.*
>
> *Raise not a marble dome*
> *To keep alive my name;*
> *The triumph of my thoughts*
> *Will then assure my fame.*

But eight years after his death, in 1879, he got a statue anyway. It resides in Eötvös Square near the Danube. If it were up to me, every guidebook would feature József Eötvös and not just his son Loránd, a renowned physicist, after whom a major university is named in Budapest.

. . .

THE ENTRY QUOTING EÖTVÖS IN AMÁLKA'S BOOK DESCRIBES
our relationship to ourselves and our hearts:

> "The human heart is a sea of emotion; and if the danger
>   that
> whips up its waves is past, it swells in a storm of its own
>   making."

This quote comes from Eötvös's first novel, *The Carthusian*
(1911), which he penned at age twenty-five.

Eötvös included *The Carthusian* in a larger work called *The
Flood Book*, which he paid to publish for the benefit of his friend,
a book publisher, hit hard by the 1838 flood of the Danube.
The Carthusian brought Eötvös fame and established him as a
respected author.

For me, Eötvös's romanticism in *The Carthusian* rang with
the purest of sounds. At an introspective moment in the novel,
the main character speaks about the chaotic nature of the human
heart. That quotation was passed down to Amálka, around
which she drew a daisy, an ear of wheat, blue corn poppies, and
an oversized red poppy with a dark center, stems dangling in the
air. They often bloom together in fields and they soar above
the entry. That's what Amálka's drawing was meant to do. I
shared all this with Phil, and he liked knowing about it just as
much as I did.

We spent a long time discussing how Eötvös knew that
people are an ever-seething sea of emotion. Phil said that
sometimes that is due to the troubles of the time, but even
without them, people work themselves into emotional turmoil
all on their own. That is their nature. I had a less poetic way of
saying it: Basically, we screw ourselves up even when things are
good. That appears to be the power of the mind: either we
control it, or it makes us miserable. I hadn't expected the
Hungarian book to be a source of Buddhist philosophy.

Sometime afterward, Phil took me to a place that should have reminded me of very happy times. The Statue of Liberty stood gleaming in the distance, the East River around it invigorating with its waves from the winds and boats and water taxis ferrying hordes of tourists. I was enjoying it, but at the same time I was fixated on the frustrations of work that day. The next morning, I realized the truth of Eötvös's writing: the challenge is to be a reflective person and not let any of my daily problems overtake me. Maybe Eötvös was really at Steamers Landing in Battery Park City when he wrote those lines in *The Carthusian*—at least in spirit.

CHAPTER 9

An Era of War

ALL OF THE MESSAGES IN AMÁLKA'S BOOK COME FROM THE
first decade of the twentieth century, when turmoil was brewing
inside the Austro-Hungarian Monarchy. The social environment in Szolnok quaked with rebellion in the air. A socialist
labor movement by railway and sawmill workers was causing
chaos between 1902 and 1905.

I let history overlay the truisms, creating the image of a
young girl growing up in a historical framework. Conjecturing
what Amálka's life must have been like was the only way I could
envision her, and it amplified the meaning of the book for me.

The world around Amálka was blossoming from 1906 to
1909. She was showered with flowery advice of love and hope
and bees lingering on sunny days.

Institutions of music and education sprouted up in Amálka's
Szolnok. The town was embellished by the construction of the
Szolnok National Theater in 1912. The government opened a
boys' middle school that year and a girls' middle school followed.
The city's growing economy demanded the development of busi-
ness education and soon a high school specializing in commerce

emerged. Promise was in the air and in these busy times, she set the book away. There were no entries for five years. It's possible that public times on the surge supercede private moments.

But progress was not to last in Amálka's world. On July 28, 1914, Austria-Hungary proclaimed war against neighboring Serbia, setting off years of horror in Europe. Hungarians look back to the pre-1914 era as a happy period. Silent were the guns of war.

Amálka's hometown turned on its head in 1914. Boys coming of age and men, many of them from Szolnok's workers' movement, were drafted into the military. Amálka must have felt the effects of this on the men in her circle of family and friends. She sporadically recorded private joys but nothing in 1915, as the world plunged into war.

Tragically, the war cut short Szolnok's cultural and educational progress. Schools eventually were converted for military use. The town itself became a military objective as Hungarians and Romanians fought near the Tisza River.

Where did this leave Amálka?

In 1916, she attended a wedding. While a wedding is a happy occasion, Amálka's friend Anna characterizing herself as sad was shocking in a memory book. I can only speculate as to why Anna had said it but it sounded like the crackle of a thunder at a wedding reception.

One of the later pages shows the faint outlines of a rough wooden fence, wanting to be an entry. The author seems to have been interrupted just as she began. But her thin pencil lines speak to the whole of the book. Amálka had fewer good times than she might have anticipated, her life, a painting interrupted. She could not have foreseen how World War I would crush the happy times in Szolnok. For Hungary's nearly four million soldiers, 56 percent were killed, wounded, or captured.

Amálka's book, almost empty through the years of World War I, is telling. Leafing through the book, it struck me that of one hundred pages barely one-third is filled. The number of events that she and others recorded each year serves as a little index of her happiness and reflects both the evolution from childhood penmanship to adolescent romances to a deep saddening at the end.

The armistice between the Allies and Austria-Hungary was signed in November 1918. Soldiers returning to occupied Szolnok at that time came home to find their families suffering. Food was scarce, so was housing. Civil society had broken down in this once flourishing city, so recently known for its industry, railways, culture, and historical landmarks. Amálka had to have shared in the misery engulfing the region as armies tangled in a deadly embrace. The flowers she drew so delicately now lived in a forest of fire.

But her life went on somehow because the book goes on. The entries in 1918 advise about handling loss and retaining hope.

I gulped thinking about the watercolor in Amálka's book of a solitary fisherman in a flat-bottom boat. It looks like a scene from the Tisza River, which an old Hungarian proverb describes as three parts fish and one part water. There must be truth in it: "The slow muddy waters of the Theiss [Tisza] seem to suit the fish better than those of any other river in Hungary," penned Hungarian-British writer Louis Felbermann in *Hungary and Its People* (1892). I could almost see the ferryboats hauling peasants and farm animals across the Tisza. Amálka and her family must have traveled it, too. It had to be wrenching to see Hungarians and Romanians battling on the gentle Tisza River in the summer of 1919. All manners of privation, from lack of food and supplies, and general barbarity ruled. There were not even enough gravediggers.

By fall 1919, President Woodrow Wilson, Prime Ministers Georges Clemenceau, Lloyd George, and Vittorio Orlando, of the United States, France, Britain, and Italy, respectively, had forced enemy armies to withdraw from Hungary, including Szolnok.

"Hungary in 1919 presented a sort of unending, formless procession of tragedies. . . there marched liberalism, revolution, socialism, communism, imperialism, terror, wanton executions, murder, suicide, falling ministries, invading armies, looted hospitals, conspirators, soldiers, kings and queens—all with a constant background of starving women and children. . . . But had there not been a magnificent toughness in the Magyar spirit, the race would have collapsed," wrote Herbert Hoover in *The Memoirs of Herbert Hoover Years of Adventure 1874-1920* (1952).

Amálka's book has one entry in 1919 and then nothing.

CHAPTER 10

Incubating

DURING MY SPARE TIME IN THE FALL OF 2006, I CONTINUED reading history books and thinking about the people in the book who had survived into my time. Even though I had no details about the intimate lives of the people who signed their names in Amálka's book, they lived at a seminal moment in history—an age of crumbling monarchies. This compelled me to delve into the political events of a century ago, of which I'd known only fragments. In this way, I wasn't bound by the details of particular people but rather immersed in a cultural wave pegged by a few facts. Learning of those times would require stripping away the layers between them and me.

Where to turn for detailed information? It seemed logical to me to reach out to one person who had helped me with school projects when I was growing up: the research librarian at the public library in West Orange, New Jersey. She had saved me on many assignments and I hoped she might come through again. After a series of calls, I heard her voice. She politely declined, citing other commitments, but ties run deep in the suburbs of New Jersey. She took my address down in case she had time.

Later, I got a letter suggesting a few books. I had found much to read myself but these would add importantly to my various tomes. The works imbued me with the knowledge of Hungarian society during Amálka's time. And here again the book and my imagination gave me a means to live in her times.

Amálka's book is the ultimate travel story—time travel by my own hand. In the early 1890s, while America was developing rapidly on the strength of steel mills, oil wells, and wireless telegraphs, the Austro-Hungarian Monarchy remained to a large extent locked to an archaic system in which two-thirds of the population were subsistence farmers. It was a system of haves and have-nots, with almost no mobility.

From their entries, it appears that most of Amálka's friends worked as civil servants and middle-class professionals such as doctors, lawyers, and railroad officials. It's doubtful that she would have been mingling with the Magyar nobles, getting their livelihood in government or the army, and I didn't see any sign of that in her book. It's also unlikely that she associated with the highest classes, the two thousand or so magnates owning about a quarter of Hungary, although the people around her might have been multilingual, an attribute of Magyar magnates.

Because the book records that Amálka helped at harvest, it's also improbable that her family and friends were rubbing elbows with the haute bourgeoisie, the very richest bankers and successful merchants.

She may have known some of the gentry, the small landowners and others of lesser social position. But they accounted for only a small percentage of the population, since most Hungarians toiled in the fields as late as 1910.

Americans would recognize the people in Amálka's group as intellectuals rather than as members of the political intelligentsia. In Central Europe at the turn of the twentieth century, the intelligentsia was an emerging social class of people whose educational and intellectual skills blended with a specific political awareness.

Clues to social change are evident. The doctor, the railroad employee, and the educated laymen with philosophical bents signed her book as equals in her eyes.

It would seem that Amálka's social circle hovered between learned professionals quoting such Hungarian giants as Eötvös and Vörösmarty and a rural mix of railroad engineers running the hottest technology of their time. She was a girl whose grandparents were most likely farmers—but freemen, not serfs. Her parents almost certainly were middle-class emerging technocrats with friends who were artists and, in the modern meaning, intellectuals.

Amálka's artistic abilities could well have saved her from the most menial jobs of her generation. Being an art school teacher would have been a good fit for Amálka, and her drawings suggest that it was a profession she may have chosen.

PART II

CHAPTER 11

Planning Our Return

THE SPRING OF 2007 CAME. PHIL AND I BEGAN TO THINK ABOUT what we might do in the week he had off. I knew what I wanted: to go back to Hungary using the book as a guide to see every place mentioned in it.

Reading relentlessly about curious and audacious adventurers exploring Central Europe ultimately had an intoxicating effect on me. I thought about what they had seen and what it looks like now, even if only shadows remained for the imagination's eye to see. Amálka lived among those artifacts.

I peered down a microscope into time. Her time, my time. Amálka's life loomed larger as the magnification increased. Colors in her little book became three dimensional. My life slowly absorbed a mother's passing, a divorce, a new marriage, a new home. I looked at my life, another page in Amálka's book, a best thought, a best time, a springtime flowering with hope. And here we were back to Buddhism again, the long way—through Hungary.

Planning our vacation, we turned to our globe-trotting travel agent Pam, who has been to every continent but Antarctica. Pam knew someone in Budapest from a trip she had taken some time ago. A few weeks later I found myself in touch with Richard Bogdán, an expert in Hungarian travel.

When we connected via e-mail, Richard wrote that he understood the search for locations and people. I said we were trying to reconstruct Amálka's life, especially in Szolnok, since she appeared to have been from there.

I mentioned that the book had artwork. A quick Internet search for Szolnok and art had brought up an art colony. Richard confirmed its existence.

Weddings and other events mentioned in Amálka's keepsake album might help us figure out her last name, especially if she proved to be Catholic because there might be church records. I soon realized that after forty-five years of Communism, there might not be many church records left.

I outlined where we hoped to go—and all in a week: Budapest, Szolnok, Pécs, Novska (in Slavonia, on the southern border of Croatia and next to Bosnia-Herzegovina), and Oradea (in Romania, just across Hungary's eastern border; formerly Nagyvárad). Richard's response was polite but direct. He said I was planning the impossible, trying to go to three different countries in five days. He suggested we skip Novska. I agreed.

By spring, the frigid New York City winter had eased and we had put together a realistic itinerary, although it needed tweaking. I had forgotten to account for the time change between Romania and Hungary, so we added an extra hour for driving and allotted the time for train connections.

A logical plan came together: no connecting trains on the same day; Budapest, day one, then Pécs, day two, both by car, not train; Oradea, day three and half of four, by train; the art colony in Szolnok, half of day four, van; then back to Budapest, day five, van. We were going to follow Amálka's trail, which in the 1900s would have involved the railway and horse-and-buggy. But our journey would be done at light speed. Before we finished out our plans, my friend Min decided to join us.

CHAPTER 12

Scoping Out the Problem

THE TRIP WAS GETTING CLOSER AND MY E-MAILS DESCRIBING Amálka's book weren't quite cutting it. A picture's worth a thousand words or, in this case, a thousand e-mails. I e-mailed Richard scans of the first few pages of Amálka's book.

I quickly got an e-mail back. He called the inscriptions to Amálka "greeting poems."

As we went back and forth, we both agreed that this intimate keepsake had not been intentionally discarded. Most likely Amálka died and it ended up on a relative's shelf for a century until that person died. Then I bet someone tossed it in a heap of nondescript books to be sold. The soft brown cover of Amálka's book easily belied its beauty.

When I mentioned to Richard that the shopkeeper said she got Amálka's book at a "free market," he thought she meant flea market. In subsequent e-mails, I sent Richard additional pages with lists of names, dates, locations, and other possible connections.

Good news was not forthcoming. He checked out all the material, searched the names in Hungarian Google and other databases, but there were no matches.

The city names were good for travel, but not helpful for finding anything out about the owner of the book. I didn't expect Nagyvárad to shed light on Amálka's artistic endeavors because that's not really implied in the book. Her book refers to people visiting the area at harvest time.

About Novska, zero information related to Amálka.

Regarding Pécs, Amálka had visited this town but we had no way to make any family connections. We continued searching to find something tangible in Amálka's memory book.

The entry for the engagement of Gizuska was the most detailed. Gizuska's family name was Lindner, a common Jewish surname in Hungary, which meant that her marriage might actually be recorded in a Jewish archive. But even that wouldn't be easy, since many documents were destroyed during World War II.

Another possibility existed. A cross-link turned up in the text. A person named Valéria went ice skating with Amálka in the winter of 1908–1909. Could it be the same Valéria who married János the year before?

CHAPTER 13

Forging Ties

10:10 A.M. IN NEW YORK CITY: RICHARD CALLED WITH NEWS. We exchanged a few pleasantries and quickly launched into a discussion about the book. After creating a timeline and cross-checking it with the text, he said that Amálka appeared to be a young girl at the beginning of the book. By 1918, however, the tone had changed. She was either in love or engaged to someone, which at that time in Hungary would likely have happened at seventeen or eighteen years old.

The professor's translation of Amálka's keepsake dovetailed with Richard's assessment. Richard added an interesting twist. The personal tone of the later entries could only have been written by someone close to her; otherwise it would have been insulting. At the turn of the last century, the language tended to be formal.

Back then, a husband would have called his wife *édes felesé-gem* or *asszony*, which translates as "my sweet wife" or "madam," a formal and respectful reference to her. A peasant woman in particular, would have addressed her husband as *uram*, "my master."

Uram is in use today by older Hungarian women and occasionally by younger women. City girls, however, would mostly use *uram* jokingly.

Nevertheless, "my sweet wife" should be uttered by every husband today.

Richard said that he'd had some luck with the name Lindner. The railway's archives listed an employee with the same name as the person in Amálka's book. But again, there were many Lindners, so that information was not as helpful as we had hoped.

As for the Olympic medalist, it was simply a coincidence that the person who wrote in the book shared the athlete's last name.

I explored a few other angles. Color photos of her artwork could be checked against any painter named Amálka. They could also be shown to shop owners and art historians to see if anyone could connect the names and the paintings. Richard said he could handle that and also look at the names again, some of which were Jewish: Friedner, Gauz, and Roth. In those days it was uncommon for Christians to have many Jewish friends and it would have been especially unusual in a place like Szolnok, in which the Jewish population was small. All of this was how people really lived, separated by classes and religion. I paused.

"We need to return to Hungary," I said to Richard. "Maybe we'll pick up a clue going to Nagyvárad. We want to go to Pécs, and if the only thing Amálka's book achieves is to bring us back to Hungary then our journey will be very successful."

. . .

RICHARD AND I SPOKE AGAIN and I casually mentioned being busy with family and friends. Richard replied that he was expanding his family.

"I am practicing, visiting all my friends who have kids and playing with them to get used to the fact I'm going to become a father soon."

"Do you know if the baby is a boy or a girl?"

"We just found out yesterday the baby is a she."

I was happy for Richard but wiped away a tear for the daughter I didn't have.

. . .

OUR CONVERSATION RETURNED TO THE TRIP. ON DAY ONE WE'D visit the Hungarian Parliament and then go to the New York Café, the historic watering hole for intellectuals and artists at the turn of the twentieth century.

I looked forward to seeing the early Christian cemetery in Pécs, a World Heritage Site, and even to sitting for four-plus hours on a train to get to Oradea for a few days of excursions. I love train trips filled with conversation, books, and snacks—or rather "chipmunk" food. I count my pleasure by the number of crumbs.

From Oradea, we intended to head to Szolnok, after which we'd return to Budapest. Richard announced that for the last night he had arranged a night cruise on the Danube so we could enjoy Buda and Pest illuminated against the dark night sky. Then, he added, "They serve champagne."

"Phil gets seasick very easily," I said.

"You can't be seasick on the Danube."

Spoken with Magyar confidence, I thought. But Richard was right. Phil had ably survived the rapidly moving hydrofoil from Vienna to Budapest, gliding past every viewpoint. A night trip would surely be worth the effort, but I decided to pack some seasick pills just in case.

. . .

SOMETIME LATER, RICHARD AND I CONTINUED OUR DISCUSSION about Amálka. The art historians confirmed the likelihood that Amálka became a teacher, given the art and the text. They also provided some context for Amálka's book itself, explaining that it is an enduring tradition in Hungary for girls to collect advice and commemorate events in an *emlékkönyv*, a memory book. It is also known as a keepsake album. On special occasions, it is customary for the owner to ask friends, relatives, or guests to write something or draw something in her book. This could require that they hold on to the book for a while before returning it. Other times a girl may just collect signatures to remember a special experience, like a day of ice skating. Some women continue to collect entries as adults but Amálka didn't. Her book cuts off in 1919, when she was possibly about eighteen years old. Maybe Amálka elected to stop it or maybe she perished.

I suppose a memory book or keepsake album from the turn of the twentieth century could be compared to the high-school yearbook of an American student, full of comments and signatures of friends and schoolmates. But having owned a yearbook, I can attest it may be the antithesis of sensitivity and art.

Margaret Fletcher in *Sketches of Life and Character in Hungary* (1892) gave an example of how cultured Hungarian ladies used memory books. Countess Anna asked her to contribute a bit of poetry to her "album."

> It is hardly necessary to say that the ladies of Branyicska were cultivated. The memory of Countess Anna, in particular, was a storehouse of poetry, and one evening she innocently put me to great embarrassment by asking me to write a typical English verse in her album. I consented, and sat down confidently, pen in hand; but the moment I tried to select from one of the many touching and appropriate fragments with which I believed my mind to be stored, they became foggy and eluded me, all except one verse, which persisted in occupying the foreground of my mind:

> "It was a summer evening,
> Old Caspar's work was done," etc.

My whole nature rose against recording this as a national specimen, and I asked to be allowed to defer writing till the morning. I got into bed in an abject state of mind, and for the better part of the night wrestled with my memory and endeavored to throw old Caspar. I mention this trifle as a warning to all intended travelers in a romantic country, to provide themselves with a little pocket book of lines likely to prove suitable. Ever since that terrible night, ever since the shameful hour next morning when I patched together some disconnected scraps and signed them with an illustrious name, I have vowed never to travel without such a book.

Amálka's friend Márton Fekete had been prepared. He had not only written something but had borrowed the book for a while to paint the seaside scene of one boat at shore and another languishing in still waters. Márton signed and dated it: Szolnok, March 6, 1914.

In general, the art historians called Amálka's watercolors high-quality amateur paintings, though one or two bordered on professional. In their opinion, the various watercolors were painted by different people, and some came from men. Hungary at that time, they told Richard, had very few women painters. Further research suggested they could be listed on one hand: Countess Nemess, Ida Konek, Wilhelmina Parlaghy, and Madame Sikorska (Júlia Zsolnay).

Amálka was not a renowned Hungarian painter. I didn't expect her to be anyway. The times provided all I needed to know, and when I recalled the saying "Fame is fleeting," I thought of the notable people of her time who we have never heard of either. Oddly, Amálka was living on and they were not. She was less anonymous than I thought and a courier of grand ideas coming through the ages. Richard pointed out that Hungary has a very illustrious "Anonymous" in its past. In the early 1200s, a nameless monk collected ancient stories and recorded the history of the Magyars. There's a statue of him in Budapest.

. . .

AN E-MAIL FROM RICHARD POPPED UP IN MY INBOX. ALONG with details about the trip, he had no guarantee of an English-speaking guide in Romania. Somehow another complication wasn't unexpected.

CHAPTER 14

Back in Budapest

"For is not Paris the metropolis of the universe where art and literature are concerned?" declared H. Ellen Browning in *A Girl's Wanderings in Hungary*.

Paris has been the jumping off point to explore Europe for centuries. For myself, I had wanted to get there for a long time and decided to do so the week before landing in Budapest with Min.

As much as I wanted to see Paris, I found Amálka's Hungary tugging at my heart. Browning in *A Girl's Wanderings in Hungary* called the Budapest of the 1890s one of the "loveliest cities in Europe" and challenged her readers by saying that "if there should be any mortal so ill-advised as to question this statement, let him go there and see for himself."

. . .

Min and I had a whirlwind week of trekking to every museum and café possible and by the time we converged with Phil, we were excited to move on. In the airport in Budapest, Richard stood by the gate, holding a sign bearing our last name.

We said hello and all shook hands.

How times have changed. If it had been the turn of the last century, his greeting could have involved his kissing my hand and perhaps saying, "*Csokolom a kezet nagyságos kissasszony!*" ("I kiss your hand, honorable damsel!"). That's what H. Ellen Browning wrote in *A Girl's Wanderings in Hungary*.

"Wait," I said, fishing out a baby gift that I had carried thousands of miles and had fretted over with two women at a trendy Tribeca store.

"For the baby, your wife, and you," I said, handing him a crushed pink-and-white tissue-paper package miraculously in one piece.

"Thank you," he said, taken aback by my informality but pleased with it nonetheless.

Once we dropped everything off at the hotel, we promptly set out for the Parliament building, which had been completed in 1904, two years before Amálka started her keepsake album. Even if she had lived seventy-one miles away in Szolnok, she must have known about it—any educated person would have— since it was the largest structure in Budapest and was rushed to completion for the Millennium celebration. Hungary was founded in 896 and the Parliament had to be suitable in 1896.

To me, Hungary's Parliament is everything that we think of as Gothic or romantic: its vaulted dome—a Baroque cupola— dominates the skyline like a Prussian soldier's helmet sur- rounded by lesser medieval spires. Its presence on the Danube reminded me of the stately seat of British Parliament but Hungary's Parliament, with its sharp points and angles, looked militaristic and not like a library. This was imperial in size and form, accented with a blood red roof.

We entered the building and passed through security where we were given wristbands with a red button to track our where- abouts. We started at the royal staircase, with regal red carpet rolling down its ninety-six white marble steps, softly illuminated by turn-of-the-century orbs.

From every angle, dynastic paintings stared down on us, reflecting heroic scenes of Hungarian law and history. These blended with the building's eclectic mixture of Neo-Gothic, Renaissance, and Art Deco styles. The Art Deco made me think back to Amálka's book.

At the top of the steps stood the Dome Hall, richly decorated with statues commemorating Hungarian history. Standing before me I faced Amálka's culture, a cauldron of royalty and the church. I didn't see a picture of Emperor Francis Joseph who reigned in Amálka's time. I was about to tell everyone some poignant historical facts about him when the sight of the Crown of Saint Stephen silenced me. The Habsburgs coveted it for over four centuries. The crown rested beneath a colossal four-ton chandelier, still ready to rule.

William Pitt Byrne, in describing the royal treasures of Hungary in *Pictures of Hungarian Life* (1869), wrote that "the feeling they inspire may almost be called the poetry of worship, and one scarcely realizes its depth and power until one hears a Magyar speak of these."

Hungarians through the centuries have felt that the king, the crown, and the land are one.

Like so many things, beauty and value are in the eye of the beholder, and there have been naysayers with regard to the crown, including some socialists and politicians. They would agree with the 1840s traveler Johann Georg Kohl who said, "the extraordinary, the preposterous value set on the crown is one of the most curious phenomena in Hungarian history and legislation." Such was his view in his book *Austria, Prague, Hungary, Bohemia, and the Danube, Galicia, Styria, Moravia, Buckovina, and the Military Frontier* (1843).

The crown stands for the strength of a people and not the government, much in the way the Washington Monument inspires Americans. It has been lost, dented and yet survives. Its force will not be denied, even if the crown disappeared once again to follow its destiny. The memory of this object overpowered its physical presence. Much blood has been shed in its name, giving it an aura beyond its symbolism of the monarchy.

Respectfully, I stepped near the glass encasement and tilted my head from side to side.

. . .

AFTER TAKING A LOOK AT THE NORTH WING OF THE HOUSE (the South Wing is for the Hungarian Assembly), we walked toward the exit, dropping off our electronic bracelets for another eager group. If they were lucky, they might see the ghosts of legislatures past in heated argument and hear the shouts of *Halljuk! Halljuk!* ("Hear! Hear!") to quell a filibustering speech.

Jumping in the car, our group passed the Inner City Parish Church, and hustled over the Freedom Bridge, crossing the Danube. On the Buda side, we chugged up a hill and confronted the Gellért Bath and Hotel, sitting at the base of a hill with multiple thermal hot springs. We wanted to go in but didn't feel like spending fifteen dollars for the three of us to visit just the lobby.

We ended up at the Rock Chapel, formerly an ammunitions storage dump during Communist times. When politically open times arrived, the chapel reverted to its original use.

Outside the building, a Gypsy was selling handmade pillow covers, little cloth bags, and tablecloths with distinctive red embroidery in traditional Hungarian patterns. I wanted to buy one but decided to wait until we got to Transylvania.

Moving on, Richard took us to the Citadel atop Gellért Hill. We parked close to the peak and walked the rest of the way. A path lined with souvenir stands led to the lookout with a panoramic view of the city and the Liberty Statue, a Soviet-era monument.

The inscription on the 1947 statue read that a grateful Hungarian nation honored the memory of the liberating Soviet heroes. At the end of the Soviet era in Hungary in the late 1980s, the statue got a new plaque—this one recognizing all those who lost their lives for Hungary's independence, freedom, and prosperity.

. . .

THE NEXT DAY WE FOUND OURSELVES STARING AT THE OPERA House, built from 1875 until 1884 at the then fabulous cost of six million crowns, the currency of the time. I could imagine Amálka and her family taking in an opera and then walking down Andrássy Street, the latter of which we did next. The street itself is a World Heritage Site. The wide boulevard is guarded by rows of ash, plane, and sycamore trees. Palatial buildings lie on either side, placed there for posterity a century ago, now historic monuments to their creators. Andrássy Street, like so much of Budapest, was built in 1896 in time for the Millennium celebration. The street has maintained its dignity and grace, especially on this summer day, when I could see the leaves on the trees moving in a slow waltz.

Nearby, a mixture of new and old emerged: a residential area known as "Pest Broadway" because of the many theaters around, and Liszt Square with its hip restaurant scene. We ran away from the House of Terror, occupied by Hungarian Fascists in the late 1930s, the Nazis in the 1940s, and then the Communists and the State Security police in the 1950s, chased by the shadows of a guilty history, hoping Amálka had outrun it, too.

We followed Andrássy Street straight to Városliget, a city park in Budapest and the site of many events at the Millennium Exhibition of 1896. A canopy of green trees hanging overhead like a porch awning shaded us, swaying as a light wind kept us cool.

In Amálka's time, paths carved out of the forest surrounded by lush green fields of grass, gardens blossoming in purple violets and white daisies, and a lake with swans created an idyllic scene.

"Both men and women were jaunty in top boots and each feminine head was bound in a brilliant handkerchief," British traveler Margaret Fletcher wrote of her visits to the park with the resplendent lake in *Sketches of Life and Character in Hungary*. This body of water was used for ice skating in the winter and was even frequented by the dashing Count Gyula Andrássy, who helped broker the 1867 Compromise between Austria and Hungary, producing the Austro-Hungarian Monarchy, which is often called the Austro-Hungarian Empire.

The lake continues to be used for recreation. The skating club's tall, classically designed stone "Ice Pavilion" from the turn of the twentieth century continues to offer skaters a place to change their boots and warm up. Amálka and about a dozen of her friends, including Janka, the one who signed "kisses from the ice," enjoyed the sport. The odds are good that Amálka knew about the skating club and, given its popularity, got a chance to skate there at some point. But I couldn't be sure.

Soon the statue of a hooded man, his face half hidden and protected by the shade of the trees, presented himself to us between the leaves. In one hand he held a pen, in the other an open book. A plaque in capital letters showed his name: ANONYMUS, and the notation GLORIOSISSIMI BELA REGIS NOTARIUS—Latin for "the Chronicler of the most glorious King Béla."

"Did he ever write his name down?" I asked.

Richard stopped and thought for a moment.

"Just 'Master P.,'" he replied.

Graced by Master P's dark bronze figure in a soft Hungarian afternoon, Min and I sat at the base in front of the ponderous statue. As Phil peered into the camera lens, Amálka and the friendships that surrounded her drifted in the air. Like golden honeybees, we lingered a while at our pleasure, rather than rush through the park.

We sauntered on toward the Romanesque–Gothic and eclectic Vajdahunyad Castle, inspired in part by János Hunyadi's castle in Transylvania. Hunyadi beat back the Turks in the Middle Ages and fathered one of the most revered Hungarians kings, Matthias Corvinus. I fumbled with the video camera.

Our group strolled on for a better look at the park's artificial lake created to represent the moat of a castle. We passed sunbathers, picnic-goers, and sports enthusiasts on the verdant grass. Cars were parked randomly on the hard dirt in some places. In Amálka's time, they didn't have to worry about this.

Not far away from the park was the Neo-Baroque Széchenyi Bath, whose thermal pools are over a century old and remain in use today. It's named in honor of Count István Széchenyi, with many monuments to his credit.

We walked inside the building to see the bathing pools. The crisp, clear water, set against the bright yellow walls practically begged us to leap in with our clothes on, but we restrained ourselves. In Amálka's time, thermal baths were equally appealing and very affordable and she must have known about them.

The day was young and we traipsed on toward Heroes Square, chatting about languages we had learned in school. It turned out that Russian used to be compulsory in Hungary, and German, French, and English could also be part of the curriculum. The usual language choices in today's Hungary are English, German, and French. Foreign languages were taught during Amálka's time as well.

Defenders of the culture stand memorialized in Heroes Square. This vast central square sweeps to the edges of historic buildings and statues of revered Hungarian leaders. If Amálka visited Heroes Square at the turn of the century, it would have looked much different to her eyes. The right colonnade originally sheltered statues of five Habsburgs, including Emperor Francis Joseph. In World War II a bomb hit the colonnades, leveling them. The statues of the Habsburgs became a pile of rubble. No one saw any reason to reconstruct them. Why honor those who denied them their freedom? In place of the Habsburg statues the Hungarians erected notable leaders such as Count Lajos Kossuth (1802–1894). His ideals about Hungarian autonomy from Austria resonated loudly in the mid-1800s and he was a flame in the Revolutionary torch of 1848.

The name Lajos Kossuth continues to evoke patriotic feelings. I figured that if I ended up at a place bearing this politician's name, I would definitely not be in Austria.

Phil and Min took on their photographic chores. I just spun around taking a 360-degree view of the square being set up for a concert that evening.

"What's this about?" I asked, thinking that it was related to the revolution of 1848.

"The last Russians troops left in 1991 on the nineteenth of June, so the last weekend in June we have the Budapesti Búcsú," Richard said, translating the latter word as "good-bye," or "taking leave of." "It's not a state holiday, but everyone knows when it is."

The Soviets occupied Hungary after World War II. Without international support, the Hungarians rose up against them in 1956 and forced the Soviets to ameliorate some conditions in the country. Economic reforms in the late 1960s, including an expansion of tourism and private industry—small shops and manufacturers—helped to reduce the poverty in the country.

The Museum of Fine Arts in Heroes Square offered a welcome respite from the very heavy history of Hungary. Paintings from Amálka's period, works of Austrian, German, Finnish, Swiss, and French artists, lined the walls. We stood silent in front of the art and then headed for a café, itself a form of art.

Immersed in gold, marble, and red furnishings, The New York Café harkened back to old Budapest. We easily lost track of time and we hoped it would never close. Others have, too. Writer Ferenc Molnár, a frequent guest, is said to have thrown the keys of the café into the Danube to ensure that it never closed.

Hurrying on, things took a solemn turn at the Dohány Street Synagogue in Budapest, the largest in Europe. The structure, built in the mid-1800s, served about seventeen thousand Jewish residents in Buda and Pest. By Amálka's time at the turn of the twentieth century, that number had grown to 160,000.

Today about 11,000 people attest to being Jewish in Hungary. This compares with around 3.9 million Catholics and 1.4 million Protestants.

Outside, a metal sculpture of an upside-down menorah in the shape of a weeping willow had the names of the dead engraved on its leaves. In front of the tree next to a fence the plaque read:

TO SAVE ONE LIFE IS TO SAVE THE WHOLE WORLD.

Standing there, I reflected on the way a single life, known or unknown, can hold one's attention in the face of sweeping history. Amálka's religion and class remained unknown. In her time, Jews constituted almost a quarter of Budapest's popula-tion, but the general impression I had from her album was that religious issues crossed social lines.

We walked around to the front where a group of elderly Americans were filing out of a tour bus, the sun reflecting off their big, black wrap-around sunglasses. The horde of people in their golf hats prompted us to move on.

Our next stop was a familiar one: the Labyrinth of Buda. I thought of the day I had been there in 2005, a little frightened. This time we walked through just a part of it and it didn't seem to be as dark as the last time. We exited to the light of day.

"Now look around," Richard said. "That is Saint John's Hill, the highest point of Budapest. It's why the city can't be extended."

Which of these hills might Amálka have climbed? Was it to the north, frigid in winter, or to the south, sunny and pleasant in summer? Did she gaze at wild figs growing on those southern slopes or skip among the vineyards, waiting for her parents and friends while they enjoyed wine and black caraway bread at one of the local inns? That's how it was in her time.

Richard could see from our faces that we needed a coffee break. He suggested the Ruszwurm, a quaint pastry shop with customers spilling out the door. There were small tables in front of the place and Phil and Min vigilantly manned one while Richard and I went inside.

"Would that be good?" I asked, pointing to what looked like a cookie.

"It's a biscuit and dry," Richard said. "I would recommend you have Ruszwurm Krémes which is a cream-filled dessert. It's what they're known for."

Reinvigorated, we walked toward the thirteenth century Matthias Church with soaring vaulted ceilings decorated in gold, sitting at the nexus of Eastern and Western religions. It dates from about the same time that the fortifications of Buda's Castle Hill took place. Frescos and stained glass adorn the church. Mary rises above the altar, bearing the crown of Hungary. Against this dramatic backdrop, royal weddings and coronations of splendor passed through its doors.

The church is an explosion of religious fervor for more than one religion.

"It once served as a mosque during the Turkish occupation before Francis Joseph's reign," Richard said, before we departed the church.

Outside, the construction underway sought to reverse the passage of time by stabilizing the church walls and foundation, which were made of limestone, absorbing water.

Where to look first? The roof. When reconstructed after a bomb destroyed it in World War II, the roofers used iron nails, instead of copper, which over time rusted and cracked the tiles. All quarter of a million of the tiles had to be replaced with Zsolnay tiles from its factory in Pécs, Hungary.

Richard pointed out that the old tiles were being sold.

"I'm going to buy one," I announced to the group.

"Are you going to carry that?" Phil asked.

"Absolutely," I said, not realizing how heavy one small tile could be. It actually weighed seven pounds, but it felt like seventy.

"Let me carry it for you," Phil said.

"No, it's okay," I replied.

Bravely carrying the tile, I followed Richard to the Hungarian National Gallery.

"Let me take you to the section that deals with Amálka's time period," he said.

Paintings by the impressionist Pál Szinyei Merse, among others, evoked the past.

"Many of them have a dark look to them and maybe that reflects the time," Min said, walking past landscapes, forest and river paintings, midnight scenes in deep hues.

"Stunning," I replied, wondering which wall I would hang it on at home.

Phil nodded in agreement.

To be honest, I'd never heard of these artists but I bet Amálka had. Amálka's artwork was not even remotely in the league of these painters. But because of her we were brought to this museum to immerse ourselves in fine art.

We were the last to leave, heading down the funicular, over the Chain Bridge and to our hotel. After a brief rest, we set off for dinner at Menza in Liszt Square. We couldn't keep it simple and take Richard's directions. We walked, got lost, but ultimately stumbled onto the restaurant.

Liszt Square felt like a piece of New York City's Greenwich Village, with its chic restaurants, friends huddled over drinks, and a lone policeman to keep order in this laid back place, if needed.

We missed the concert in Heroes Square but we didn't fret. The remnants of Amálka's era were slowly seeping into our minds.

Whatever we had learned in Budapest about Amálka was just the start. To truly understand the commotion and wonder of her times, we needed to follow British writer W. B. Forster Bovill's advice in *Hungary and the Hungarians*: "Visitors coming to Budapest must not imagine for a moment that by coming to Budapest and exploring its environs that they have seen Hungary and the Hungarians. Not so. What you have seen is a cosmopolitan city . . . the keyboard of Hungarian activity, intellectual, commercial and political. But Hungary and the Hungarians you have not seen. These live beyond beaten tourist tracks."

THE CROWN OF SAINT STEPHEN

I suspect that Amálka never witnessed this golden, bejeweled crown with the bent Roman cross on the top. The bend in the cross has been the subject of eternal debate and conjecture. The explanations: It was damaged in transit from Pope Sylvester I to Saint Stephen; bruised when a king wore it in battle; stuffed into a too small iron chest; fell from the head of a monarch; dropped being placed on the head of a king; injured when stolen and buried by the daughter of a count.

Lady-in-waiting Helene Kottanner in the fifteenth century also may have had a hand in bending the cross. She stole the crown, concealed it in a pillow, and ultimately delivered it to Queen Erzsébet so that her three-month-old son László could be crowned the Hungarian king. King László reigned from 1453 to 1457.

Amálka would have heard these old tales, too. Although the bend in the cross remains a mystery, many a brawl ensued over the crown down through the centuries, since whoever possessed it would be king.

In the mid-nineteenth century, the crown lead a continuing adventurous life. After the Hungarians' failed bid for independence, Hungary's prime minister buried the crown near Orsova on the banks of the Danube.

The Austrians learned the crown's location a few years later and dug it up. After that, the crown was "jealously locked up, sealed and guarded and never sees the light except when required to figure in the ceremony of a coronation, when its iron case is opened, in the presence of official personages, with great precaution, and under prescribed regulations most strictly observed," wrote Byrne in *Pictures of Hungarian Life*.

The last two Hungarian kings coronated with the sacred crown were Emperor Francis Joseph in 1867 and Emperor Charles I in 1916.

The crown's movements continued during World War II. Right before the war ended, Hungarian socialists secured the crown and passed it to the US army so that it wouldn't fall into Soviet hands. Years later, the Americans wouldn't even acknowledge that they had it, causing all sorts of speculation regarding its whereabouts.

Ultimately, the Cold War had thawed enough for the crown to be given back to the Hungarian people in 1978 by then president Jimmy Carter.

I visited the Jimmy Carter Library and Museum in Atlanta, Georgia. I proudly pointed out the replica of the crown sitting in a glass display to my girlfriend. With its bent cross, one could easily see its medieval thoughts. Hungary gave this reproduction to the United States on March 18, 1998, in gratitude for the return of the original crown. It was a moment of pride for both countries.

CITADEL

The citadel in Budapest would be best-suited for an observatory, and that's exactly what was built on the hill by the royal university of Pest beginning in 1813. But I didn't see anything that even remotely looked like it housed a telescope. The observatory became damaged during Hungary's War of Independence in 1848. After that, it was taken down by the Habsburgs, who built the citadel in 1854.

Think of a chess game. With the Austrian citadel hanging over their city, the Hungarians always saw themselves in check. Even after the Compromise of 1867 between Austria and Hungary, the Austrians wouldn't give it back. The keys were eventually handed to the Hungarians in 1897, but it wasn't until two years later they got full control. In Amálka's time, the Hungarians wanted to demolish the citadel, but only some of it ended up being taken down. One idea was to put a museum in its place. But when World War I intervened, the citadel became militarily important again as a fort.

Ironically, when the Austrians pointed heavy artillery at the Hungarians in the mid-nineteenth century, it was purely ceremonial. It wasn't until the mid-twentieth century, during World War II, that the citadel's cannons were fired in hostility on the streets of Budapest. The Soviets, Germans, and Hungarians fought bloody battles around it in early 1945.

MILLENNIUM

Effort was made to complete the Parliament building before the Millennium celebration in 1896 in homage to the Hungarian conquest by Árpád and his warriors battling their way into the fertile plains surrounding the Danube and Tisza Rivers in 896.

Over the next four hundred years, Árpád's offspring fought for the land, made peace with the Holy Roman Emperor and embraced

Christianity; developed a feudal class system; clashed with the Mongols; and reorganized the country to better defend themselves against invaders. Love of the land in Hungary runs blood deep.

Thinking about this Magyar lore brings me back to the Parliament. It marked the beginning of the modern era in Budapest, one that included new buildings, gas lighting, and a subway, which drew the attention of New York City subway designers. Hungary's Millennium was a coming out party, and Europe took notice. The Times of London on April 24, 1896, gave the Millennium Exhibition some good ink, recommending Britain's railways as an easy means to the big event.

VÁROSLIGET

What moving pictures I would have taken at Városliget Park if I could have traveled back to August 5, 1278. Then this park was known as Rákosmező, Field of Rákos, where the earliest legislature of sorts—the Diet—assembled. About one hundred thousand armed noblemen, with an entourage of prelates, settled disputes by argument and battled during trials. One minute, a discussion; the next, an all-out brawl.

With my camera rolling, I might have been able to capture the moment when men "threatened to surround Pest and Buda, and force the consent of the Crown to their wishes by starvation; sometimes with boisterous loyalty they declared themselves ready to die for their King and country, and with freshened zeal rushed from the council to the battlefield." That's how John Paget described governance in *Hungary and Transylvania*.

By Amálka's time, civilization had nearly overtaken the sword, but the land remained largely agrarian and the government and its administration had moved indoors. At the turn of the twentieth century, Vajdahunyad Castle in the park housed the forestry, fishing, and game sections of the Royal Hungarian Agricultural Museum. The growing of crops and fruits, the technology of farming, bee cultures, and breeding horses and domestic animals were critical to the nation. The museum intended to provide the most advanced information on agriculture available at the time. I hope Amálka visited it. She painted fruit, and nature was among her favorite subjects.

NEW YORK CAFÉ

The café swung open its doors in 1894, two years before Hungary's Millennium celebration. Over time, it attracted Hungarian literary lions such as Ferenc Molnár and Gyula Krúdy, movie directors like Sir Alexander Korda, known for *The Thief of Bagdad*, and Michael Curtiz, who brought *Casablanca* to the screen.

An opera, *John the Valiant*, and various operettas, by Pongrác Kacsóh and Imre Kálmán, were composed there, too. After World War I, new management took over and created a food kitchen, which evolved into a restaurant for high society. With the specter of another war looming, the café closed and was repurposed as a warehouse. But in 1954 it got a reprieve and was reopened, again as a restaurant.

In 2001 the café was bought by the Italian Boscolo Group, which spent at least five years restoring it to its original splendor. Adorning the outside walls are sixteen bronze fauns, inviting you to the café itself. Inside, sinuous columns of marble support high ceilings and Art Nouveau lights sparkle everywhere. A gilded café, a gilded palace.

CHAPTER 15

The Ancient City of Pécs

WE WERE PROVERBIAL STORKS FLYING TO PÉCS, A CITY AS ancient as Hungary itself. Almost two thousand years ago, Rome built it and called it Sopianae. Hungarians may know Pécs as Sophiane. I'd actually seen various spellings of the city's earliest name in my research. Germans used to call the city Fünfkirchen. Everything seemed to have three different names. The most important thing to me was that Amálka and the people who signed her memory book had spent time there in 1907, when it was a bustling city of forty-three thousand.

At the top of one page in Amálka's keepsake is the phrase, "remembering the time we spent in Pécs, 1907." The number of friends and family at that gathering totaled fourteen, including János Molnár, the fiddler of the house, and Aunt Zsuzsika.

The entry shows a slice of life, an ordinary life but an aspiring life. It doesn't appear that these people were giants of their age, but had Phil and I met them, we would have enjoyed them. They were versed in the simpler pleasures of life.

The other entry from Pécs is advice from Katinka, saying that disappointment can lead to happiness. Everyone has experienced both at some point in life—losing someone and finding a new love.

. . .

Knowing we were destined for the Zsolnay Porcelain Factory, renowned for its innovative and artistic ceramic design, we made it a point not to be late in meeting Richard. None of us had anticipated the heavy traffic that Richard would encounter getting to us in downtown Budapest. Once we were on the road to Zsolnay, we understood his plight. Cars were lined up bumper-to-bumper on the highway into town as we journeyed south in the opposite direction. A distant memory of commuting from the suburbs of New Jersey to New York City during morning rush hour crossed my mind. Traffic jams are traffic jams in any zip code.

As we whipped down the M7 expressway leaving Budapest behind us, the conversation quickly turned to the Hungarian language and how the ending on a word can change its meaning. Phil's camera served as an example. Camera is *kamera* in Hungarian, and my camera becomes *kamerám*.

This is exactly the kind of knotty, intricate stuff that engages me so. Phil must have known what I was thinking because apropos of nothing, he turned around to me and said, "Hungarian is harder than you think."

I nodded, the scenery dashing behind. We were moving quickly past fields of corn, wheat, and sunflowers. Not much had changed since the early 1860s, when D. T. Ansted recounted a similar view of these fields in his book *A Short Trip*.

Min commented that she'd never seen anything like these dinner plate–sized sunflowers, and neither had I. They swayed in the breeze, soaking up the warm rays.

As we drove, it became apparent that cars, not sunflowers, were the major difference between Amálka's time and ours. We passed a man clad in a plain shirt and brown pants in a cart being pulled by a white-and-brown horse. He was collecting metals and garbage and Richard said that he might be a Gypsy.

This scene was exotic for a New York woman accustomed to dealing with hard cement, little grass, and lots of harried people juggling papers and coffee in their hands.

Soon I found myself marveling at storks in big nests at the top of telephone poles. A horse cart overflowing with hay rolled along the road beneath them. A brave woman furiously pedaled her bike past cottages and laundry on clotheslines, billowing in a gust of wind.

In Amálka's time, cycling was a novelty yet to be enjoyed by women in Hungary. Rough roads made those old bikes with a high seat and huge front wheel no pleasure to ride. But Amálka dried her clothes outdoors, as many Hungarians do today.

They had nature and so did we on this warm summer day driving to Pécs. Green fields, then trees shading us on our way to this historic city.

Before we knew it, we were pulling into a parking spot at the Zsolnay factory just six minutes before the tour started. Rushing out of the car, we darted to the entrance looking for a small group waiting for us.

A friendly woman with red hair and fair skin chatted in English and Hungarian with three other tourists. I struck up a conversation since they were motivated to get here, too.

"We're on a bit of a world adventure," said a woman with a distinctively Australian accent. She then proceeded to provide a list of travel destinations starting with Pécs, Prague, Copenhagen, Berlin, Brussels, Paris, and Beijing over six weeks.

She explained that her father was Hungarian and had been in a prison camp. I assumed it was World War II since she and her sister looked to be about ten to fifteen years older than me. He was "sent home to die, but he lived," she said. "They weren't given much to eat—soup, burnt toast, you know. The conditions killed off a few of his friends."

I was humbled.

"He came to Hungary some weeks back," she said.

I figured they had connected with him before coming to Pécs.

A young Hungarian girl from Pécs accompanied the two Australian women. They had hosted her in Australia through an exchange program.

As we stood outside the factory in a small courtyard embellished by Zsolnay tiles and sculptures, the Zsolnay guide held up a leaf.

"Does anyone know what this is?" she asked.

No one did. Our silence gave away our ignorance.

"It's a ginkgo biloba leaf, the central theme of our Autumn line," she said, handing it to me. She promised to show us some finished pieces with this motif.

Our Zsolnay guide said that Pécs's status as an important industrial center in the nineteenth century was augmented by the Zsolnay Porcelain Factory. The Zsolnay founders created a special glaze, now the hallmark of the products.

"Only three men know the whole production process, from start to finish," she said firmly.

Many people must know Coca-Cola's secret formula, likely more than three. How many knew Amálka's secrets?

"Now we see some artists," she said.

We entered the factory to see women in a row painting porcelain cups, delicately dabbing the brush on a paint palette nearby. No automation to be seen. Instead, the women employed a very old technique, requiring precision. Their hands were rock steady, as if they were making an intricate microchip that would be rendered useless with a single jagged line. The cups sat patiently on racks, like good soldiers in formation. We quietly walked past.

Our questions sprang like weeds.

"How many plates can be made in an hour?"

"Five hundred."

"What's the composite color?" one member of the group asked.

"That's a secret," the guide affirmed.

"Are you available in the US?" I asked.

"No more in the US," she said.

"Where do you get the artists?" Min enquired.

"Artists get three years of a special school before they begin working here," she said.

Phil asked how long it took to make a vase.

"Two months."

In a world where so much is machine made in minutes and seconds, this sounded like an eternity. But the end product, I thought, is worth the wait.

The hundred-year-old advice from traveler W. B. Foster Bovill in *Hungary and the Hungarians*—"If you wish for a real Hungarian souvenir, buy a piece of Zsolnay ware. It is not cheap, but its quality is unrivalled"—is valid.

I purchased a plate, flowers and nuts erupting from porcelain purity. It was hard not to buy another, but I had hit my limit. The delicate plate and my weighty tile were all I could hand-carry back home.

A little green envy ran through me, though, when I read that a Hungarian countess had given the twenty-three-year-old British adventuress H. Ellen Browning a tea set equivalent to a masterpiece of art. "The pâte itself is almost as thin and transparent as an egg-shell whilst the sprays of flowers painted on it are of the daintiest and most delicate description; and a set of dessert plates painted with peasant-scenes is a source of admiration to everyone who sees them," wrote Browning in *A Girl's Wanderings in Hungary*.

Since Browning uttered those words in the last century, political turmoil, World War I, economic crisis, World War II, and nationalization overwhelmed much of the culture of Hungary.

The factory was not exempt from the turmoil. Nationalization brought the need for large-scale industrial production, an affront to Zsolnay's artistic heritage in Art Nouveau. The factory survived with a focus on industrial porcelain but in later years was able to return to its roots.

The Sultan of Oman asked Zsolnay to re-create objects he'd seen in museums. Initially the factory's artisans were apprehensive about the request, especially because they had no documentation on the techniques used to produce those historic styles. The factory took on the challenge anyway, relying on its artists and better materials and techniques to get the job done. The final products turned out to be better than the originals. The Sultan placed another order.

Our guide said that a temporary exhibit displaying a few of the Sultan's pieces had been set up in town. I was sure the Sultan's pieces had embellishments beyond the delicate eight hundred dollar red and gold bowl Phil admired but didn't buy at the factory's shop.

As we left, I asked how many Americans visit the factory a year.

"About one hundred to two hundred," she said.

· · ·

IT WAS NEARLY NOON. BEFORE WE GOT ON OUR WAY, WE PEEKED in the window of another part of the factory filled with brightly colored stoves and fireplaces made from Zsolnay tiles and porcelain.

Driving to Kossuth Square, we parked and hopped out at a local restaurant, an appropriate choice given its Zsolnay wine fountain. The only problem was that the place was closed, so we took to the winding medieval streets, walking past worn buildings with brightly painted old doors, on our way to Jókai Square, ending up at a pizzeria.

McDonald's was an option in Pécs, too. Although the familiarity of Coke and McDonald's spoiled some of Pécs's historic aura, the city is run by its citizens and if they wanted an international cuisine, we tourists would just have to live with it.

After lunch, we walked to Széchenyi Square. Richard raced off to put change in the parking meter. As he left, he joked that if he didn't come back, we knew our way back to Budapest.

Min and I laughed, thinking about Paris, where the maps left us in a worse circumstance than if we'd relied on mere wit. This was one of those moments when Phil abandoned us to take pictures, not wanting to know the inside joke.

Richard returned to find us giddy and ready to move forward. I missed a step heading to the Inner City Parish Church, bruised my toe, and limped into the thirteenth-century structure that became a mosque when the Turks captured and occupied Pécs in the sixteenth century. By the late seventeenth century, Pécs was freed from Turkish occupation, paving the way for a re-Christianization of all the churches. Amálka had to have stood here since it is one of the town's most historic structures.

I looked at the altars, crosses, and images of Christ and Mary along the Moorish yellow and red arches. A niche painted in orange, yellow, and light blue with a low standing white marble holy water font made me pause. Arabic script decorated the wall. The brightly colored Turkish remnants overwhelmed the Christian symbols. Richard said this was a consequence of the Communists restoring the church as a museum and wanting to humiliate the church by emphasizing its non-Christian past.

We walked around, bought a booklet in English, and lit a candle. Next the Cathedral of Pécs, also known as the Cathedral of Saint Peter.

On our way, we stopped at a fence smothered in a cluster of locks.

"Do you know what this is?" Richard asked, pointing to the locks, most rusted, but others glistening like a new penny in the bright sun. In most cases, a date could be found on the lock.

"It looks like it's something to do with couples," Min said, moving her fingers over a heart on one of them.

"Warm, but not quite right. It's for new loves. Before they are married, they take an oath," Richard said. "And they put a lock here."

"We should get a lock," I declared, quickly turning to Phil. "There's a place to buy locks."

He looked to me, raising his eyebrows, but said nothing.

"You said 'I do,' " I playfully announced to our group.

"I did," he said, squeezing my hand, flashing a mischievous look. "But that doesn't mean we have to throw reason to the wind."

Richard chimed in, "Well, it's also for newly married couples."

"Okay, now come here then," I said, tugging at Phil's shirt.

"Yes, you two, let me take a picture, right by the locks," Min said, egging us on, waving us over to the locks.

We pushed on to the cathedral of Pécs, which was renovated in Amálka's time. Again, no question in my mind, she had been here. I felt warm just thinking about it.

The cathedral ranks with those in Rome. The twelve apostles, the façade, and four towers lorded over believers passing through the entrance.

This sacred place is an easy reminder that churches have been around in Pécs since Roman times. Pécs was then known as Quinque Basilicae because it had five early Christian basilicas. The name Five Churches also may have referred to the diocese around the city, and not just the city itself. This is logical when you consider that churches would have been spread over a diocese, reaching many people in rural areas surrounding the city. The Germans called the city Fünfkirchen—or, "five churches." And here was the reason that the city was labeled Fünfkirchen and not Pécs on the 1880 map from the New York Public Library.

As I passed through the church's wrought iron gate bearing grapes and leaves on twisted vines, I realized how much of Christianity stood at this door. I thought I might encounter God himself, especially when I met a statue of Jesus, his open arms reaching down to another figure hidden among the grape leaves.

The cathedral was a gift to God. Light streamed in from the glass windows over the main altar, showing the elaborate frescos. The base of the cathedral dates back to the eleventh century with the top being added in the nineteenth century.

The oldest part of the church can be found down a set of worn stone stairs. We walked quietly past reliefs to a cold basement where plain pillars supported gilded and brightly painted arches. Hardly anything lined the walls, save for what looked like an altar. The space is used for special ceremonies, baptisms or masses, and by pilgrims. We took a last look around and quietly made our way upstairs.

Historical buildings sat near the cathedral but we passed them up in favor of getting into town to see the Sultan's Zsolnay pieces. A small, white train, trimmed in gold with a car engine, the kind you see running around zoos and estates, would take us back toward the center of Pécs. We sat back and relaxed to the hum of the train and the soothing voice of the red-headed conductor happy to have us on board.

The little train jerked to a stop. We tripped out of our seats and took a short walk to Csukás mansion at 14 Perczel Street, housing some of the Zsolnay pieces made for the Sultan.

A sultan's wealth can commandeer an entire factory, something beyond my imagination. I asked Phil for some insights, hoping he might know better, even though his ancestors were Russian peasants, not Arab nobility.

"What would you do if you had the wealth of a sultan?" I asked.

"I'd try to make the people's lives better," he replied.

"But wouldn't you want to buy a hand-painted platter from Zsolnay?"

"Why not," he said, teasing. "The people need a happy sultan, too."

An elaborately decorated façade with two vases and what looked like a crest adorned the Csukás mansion. After Richard had a few words with the Hungarian woman on watch, we entered. The platters and vases decorated in gold and red were busting with brilliance.

I desperately wanted to pick one up and hold it to see its luminous colors in the light. I did not let desire overwhelm reason. Someone actually might see a chip if I inadvertently put it down the wrong way. These objects, destined for a palace, deserved to get there in one piece.

Time to go, but not before I signed our names and city in the guest book. It pleased me that we were the only New Yorkers visiting that day.

"Now we're going to get mail from them," my husband said, joking.

"What's so bad about that?" I replied.

He shook his head and resumed his photography.

Hitting the road, I scanned the patchwork of light and dark green fields and the mustard yellow and brown sunflowers through the glass. I cracked the car window slightly and a light breeze cooled my face and neck.

• • •

Since Richard had spoken so highly of Siófok on the southern shore of Lake Balaton, we changed our plans. Instead of racing back to Budapest for dinner, we'd take a detour to the Hungarian Sea. Balaton was affectionately called this in Amálka's time and mine because Hungarians lost their access to the Adriatic Sea after World War I.

Navigating the streets around Siófok, we found a parking spot near a construction site. Once on foot, we glided past hotels and faded mansions, now the property of corporations and the wealthy, heading toward the promenade. Bikini-clad teenage girls and shirtless young men carrying soda and water bottles sauntered down a path lined with restaurants, shops, and arcades. I saw a young girl playing the way I did as a child in Keansburg, New Jersey. Winning a cheap trinket was a source of huge pleasure back then.

Young couples pushed baby carts and older people moseyed along at a regulated pace. Life is good, I thought, for the people who can enjoy this lake, the largest in Central Europe. Hungarians love it and so do the Germans who would reconnect with their relatives there during the division of Germany. When it gets cold enough, there's ice skating on the lake.

We strolled to an area of the beach that was free rather than pay to get closer to the water, which we couldn't go into anyway. Teens stood two hundred feet out from the shore under the hazy sun. A windless day without a ripple in the water, it looked very much like the scene described by Gedeon Mindszenty (1829–1877) in Amálka's album.

. . .

HUNGER WAS SETTING IN. ON THE FRONT WALL OF A RESTAURANT, a comic sheepherder, his long mustache ending in curlicues, looked down on us. Next to him, a boiling pot of goulash gave us the feeling that a hearty meal was near. Plus, the word "restaurant" stood out among the Hungarian and German words.

The establishment turned out to be known for fish. Thus, we ate fish on this balmy and peaceful day on the shore of dreamy Lake Balaton. Now I know why the nobles and the rich wanted Lake Balaton for themselves.

ZSOLNAY

A málka had to have heard of the renowned factory founded by Miklós Zsolnay in 1853. It quickly evolved into a center of innovation in ceramics and art, achieving international recognition at the Paris World Exhibition in 1878. By the end of the nineteenth century, the factory met a great deal of success, having created, among other things, a metallic luster glaze first displayed at Hungary's Millennium Exhibition of 1896. Finishes identified Zsolnay products but so did styles. At the turn of the century, Zsolnay joined the emerging Art Nouveau trend. It was during this period that the façades of many of the country's most important buildings were embellished.

LAKE BALATON

Wealthy families built summer homes in the late nineteenth and early twentieth centuries around Lake Balaton. Back then it was not widely enjoyed by the general public, but as hotels sprang up over the years, so did visitors.

When the Communists came to power in the mid-twentieth century, Lake Balaton became a holiday place for everyone. For example, a cheese factory might have a villa at Lake Balaton. If one of the workers qualified in the factory manager's eyes, that employee and his family would have an opportunity to vacation at that villa in an organized holiday.

CHAPTER 16

All Aboard to Várad

We returned to Budapest from Lake Balaton in the evening. The next morning, before the train to Oradea, we squeezed in time for the Gerbeaud Café in Vörösmarty Square, its sweets, cookies, and teacakes being local favorites in Amálka's time.

We were in good company. Emperor Francis Joseph, his wife Empress Elizabeth (known as Sisi), Hungarian statesman Ferenc Deák, and composer Franz Liszt were all unable to resist the Gerbeaud. Gerbeaud was even exporting his products to the Turkish sultan. The Turks apparently had acquired a taste for Hungarian pastries.

I assumed that Amálka and her group did, too. I imagined that I would be tasting one of her favorite treats when I ordered the light apple dish in vanilla sauce and whipped cream, plus a cappuccino. It was fun to be romantic about her. After all, that's why I was here in Hungary, reliving fragments of the past and filling in the empty spaces where needed.

"It looks like it's going to be a good day for our journey to Oradea," I said.

"You like adventure, you're going to get one," Phil replied.

Before we left, we picked up a few cheese pastries for the train and went back to the hotel. Richard arrived and we moved on to the Eastern Railway Station (Keleti).

"My wife will be picking up the car there," he said.

Waiting for his wife, I asked if the station had changed much since Amálka's time.

"The train station has undergone various reconstructions over the years, especially to repair damage from World War II, but the look and feel of it is essentially the same as it was at the turn of the twentieth century."

A woman with light brown hair, fair clear skin, and a full belly waved to Richard and walked toward him. Phil, Min, and I stood nearby.

"I'm Julia," she said. "It's nice to meet you. Thank you for the gift and thinking of the baby."

Julia exchanged a few excited words with Richard. At the end of their conversation, she wrapped her arms around his neck and kissed him good-bye. He blushed.

Clearing his throat, he said, "Okay, we are ready. Let's go."

With only a backpack slung over Richard's shoulder, he proceeded to show us inside the station. After finding our track, we walked toward the train. Richard had booked a private first-class compartment for our group. He got the seats at half price. We were happy about that.

Climbing into the train, past a sliding-glass door, we plopped ourselves down on well-worn but comfortable red, velvety seats with white cloth-covered headrests, a luxury in an earlier era. I guessed that the decor dated back to the 1950s or 1960s. We hoisted our luggage onto the metal rack above the seats to make room.

Phil stared out the window at the narrow gauge of the tracks and the old cars sitting on them. "Looks like 1870s steam trains," he said, but Richard explained that the first train tracks in the country were actually vintage 1846.

The date struck me because it meant that Hungary was beginning to modernize even before the Revolution of 1848, but clearly not fast enough. Even now, the train didn't strike me as particularly modern by European or American standards, but then again, this was clearly the legacy of the Soviet occupation, which lasted forty-five years. I thought back to the little wicker seats on trains churning through suburbs of New Jersey in my youth. When they became modern, they lost all their charm. If Amálka and her folks took the train, they would have had the harvest on their minds.

On October 8, 1907, during harvest time, Amálka visited Nagyvárad with her grandmother and a number of other people whose names suggested that they were related to one another. Their free-floating signatures randomly adorning the page like confetti speak to the happiness of the day. If they were rich enough, they might have taken the railroad to participate in the harvest.

In our mechanized time, it's hard to appreciate the social significance of the harvest and how important it was to get there. In Amálka's time, it brought families and friends together, reaping corn, making wreaths, and generally having a good time. Most harvests ended with a festival with dancing and singing, which goes a long way to explain why Amálka recorded it as a special event in her life in 1907. Her family obviously stayed in Nagyvárad because a few pages later the book had another entry. Then, in 1908, although there is no mention of the month, Amálka traveled back to Várad, the Hungarian nickname for Nagyvárad, along with several of the same people who made the first visit, including her grandmother. Their names appear like kites hanging in midair in the album. A line in pencil separates the names from a watercolor of a peach and grapes at the bottom of the page. They had to be attending another harvest festival.

"So many names appear again," I remember Brigitta telling me when we had looked at this page together several months earlier. Then she looked up at me, her eyes glistening, and said, "It shows the closeness of family and friends."

My reflection stood in the window of the train, passing endless plains of wheat, corn, and sunflowers. The landscape looked like Nebraska, with cornfields bumping against the sky at the horizon; it was all very rural and looking much like it had when the first railroad came to the countryside in the mid-nineteenth century.

Soon enough, the sign for SZOLNOK came into view and the train slowed to a stop at the station. We peered through the windows at the Stalinist-style low buildings that looked abandoned, but a bike standing outside a door revealed that the buildings were in use. In the distance, a lone high-rise rose. It looked like an apartment building, boxy in style, like so much of the Soviet-era architecture we had seen elsewhere. But Szolnok was not our destination now, and soon we were chugging past nondescript car garages and open fields where horses and cows milled about, in their conventional way.

The Ady Endre Intercity speed train made eleven stops on our five-and-a-half-hour journey to Oradea. It was slow going at times, given the manual signaling and the fact that occasionally the train simply stopped for no apparent reason. The same thing probably happened to Amálka on the train from Budapest to Nagyvárad. Baedeker's *Austria*, a guide of that era, said that it took eight and a half to thirteen hours to get from Budapest to Cluj via Oradea. The mere range in the estimate showed me the uncertainties of turn-of-the-century travel.

We didn't care; we were in our own space in another century. We munched on our food, read, chatted, and had another "chipmunk" experience.

As we approached the Romanian border, we quieted down. The landscape appeared even less developed than in Szolnok, with fields of yellow and green crops stretching into the distance.

"Passports, please," Richard said, collecting them.

Two Hungarian border patrolmen in full uniform came to the door of our compartment. Richard surrendered our passports and we sat quietly while one officer fiddled with a box strapped across his shoulder. It looked like an old portable radio. It apparently had a satellite connection to a customs database.

If everything is okay, your passport gets handed back to you in a matter of minutes and you are allowed to proceed. But if there's a problem, it would come up here. Traveling between borders could take time if there were any issues with the satellite.

As one of the border patrolmen played around with the gizmo to get a satellite connection, the other one quizzed Richard. We assumed they had to be wondering why two Americans, a young Asian woman, and a Hungarian were traveling together to Oradea. I couldn't blame them for it. Most of the other passengers looked like locals. There weren't a lot of "us" in sight. I had a feeling that it wasn't unusual for travelers to feel a little alone on this journey.

Finally, after the border guards had a brief discussion with Richard and we had been fully checked out by satellite or whatever that box was connected to, one of the officers said okay and handed back our passports. We were free to move forward into Romania, where our passports got checked once again by polite but stern guards.

The train came to a complete stop. We gathered our belongings, got off in Oradea, and began looking around the platform for our Romanian guide. I didn't see any likely suspects and neither did the others, so we walked through an underpass that was odiferous even by New York City subway standards to the front of the station.

No sign of our Romanian guide.

Beggars missing teeth and shoes, and Gypsies in bright clothes grazed my shoulder. A Gypsy woman cradled a baby swathed in a colorful sling. I faced a shoeless young man with a dirty face, searing blue eyes, and filthy clothes, his pants cut off

slightly below the knees. He looked at me. I speculated as to
what he was thinking. We were another set of invaders I
suppose, but we were innocuous. I wanted to say, we're just
curious about Amálka, that's why we're here, but I knew he
wouldn't understand. Other men of modest means with tidy
clothes and clean shoes milled about. I closed my eyes for a split
second and exhaled. Amálka's keepsake is replete with advice to
do good. But in the world created by leaders like Romania's
former President Nicolae Ceauşescu (1918–1989), president of
the Socialist Republic of Romania and a tyrant, it was not
possible to avoid the bad.

Still no Romanian guide. We leaned from side to side, looking around, checking that we had everything. Phil's eyes were
trained on the distance. He and Richard were brewing a Plan B
for our group.

Then, out of nowhere, a slightly built man with a head of
gray hair appeared holding a sign for our group. The Romanian
gentleman pointed to a small black car. We slipped into the cool
air-conditioning where a young man began speaking in
Hungarian to Richard. He advised us to stay in a group while
walking around. We nodded in agreement.

With the quick turn of a corner, we arrived at the Hotel Continental Oradea and poured out of the car with our bags. Inside,
the blue couches and silver railing seemed retro by American
standards. But we were relatively confident that the accommo-
dations would be adequate since there seemed to be foreign
business people milling around in the lobby. One of the hotel's
primary features is a large thermal spa.

The attractive women at the check-in counter wore smart
blue outfits and acted very businesslike in managing customers.
Once everyone in our group had keys for their rooms, we set
about trying to find a restaurant for dinner.

The clerk at the front desk seemed the ideal person to ask for
a recommendation so Richard asked her for one.

"Our hotel restaurant," she replied stoically to our guide.

Clearly, it was her job to recommend the restaurant here, but we wanted to try some of the local food.

"Do you have a favorite restaurant?" I asked.

"Yes," she answered tight-lipped.

"Will you tell us what it is?"

"No," she replied.

I just shook my head.

"I can tell you my favorite," chimed in an enthusiastic businessman standing behind our group. "Scorilo."

The woman at the front desk ignored the conversation and returned to her work.

"Scorilo?" I asked. "Where is that?"

The man turned toward the front door and began pointing to where we should go. Richard repeated the instructions, saying, "You go out and make a left at the corner . . . and then turn right."

Realizing that we were not comprehending his gestures, the man asked, "Do you have paper? I will draw you a map."

With that he fashioned a straightforward route to our destination. As he drew, his story came out. He was born in Romania but had lived in the United States for many years working as a businessman in Detroit. Periodically, he returned to Transylvania.

"It's the best place in Oradea," the businessman said. "I go there every time I'm here."

He was nodding his head, as satisfied as if he'd just eaten a meal there himself. He handed me a simple map of sticks and dots designed for a child. We were to head north from the hotel a few meters, then take a left at the first fork and look for "Scorilo" on the left. Follow the little sticks and dots. How could we go wrong? We agreed to trust his judgment since he was so adamant about the place. Then we retired to our rooms.

Min's room was right off the elevator. Phil and I made sure she got inside. We slowly walked down a very dimly lit hallway to find our room at the end on the right. Pam hadn't taken any chances when she booked the room. She chose the best available. Upon entering, a small sitting room with a television and a large dining room table complete with a buffet sat before us. In this part of the room, a small door led to a half bathroom. Wondrously, the master bedroom had a full bathroom.

The sitting room furniture was glass and brass, something I'd had twenty years earlier when I lived in Hoboken. The dining room table was a rich dark wood, but the leg bolts protruded from the outside. Overall cozy and sufficient, albeit a little antique.

"Odd, don't you think?" I said to Phil, who was rummaging through his jacket pockets to recheck our tickets.

"It's utilitarian. Obviously the maker wasn't concerned about aesthetic details," he said, resting his backpack on the buffet as I explored the bathroom, eager to freshen up.

Above the faucets, the sign read: COLD WATER IS DRINK-ABLE. HOT WATER IS GEOTHERMAL. Geothermal? When I turned on the hot water, the dissolved gases released a faint sulfur smell into the air. I could stand washing my hands and flushing the toilet, but taking a shower would be another issue. Fortunately, I didn't have to worry about that until the next day. It was seven at night and time to head out.

When our group met in the lobby, Min mentioned that she could tell the water was different from the water back home.

We followed the route laid out by our new friend, the Romanian American businessman from Detroit. I scanned my surroundings—a loose dog, concrete buildings, a mixture of dilapidated and reasonably maintained structures, local businesses, some dirty angels decorating a window, and a Red Cross tent pitched in front of a shopping mall; across the street, a small stone building with Roman arches for windows and a much larger one for the door and vents on top of its red roof. Richard said it looked as though it was originally Hungarian. To us it would be a rags-to-riches princess with a little gentrification. An owl hooted and birds chirped. It seemed surreal and eerie in the twilight.

Gray buildings, very little grass and no flowers, just hard dirt, beaten sidewalks, and cracked walls were in my line of sight. I looked around again. So did Min, Phil, and Richard. Maybe we had missed the restaurant? The men were formulating a Plan B again.

We trudged on, dusk turning into night. Just when we thought we were lost, an arched doorway with an iron gate beaconed to us. The top of the gate bore a decorative letter "S" inside a circle. It looked like a monastery, which it really had been. Constructed in 1703, it served as a bishop's residence, then later converted to a restaurant and hotel. In our haste and hunger, we followed the music, missing the hotel's main dining rooms inside and ending up at their terrace restaurant outside. It looked a lot like an American restaurant/bar.

Our eyes brightened. An oar, a wheel, dried corn, and goulash pots decorated the walls. Two young men, one playing a keyboard and the other singing, entertained a crowd, noisily laughing and talking.

The waiter pointed us to a table across from a swamp cooler that had been connected to a man-made waterfall cascading into a small pool surrounded by plants. A fan attached to the cooler blew a mist of chilled air on the guests who sat under a tin roof. Every seat was taken.

Before we even sat down, Phil made sure we could pay by credit card—yes, was the answer—because we didn't have any of the local currency.

Romanians use lei. One US dollar is 2.5 lei, and ten US dollars is 25 lei. That may be so, I thought, but I had brought a small stack of single-dollar bills and found they were universal in their appeal.

Our wooden table was made from several tree logs. Moving the chair tested my strength. Both the table with its brown-checked cloth and the sturdy chairs befitted the outdoor decor. A television on the wall alongside our table gave us a close-up view of the musicians in the front room.

We opened the menus and scanned the varieties of foods.

"They're known for their venison specialties," Richard said, after having queried the waiter on what would be best to order. Wild boar, stag, and small pig were being contemplated when the waiter came to take our drink order.

Any conversation about Amálka had to wait as the singer belted out "Way Down South," "Just a Gigolo," and "Everything."

Food and lots of it topped the music. Bruschetta and thick, large slabs of salmon on bread overwhelmed the dainty portions doled out in upscale New York City restaurants. I ordered pheasant soup, which I'd never had before. My taste buds flashed with memories of turkey soup. Chunks of potatoes and carrots floated in the hot broth.

The men in our group ordered goose leg and goose liver and the restaurant delivered what looked like a steaming whole goose and a Titanic-sized potato in aluminum foil. Phil sat there, not sure where to begin. My selection, the steak of a roe, a small Hungarian deer, landed in front of me smothered in large grilled vegetables. Min teased me, saying that I was eating Bambi. The menu had many varieties of meat, undoubtedly the result of liberal hunting rules. We joined in the general reverie, eating with gusto. Phil ordered another beer.

We all agreed: Scorilo would be highly ranked if it were situated anywhere in the United States. In New York City we wouldn't even be able to get in.

Min and I split dessert, Somlói Galuska, a walnut cake of Hungarian origin. The men were drinking Jägermeister, a digestive aid, which Richard called a "hunter master's drink."

A young woman in a white blouse and a long embroidered skirt approached us with flowers. Now, I really felt like a time traveler. My husband performed the protocol automatically, buying two roses, one for me and the other for Min.

The meal ended. I guessed the price at a small fortune but it turned out to be quite reasonable.

A vision of Amálka and her family came to me. Even though Hungary had transitioned from a largely agrarian economy to an urban existence, the women of Szolnok, regardless of education, clung to old traditions, eating at home, tending their vegetable gardens, and feeding their chickens. If mothers were doing this, daughters were, too. This practice didn't end in Szolnok until after World War II.

For us, though, we were especially grateful to the businessman for the tip that got us to Scorilo. Our waiter, wearing an orange shirt and black pants, had been an attentive and formal young man. When we asked, he called a cab to take us back to the hotel.

Walking toward the street, I noticed a good-looking young Romanian in a tight black top and dark jeans standing at the wrought iron gate to the hotel. His eyes followed us, his lips pursed. When we walked by him, we simply said thank you in English out of courtesy and he nodded his head without expression.

Packed in the taxi, we gave the driver five euros and he didn't turn on the meter.

We got out in front of the hotel. A thin sheath of darkness and stillness enveloped us as we breathed in the summer night air. Phil and I looked around. I lowered my head, worried for Romania. The world isn't as disconnected as I once thought. When I was young, I was preoccupied with my job and other daily tasks. The world was somewhere "out there." Now a part of the world that had seen so much shifting over the centuries was beneath my feet. A young Hungarian girl was showing me the fate of Central Europe. I picked my head up, reached for Phil, and walked into the hotel following our friends.

It had been a long and busy day. Phil fell asleep right away and I didn't have the heart to wake him. I wanted to ask whether the pitiless leaders I kept running across were products of nurture or nature. Compassion had not risen with their ranks. Why? And I had questions about Amálka, too.

But there would be no answers that night. I opened the nightstand drawer next to the bed and found a copy of the hotel's guest information book *Welcome to Romania.*

The historical timeline in this book grouped the ninth through the fourteenth century as a single uneventful period in which Transylvania, Moldavia, and Wallachia were created. I looked the book over again and realized what was missing: details about the Hungarian role at the start of the eleventh century. The decision to de-emphasize certain parts of history in favor of others didn't surprise me; many countries have done this for ages. Nothing wrong with that really, but I was also happy that the *Encyclopedia Britannica* from the turn of the twentieth century had given me a broader overview of the region's complex history. In all likelihood, the encyclopedia's overview matched what Amálka would have known because it included the Hungarian experience starting with Saint Stephen in the eleventh century through World War I.

In 1914, Hungary aligned with Germany and became part of the losing side in World War I. In retribution, the victors in the Peace Treaty of Trianon in 1920, stripped Hungary of Transylvania, home to millions of Hungarians. Hungary's virtual death at Trianon led to the flags in the nation being hung at half mast. Hungary regained Transylvania for a short time during World War II, but it reverted back to Romania at the end of that war. That was over fifty years ago. I had a feeling that these ethnic issues continued to fester.

I picked up the phone.

"Do you sell the information guidebook in the room to guests?" I asked.

"Yes, at the front desk."

"Please hold one for me," I said.

I turned out the light.

GERBEAUD CAFÉ

Founded in 1858 by Henrik Kugler, the café's name actually comes from its second owner, Emil Gerbeaud, who took it over in 1884. Just before the start of Amálka's memory book, the Gerbeaud employed one hundred fifty people.

World War I and Gerbeaud's death in 1919, the year that Amálka's album ends, signaled troubled times ahead. The death of Gerbeaud's wife in 1940 led the family to sell the café at auction. It went through various management changes and identities over the intervening decades. Then in the late twentieth century plans emerged to revive the glory of the Gerbeaud Café, so synonymous with the good life in Budapest. By 1984, the Gerbeaud name was back on the building. Today the café carries on a nineteenth-century Budapest tradition, when nearly every street had a large and excellent coffeehouse.

ELIZABETH, EMPRESS OF AUSTRIA, QUEEN OF HUNGARY

Elizabeth Amélie Eugénie, a Bavarian duchess (1837–1898), married her cousin, Francis Joseph, becoming Empress of Austria.

She served as Hungary's emissary to the Habsburgs, facilitating the Compromise of 1867. Elizabeth assumed the throne of Queen of Hungary upon the coronation of her husband. Beloved by the Hungarians, she mastered their language.

Elizabeth was a renowned beauty but eccentric. She had long brown hair down to her ankles that took hours to be groomed and styled into braided masterpieces. Smart and multilingual, Elizabeth was also entitled, rebellious, fiercely independent, and trapped by her fame. She got an anchor tattooed in the most discreet spot she could think of—her shoulder. On top of everything, she was a world-class equestrian and adventurer. She liked to travel but her unprotected roaming would tempt fate.

Many people warned Elizabeth to allow the monarchy's security apparatus to fully protect her. Oddly, the last English language book she read was none other than *Corleone* by F. Marion Crawford, according to Edward De Burgh in *Elizabeth, Empress of Austria: A Memoir* (1899). De Burgh wrote that her English reader Mr. Barker chose this Mafia story "to make the Empress familiar with the murderous machinations of blood-thirsty wretches, hoping it might lead to her taking more care of her personal safety."

Sisi's free spirit would not be tamed. On Saturday, September 10, 1898, while walking near the Hotel Beau Rivage in Geneva with her Hungarian lady-in-waiting and a footman trailing her in the distance, an anarchist stabbed her in the heart.

All of Hungary mourned. Sisi was as close to a patron saint as one could have been back then.

Mark Twain, living in Austria at the time, commented on Elizabeth's demise in *What Is Man? And Other Essays* (1919).

"And whether with a crown upon her head or without it and nameless, a grace to the human race, and almost a justification of its creation."

KELETI

The Keleti station was completed in 1884. Amálka's relatives surely knew of its construction because trains were a major advance from horses and carts. The train must have seemed like a rocket ship to them—traveling fifty or so miles in two hours, versus fifty miles a day in a country cart. By 1906, the starting year of Amálka's book, railway travel in Hungary had exploded, jumping to 96 million passengers from 13.45 million in 1887, according to Percy Alden's *Hungary of To-Day* (1909).

SZOLNOK

Looking at the countryside cast me back to the mid-nineteenth century, imagining how Amálka's town must have looked. British diplomat A. A. Paton, after arriving by train in that era, called Szolnok a simple village of twelve thousand people, good-natured and honest in dealing. Szolnok was rural and undeveloped, cottages and farms widely dispersed.

"The ploughs here are of the rudest description, and are all of wood," Paton wrote in *Researches on the Danube and the Adriatic; or, Contributions to the Modern History of Hungary and Transylvania, Dalmatia and Croatia, Servia and Bulgaria* (1861).

"[I]n Szolnok, where there are no Germans or Slovacks, you might imagine yourself to be in a village of Central Asia . . . nothing being visible but filth and barbarism. Here and there a few logs of wood are thrown lengthways in the streets to prevent one from getting over the ankles in mud."

By the 1890s, the town had made remarkable progress, developing into an economic center, with a strong agricultural base, banks, shops, and other businesses. The population had soared to eighteen thousand people and the railroad stood at the intersection of seven tracks, making the town a very important commercial center.

During World War I, Szolnok became a battlefield for seventy-seven days and was reduced to rubble. The town revived only to face annihilation in the next war; its train station, too, was destroyed a second time. In 1944 the estimated population was four thousand people. Today, Szolnok is a bustling city with eighty-one thousand people calling it home.

CEAUŞESCU

While America was migrating from *Green Acres* to Madonna, the Romanians were being tortured and spied on by one another and the government of Nicolae Ceauşescu. It was the terror of George Orwell's *1984* in true life.

In a fascinating twist of fate, given the turbulent and fractious history of Romania and Hungary, the Hungarian priest Reverend László Tőkés in the historic, Baroque town of Timişoara (Temesvár to

Hungarians), helped spark Ceauşescu's demise.

When things started to heat up, both Romanians and Hungarians formed a human chain to protect Tőkés, placing their lives and their families at risk. The ac-

tions swelled like a rising tide, overtaking the Romanian capital of Bucharest, and the rest is history. Ceauşescu and his wife were executed by firing squad on Christmas Day 1989.

CHAPTER 17

Várad Shower

WE SPENT A PEACEFUL NIGHT AT THE HOTEL. IN THE MORNING,
I walked into the bathroom and read the sign again: "Cold water
is drinkable. Hot water is geothermal."

As we had learned at check-in, the hotel sat on an underground spring of geothermal water. The spring supplies the hotel
with hot water that also flows into the swimming pool, where
people can enjoy the water's healing properties. It saved on
electricity to get hot water this way and I imagined that electricity
was in short supply because the hallway was very dimly lit.

But the smell . . . I just didn't know if I could deal with it in a
shower. With little time to get ready, I had no choice but to
plunge into the process. First turn the water on. I tried the
handle once, twice, three times. Then I picked up the phone.

"I knew you were going to call," Min said as soon as she
heard my voice.

"I can't turn the water on. I'm going to try again, but if I can't
get it on, can I come down to take a shower in your room?"
I asked.

"Sure," she said.

"The smell, though, I don't know if I can take a shower in it."

"I think it's the drain," Min said.

"Okay, maybe it is. Let me wake Phil up. I'll call you back if I'm still stuck."

He was dead asleep.

"Honey, you have to get up. I have a problem," I said in a low voice. He reluctantly opened one eye.

I wasn't going to move until he got up and he knew it.

He rose from a comfortable bed with his eyes half closed and walked like a zombie toward the bathroom.

"What is it?" he asked.

"I can't turn on the shower. You have to help me and I don't know if I can take a shower if the water smells funny."

"It's just sulfur dioxide," he said, gaining some consciousness. He was twisting and twisting the silver dial, but nothing. I was just about to call Min when he got it to turn.

"Okay, it's on. So get in there. You'll be just fine," he said, beelining back to the bed.

I stood there frozen, the smell overwhelming me. I took a few deep breaths. Feeling abandoned by Phil, now nestled back in bed, I prepared alone for my water assault. Finally, with steam gathering, I stepped in. At first it was difficult to take the smell, but after a while I started to get used to it, and then, believe it or not, I didn't mind it. Strangely, I no longer smelled the odor and I began to enjoy the rushing hot water. I hung in there as long as I would at home. Maybe that wasn't such a good idea. When I stepped out, water was everywhere. We had extra towels and two robes to soak it up. Phil said this happened because I didn't pull the shower curtain over, but I did. I thought it had to do with the tub itself. It had a plastic-like exterior and was loosely set on a concrete base, not like the neat little porcelain tubs we have in the United States—and it moved when I did.

I dried off quickly.

Phil showered with no problem and dried himself with the only thing left, a hand towel. He just shook his head at me as we left for breakfast. We launched into everything from the eggs and cold cuts to the fresh cheese and yogurt.

After breakfast we gathered in the lobby to meet our Romanian guide and driver. Richard mentioned again about the shortage of English-speaking guides in Transylvania, and that our Romanian guide would speak Hungarian, which he would translate into English for us. If our Romanian driver had anything to share, the guide could translate that into Hungarian so that Richard could give us the story. This seemed almost easy, given the multitude of tongues spoken here in Amálka's time— Magyar, Greek, French, German, Slovenian, Serbian, Turkish, Russian, and Croatian. Imagine if we had to deal with that?

We had wanted a taste of Amálka's era, the former multilingual, multicultural Austro-Hungarian Monarchy. No complaints from me.

CHAPTER 18

Kopjafa, The Carved Biography

"IF YOU WANT TO SEE HUNGARY AND THE HUNGARIANS, BEGIN where I did, away in the Carpathians." And with that good advice from British author W. B. Forster Bovill in *Hungary and the Hungarians*, we drove toward the Transylvanian mountain range to the east of Hungary. It juts high above the plain and like the Tatra, its little brother to the northwest, gathers snow in the winter on its peaks.

I'd like to tell you that I had everything mapped out for our first day in Transylvania, but I'd be lying. I had no idea. The genteel old man who kissed my hand and Min's when we met him, however, did know. He was our Romanian guide and for the next two days, I called him Mr. D.

He shook Richard's hand and my husband's, too. His shiny, distant blue eyes made me curious about what he had seen during Ceaușescu's regime. I didn't ask.

We stepped into a Romanian minivan that could hold fourteen people. We wouldn't have to fight for a seat here. It was just us, three tourists, two guides, and a driver, on this tour.

Transylvania consisted of 21,000 square miles in the 1900s.

Then, and even now, according to our Romanian guide, it was called "the land behind the forest." Transylvania had a certain magical connotation. I could almost see Mr. D as a Romanian Merlin waving a wand, calling us farther along the Amálka trail.

We would make three major stops on our trip: the King's Pass, or Királyhágó in Hungarian, which had a special historical connection to King Matthias Corvinus; a Protestant Church in Kalotaszeg that dates back to the thirteenth century, and a visit to Cluj-Napoca, Cluj for short (Hungarians call it Kolozsvár, in reverence for the empire now gone). Cluj was backed by a semicircle of the eastern Carpathians and the Transylvanian Alps.

Mr. D loaded us up on historical details, but you'd be much less confused if I just skip to 1859, when Moldavia and Walachia rid themselves of the Turks. Those two regions came together to form Romania in 1862.

I was interested in Transylvania's history, however, because of Amálka. Mr. D had a story to tell.

The Austrians beat the Turks in the seventeenth century, reuniting Transylvania with Hungary. Mr. D emphasized the Peace of Karlowitz in 1699, which formally acknowledged that Transylvania would be ruled by Austria's King Leopold I wearing the Hungarian crown. The Turks were gone but life wasn't much better. Transylvania's assembly had been directed from Vienna since 1690, but Transylvanians never got the freedom that they wanted.

The Austrians reneged on a promise to give the Transylvanians religious freedom. The Transylvanians, the majority of whom were Protestant, identified religious freedom with political freedom.

That, plus other political abuses, led to a revolt spearheaded by Transylvanian Duke Ferenc Rákóczi II at the beginning of the 1700s, when Joseph I reigned as Emperor. The Austrians crushed the rebellion but the Hungarians negotiated their way to religious freedom anyway.

In the eighteenth century, Transylvania was a grand principality of Hungary under the enlightened Austrian despot, Empress Maria Theresa, explained Mr. D.

By the nineteenth century, the Romanians of Transylvania sought autonomy and fought against Hungarian oppression in the Revolution of 1848. This war was characterized by an exceptional level of brutality and inhumanity on all sides.

While frowning, Mr. D explained that Austria asserted its prowess, with Russia's help, and it was all over for Hungary and Transylvania. Hungary melded into the Austrian Empire. Transylvania separated from Hungary after the revolution, then formally, though unhappily, reunited with Hungary by the late-nineteenth century. After World War I, Transylvania was permanently attached to Romania. We were traveling into the region's heart and one of its most historic cities, Cluj.

W. B. Forster Bovill promised in *Hungary and the Hungarians* that by the turn of the twentieth century, "the American would find Kolozsvár more interesting than any other town in Hungary" with people in native costume and historic houses. We knew we weren't going to see any native costumes, but historic houses were on the list.

Amid all the historical chatter, I wanted to look out the window. A Gypsy family in a horse-drawn cart trotted down the highway as cars whizzed past. It was reminiscent of Amish country in Pennsylvania, although far less romantic. Fair or unfair, Gypsies in this part of the world have long had a poor reputation.

Surely Amálka and her friends passed a few Gypsies on the way to Cluj, which she likely called Kolozsvár, or the German Klausenburg, in her time. Many Hungarians spoke German, not only because it was the language of Austria but because the offspring of the original twelfth-century German immigrants, the Saxons, had grown to about a quarter of a million people by 1900. A number of other groups inhabited Transylvania during that period. The Seklers and Hungarians, along with the Saxons, dominated the political process, but they were outnumbered by the Romanians, known as Wallachians, the Armenians, Jews, Slovaks, Ruthenians, Bulgarians, Serbians, and Greeks.

Overwhelmed by history, we asked about something recognizable, the work ethic of the Romanians. Mr. D said that when the country was Communist, work ethic varied from person to person. Some worked hard, others didn't. That sounded like the United States to me. But unlike the United States, Romania based its production on central planning, not market demand. To Americans this would be a critical flaw but, as it turns out, other issues can make this type of system unsuccessful.

"The idea of Communism was to share, to give for free. But if so, the people won't pay for anything and the country goes bankrupt," said our democratically-minded Hungarian guide Richard. "It goes against human nature and then it doesn't work."

Richard had inherited Eötvös's capacity for politics. Frederick Riedl, author of *A History of Hungarian Literature* (1906), noted that Eötvös' opinion was that equality, in its extreme, ends up as Communism, and that Communism is "a form of despotism exercised in the name of the people."

The logic of it was irrefutable to me—Why work hard to make money to pay for something when you are expecting it for free?

Communism didn't leave the Romanians richer. A little less than one quarter of the population lives below the poverty level, which was evident by the look of some of the places we passed. A pervasive drabness often blanketed the scene from the road. It wasn't one specific building, person, or street.

As I looked out the window, I heard Mr. D say that twenty-two million people live in Romania. That's about the number of Texans, but unlike Texas, which conjures up visions of tall, lanky cowboys, Romania has an ethnically mixed population, with the largest minorities being Hungarians, followed by Gypsies, Ukrainians, and Germans.

Mr. D said that Hungarians account for 7 percent of the Romanian population, or roughly 1.5 million people. However, these numbers are declining due to intermarriage with Romanians and migration to Hungary and other countries. In addition, forced in-migration under Ceauşescu diluted the influence of the traditional Romanian and Hungarian populations in Transylvania.

Mr. D's enthusiastic explanations continued and with a twinkle in his eye he returned to his favorite subject, history. We passed Aleşd, the site of a peasant uprising against their landlord in 1904, marked by a memorial. I took it all in as we whisked our way through the Sebes-Körös valley.

Soon enough we saw churches and a few old mansions that had belonged to Hungarian counts. Thinking about how impressive these places must have been helped me understand the peasant revolt. The mansions were in disrepair, and the only thing of note, aside from the cars scooting by, happened to be some chickens milling around gates along the road and an old woman dragging bales of hay in a field.

We reached the King's Pass, about two thousand feet in altitude. We parked at a viewpoint in front of a grove of green trees in a pasture and a flock of sheep grazing comfortably not a hundred yards in front of us—as they must have done for centuries.

Looking at the mountain ridge that once divided Hungary and Transylvania, Mr. D reminisced as if he had been there when King Matthias's army crossed those mountains. In Mr. D's mind, Caesar's troops crossing the Rubicon on the way to Rome had nothing on Matthias's army marching across this ridge to assault the Turks. Richard later clarified that the clash to which Mr. D was referring occurred at Kenyérmező, and was one of the greatest medieval victories for the Europeans against the Turks in the fifteenth century.

Here the mountains reign. Standing quietly, gazing out into the distance, the granite peaks slicing into the sky, I was vaulted back to Matthias's time. I could almost feel the ground shaking as the troops stomped off to their destiny. Even the haze of the slightly overcast day could not cast a pall over the mesmerizing view. Mr. D just looked at the mountains.

We took a few pictures for posterity and asked questions, then got back into the van. Mr. D chatted away in Hungarian with Richard, promising to point out sites he thought were unusual. He found one right away: a wooden Orthodox church built in 1791 and no longer in use, opposite a new church, the Orthodox Church of Bucea, built in the 1970s during Communist rule.

We passed Feketetó, the site of a market since 1815. Mr. D said that people used to come to shop for the whole year. It must have been a lively scene then, but now the open space was occupied by chicks and ducks. I wasn't that interested in ducks.

It got better though. In nearby Gaina, toward the eastern Carpathians, a "bride fair" was held on the third weekend in July, at the peak of Mount Gaina.

In the early days of Romania, this area was known for shepherding, a solitary activity that afforded little opportunity for fraternizing with the opposite sex. Necessity is the mother of invention, so the locals created a fair to give young people a chance to meet and marry. Mr. D especially liked telling this story.

"Since the courtship probably had to be done quickly, girls who wanted to marry carried a box with stuff, a sort of dowry," Richard said, translating a highly animated Mr. D. "Then if the couple liked each other, they would just marry and go home together. It had to be a busy time for the priest!"

By the end of the nineteenth century, the girls and their suitors already knew that they would be betrothed, and the fair served as a public ritual celebrating and making official the marriages. The girls and their families, along with the best horses, biggest oxen, sheep, calves, poultry, and even beehives, made a caravan to Mount Gaina. This gave the brides' families a chance to show that they were "keeping up with the Joneses." The young men came with their families, too, each wearing a belt big enough to hold gold and silver.

We playfully looked for any straggling brides, and when we didn't find any, Mr. D assured us the tradition lives on, but that doesn't mean they choose the bride there.

Talking made the time fly by and before we knew it, we had arrived in the Țara Călatei region (Kalotaszeg for Hungarians), where the Gypsy in Budapest could have gotten the linens with the distinctive red embroidery in traditional Hungarian patterns that I had wanted to buy. The center of the region is Huedin (Bánffyhunyad to Hungarians) and our destination was a Protestant church.

Looking out the van's window, we noticed a number of garish Chinese palaces, half finished, lining the side of the road. Each one was larger than the last. Among the biggest was a four-story mega mansion with two bright orange columns down its center. The rest of the house was a mixture of yellow and orange with white trim. Oriental silver spires and what looked almost like a gigantic, antique silver comb in the center topped this mammoth structure. Three men appeared to be working on the building although they didn't seem to have many supplies.

"It belongs in Fantasyland," Phil said.

Mr. D knew the story of these homes. The owners, gypsies, were given money by charities to build a church, but instead of building the church, they built houses for themselves.

The houses were a good demonstration of old Gypsy proverbs. "Never despair of your luck, for it needs only a moment to bring it," and "Who has got luck need only sit at home with his mouth open," observed Scottish writer Emily Gerard when she traveled through Transylvania in the spring of 1883 with her husband, an officer in the Austrian army. She detailed her adventures in *Land Beyond the Forest: Facts, Figures and Fancies from Transylvania* (1888).

The gypsies couldn't believe their good fortune, but then they got competitive. Everyone was trying to outdo each other, which explains the size of the houses. As soon as the donors realized what had happened, they cut off the money. So the houses sat half built, our guides said.

"They could have built the church and the houses with the money if they were smaller," Phil said, as we whizzed by.

. . .

LIGHT RAIN GREETED US WHEN WE REACHED THE CHURCH IN Huedin located behind King's Pass. Once it had been known as Saint Elizabeth, but it later became a Protestant church.

A middle-aged man with brown hair and a thick mustache, dressed in light blue pants and a white shirt, hurried down the rock path to meet us. His light brown sandals over dark blue socks made me think he was German. He grinned, obviously very happy to see us.

In the introductions, we learned of his multiple roles: Hungarian church pastor, historian, and local guide. Richard was going to translate for us again as the priest was the only person in the group who really knew anything about the church.

Min looked up at the church's brown tower and I looked down at my note pad, scribbling as fast as I could. "The oldest part was built in 1255 . . . a tower was standing here in 1411, it was a bastion, and in the late 1400s the tower and the church were connected," Richard said, interpreting for the priest.

"In the mid-seventeenth century, there was the worst destruction. The Tatars and the Turks attacked here. Two thousand locals were killed and the church was destroyed," came the English translation.

We also noticed a joined pair of totem poles with emblems carved in the wood. They stood on the top of a low earthen mound.

"It's a *kopjafa*, which consists of the biography of the dead person in ancient Hungarian symbols," the priest said. The "biography" would have included their age, sex, job, social class, and information on how the person died. It's an obituary carved in wood from a time before the printing press.

We stepped into the church and stood on its uneven wooden floor. We thought there could be a crypt underneath but the priest assured us none existed. He seemed to be unaware of the painter Adrian Stokes's reporting that a crypt had been unearthed in a church that bore a resemblance to this one. I couldn't fault the priest for not knowing this obscure detail that I dug up from my research.

Three wooden chandeliers showered light on the white plaster walls decorated with red wool weavings in symbols of the sun for man and the moon for woman. An abundance of tulips and other flowers, fertility symbols, and snakes represented protection. I recognized the tree of life in the patterns. The simple wooden pews offset the colorful embroidery.

These symbols encapsulate Transylvania's deep and complex history. Well beyond folk art, they constitute pagan symbols altered and adopted by the church in the eleventh century, when Hungary converted to Christianity. That's how the snake, the sun, the moon, male and female genitalia became flowers, tulips, hearts, and wheat. The locals who embroider these complex patterns usually can't interpret them even if they know the order in which to employ them.

Tulips often adorned Transylvanian homes. People carved or painted them on wooden chests and door posts as well as embroidered onto pillows and other bedding. Adrian Stokes recounted his visit to the area in *Hungary*, writing that no one seemed aware of their religious significance; they simply thought of them as "charming patterns, peculiar to the district." Nevertheless, the travelers sensed that tulips and other symbols were deeply woven into the Magyar tradition, just as they concluded that the church's wooden ceiling paintings were done by Magyars.

Now it was our turn to see the wooden ceiling. The priest pointed out two types of painted wooden panels. On one end of the church ceiling were stylized Renaissance flowers in black, white, and pink, a faded red. A painter from Segesvár, a city now called Sighişoara, in Romania, probably did this work in 1705.

At the other end of the church, the wooden ceiling panels had an entirely different motif, a combination of astrological and Oriental styles dating from about 1780. I could see some of Amálka's drawings of winding flowers and twisting vines in a few of these works.

Heading outside, the priest said that he'd like to give us the community's cultural newsletter. The Dutch had given him a printing press so he edited, laid out, and printed twenty-five hundred copies of it. He would have printed more, he said, but lacked enough money for paper.

The priest also mentioned that his wife had written a book about the symbols. Richard bought a copy. I might have too if it hadn't been in Hungarian.

On the way, we passed the kopjafa again. Red, white, and green ribbons, the colors of Hungary, had been tied near the top. The kopjafa had two branches, one taller than the other. The tall piece was topped with a closed flower and the shorter one was topped with an open flower, signifying death and life, respectively.

Looking around one last time, I thought about how far away we were from home. I glanced down a side street at two old women, one dressed entirely in black, talking to a friend near what was likely a medieval stone house. Pennants in red, yellow, and blue, the colors of the Romanian flag, were strung across the street. In the distance, Romanian and European flags hung proudly on small poles over arched doorways. Romania and Bulgaria joined the European Union in 2007. Over the street and into the distance, telephone wires looped from pole to pole as they might have in an American city in the 1950s.

Soon it was time to go. We got back into the van and a short distance later we stopped at Izvoru Crişului (Körösfő to Hungarians). Little did we know about its tradition of cottage industries for homemade goods like baskets, pottery, embroideries on linens, and carvings, selling to tourists passing through the area. Amálka must have seen them. She was a local.

The shops continued in the old tradition, and many seemed to be part of people's houses. Handmade baskets, clothes, and embroidered linens dangled near the entranceways. Simple, loose-fitting, white cotton blouses accented with red or blue stitching stood for sale. The shopkeepers had slung rugs across the railings and hand-carved wood horses and other animals sat on small shelves. Wooden walking sticks were gathered in a tall porcelain vase.

I ran my hands over the linen and felt the delicate nature of the embroidery. I couldn't believe that such refinements came from human hands. I struggle sewing a button. But I could see the women in the shops embroidering in the finest needlepoint as customers milled about.

We asked one woman about the elaborately embroidered handmade table runners with traditional flower motifs of gold- and silver-colored threads. We offered twenty dollars for two. Without much discussion, she agreed.

Our shopping continued. The hats made out of mushrooms didn't appeal to me but I did buy a handbag from the woman solely because she was so genuine, showing us her baskets, dresses, hats, and slippers and letting me play with Dixie, her black puli, a sheepdog with characteristically long corkscrew curls.

"People tell me Dixie could be in the movies," she said in very good English.

I don't know how many movies they're casting for dogs in Transylvania, but Dixie, with her pearly white teeth and perky personality, would be my choice.

To Phil's astonishment, we had a light load as we entered the van, having picked up only a few things. The temptation was to buy. Everything was handmade and very reasonable. But how to get it all back unless I asked Phil to leave behind most of what he had in his luggage, since I was easily over quota with mine? That was a good idea, I thought. Then again, maybe it wasn't.

The road took us past the Maros River with storks flying overhead. Mr. D pointed to Borsa, a village with a pyrite mine. I want to believe that Amálka would have admired my tenacity in getting to know Transylvania.

Rested after the shopping trip, Mr. D launched into an abridged history of Cluj for his American neophytes.

Mr. D began his tale with the Romans forming a settlement called Napoca, which is where the city gets the second part of its name. He said the first writing from Cluj dates from the twelfth century.

It's very likely that my heroine, Amálka, knew the origin of the people and the city because it was an important center for learning and artistry. Its history would have been common knowledge to educated people.

Close to our destination, I looked at a father and his three sons in a cart being pulled along by a lumbering white workhorse on the shoulder of the road. This part of the road included 1970s-era housing: Uniform and standard, none stood out, similar to the way the whole of the people, rather than individuals, was supposed to be the focus in a Communist society.

Communist governments began to collapse in Eastern Europe in 1989, with the fall of the Berlin Wall, and so did their economies. Housing and employment became critical issues for Romanians and Hungarians. The old curse of ultra-nationalism flared across the region, a fire stoked by Gheorge Funar, Cluj's mayor from 1992 to 2004. By the 1990s, though, freedom and private enterprise began taking hold in Transylvania, leading to significant development across Romania, Mr. D said.

Today, the population in Cluj exceeds 318,000 people, making it one of the largest cities in Romania. Romanians dominate and ethnic Hungarians are in the minority. It has evolved since the turn of the twentieth century, when it was populated by 47,000 principally Hungarian residents.

Cluj was a cosmopolitan place beginning in the 1890s. "The streets are fine and broad," said writer Louis Felbermann of his visit to the area at the turn of the twentieth century in *Hungary and Its People.*

Writing in *Hungary,* Stokes concurred. "It is a pleasant, friendly place, with many good houses, the aristocracy of the province assembling there, in the winter months, rather than in Budapest. Most of the people one meets are dressed like those in London or Paris, and quite in the latest mode. In contrast to these, are to be seen surprising groups of peasants and Gipsies, who appear to have been left by the Middle Ages, or to have stepped out of pictures by Breughel."

Remnants of Austro-Hungarian architecture, painted in imperial yellow, remain in Cluj. A street-widening project on Boulevard Eroilor reflected the city's progress.

The Romanian driver parked in Piața Unirii square and we hurried out of the van into the busy streets. The first course of action was lunch. Mr. D ferried us to a restaurant in a turn-of-the-twentieth-century building, white and freshly painted, with small balconies. He had eaten there before and liked it but didn't realize it would be closed.

Nonplussed, he guided us to a hotel about a block away. We jogged up a narrow, winding set of stairs into a dining area, passing a concrete fountain in the shape of a small lighted cave with water flowing smoothly between stalagmites. Overstuffed, brown leather chairs with wood frames flanked each side of the fountain against the wall. The room was decorated with potted plants and fake trees at strategic intervals. A picture of the Empire State Building hung on a wall. A television with European

MTV blasted loudly.

"Must be what they think of New York," Phil remarked.

"Guess so," I said.

A sturdy woman with gray hair and a hint of purple stood near two men who sat smoking cigarettes at a table for six.

Mr. D approached her to ask for a table and a heated discussion ensued. It became clear to us, even without knowing the language, that something was bothering her. Did she dislike Transylvanian Hungarians? Our Romanian guide was an easy target: A quiet, old man who had most likely spent decades of oppression under the Ceaușescu rule. He looked visibly shaken.

Richard turned to us.

"He's afraid of the situation," he said, referring to Mr. D.

Richard took over when the woman approached us, and even though she knew he was Hungarian, she spoke normally. Then she left us.

In the meantime, an argument broke out between the woman and one of the men at the table. Soon she stomped out, the television was turned off, the cigarettes were stubbed out, and we sat down at a table, a little shell-shocked.

Ultimately a nondescript waiter sauntered up to our table and handed us menus as if nothing had happened. The service was slow, but we got a few things to eat. We had traditional pork sour broth on Richard's recommendation, along with mixed grill, veal scaloppini, and grilled chicken breast. Mr. D sat with us but had nothing to eat or drink. Richard explained that he takes his meals with his family, but I suspected that I wouldn't have been hungry anymore if I'd understood exactly what had been said earlier. All in all, the experience was odd and disquieting.

Maybe it was the kind of weird thing that is set off for no reason whatsoever other than the person having a bad day. Maybe they were annoyed that we interrupted their break, or that we were a mixed group of three Americans, one Hungarian, one Romanian of Hungarian descent (Mr. D), and one Roma-

nian (the driver). But that's what happened that day.
We ate quickly, skipped dessert, and Phil paid the bill.

TRANSYLVANIA

The name Transylvania comes out of the Middle Ages, a time when the region was known as Silvana Regio. Ultimately that evolved into Ultra Silvana or Trans Sylvana, which means "beyond the woods" in Latin.

The Hungarians called it Erdély, "forest land," and the Romanians used the name Ardeal. Transylvania also went by its German name, Siebenbürgen, or "land of the seven fortresses."

These seven German fortresses, or burgs, helped the people withstand the many invasions of the region. Cluj, or Klausenburg, was one of the fortresses. Cluj, or Clus, is derived from clusum in Latin, meaning to close or enclose. Walls once surrounded Cluj's inner town, making it a closed city.

KOLOZSVÁR

Battles have raged over Kolozsvár. The Roman town was destroyed in successive centuries as warring tribes fought for the land. The Magyars built their settlement on top of the Roman encampment around 896, Mr. D said. I could see that he was in familiar territory again, impassioned by the past.

In 1061, the Benedictine monastery of Kolozsvár was founded kolozs meaning leader, and vár meaning castle, according to Mr. D, explaining the etymology of the city's Hungarian name.

In a strategic move, the twelfth-century Hungarian King Géza II

(1141–1162) invited the Saxons to live on and defend the land. They called Kolozsvár by its German name, Klausenburg, taken from klause, an old term for a mountain pass. It was very likely given this name because the Carpathian Mountains are so close to the city.

Many of the Germans who were invited had become familiar with the area from their travels during the Crusades. Additional Germans arrived on the land under King András II (1205–1235) in the thirteenth century. They were needed because the Mongolians, or Tatars, intended to destroy Europe.

The Mongolian commander in charge of the invasion of Eastern Europe was Ghengis Khan's grandson Batu. At the urging of Russian Prince Dmitry, whose life had been spared during the Mongolians murderous campaign in Kiev in late 1240, Batu turned his sights to a richer prize: Hungary. He plundered the country, and stopped to return to Mongolia only upon the death of the Great Khan. Historians estimate that in the two years the Mongols attacked Hungary around half of the population was put to death.

CHAPTER 19

Earthquake, Fire, and Flood

AFTER LUNCH, MIN SAID SHE HAD GOTTEN A FEW LONG STARES. We tended to agree with her. We hadn't seen anyone who couldn't pass for Romanian or Hungarian since we entered Cluj. The only apparent foreigners were a Spanish couple who had been on the train with us to Oradea. They must have been European tourists on a short stay, since they didn't have a lot of luggage with them. The one thing we could reasonably conclude was that the region was not strongly multicultural, even though it had an extremely varied history and had been a cultural oasis in Amálka's time.

Heading to the town center, we got a clearer notion of the Romanian nationalist movement that had recently taken root in the region.

On one end stood the commanding bronze statue of Mathias Rex (King Matthias) on horseback, a symbol of his fearlessness against his foes, and on the other end the antithesis: a small fence surrounded by a pitiful archeological dig with a few old stone pillars. Mr. D said that Funar had commissioned the dig to show that the small hill was an archeological site containing Roman ruins, which would support his claim that the statue should be removed. Phil asked about the pieces, noting that they were strewn oddly in the pit. Mr. D said that most people thought they were brought in from somewhere else. We went on.

Mr. D continued to regale us with tales to help explain Transylvania's sense of autonomy, especially when it was a dukedom in the sixteenth century. It was independent enough to have its own mint, producing gold forint coins with portraits of Transylvanian dukes that were recognized as legal currency by France, Poland, and the Sultan. Transylvania was trapped between the Turks and Austrians in this period.

Our next stop was the thirteenth-century Franciscan Church of Cluj, originally Romanesque, then Gothic, and finally Baroque. The Madonna, Saint Stephen, and Saint László are represented inside the church. Over the altar the Hungarian words Istenem A Mindenem! proclaimed "MY GOD IS EVERYTHING TO ME."

A young woman in a plain white blouse with shoulder-length brown hair in a ponytail was on her knees. Would Amálka have looked like that? Would I have even noticed her? She must have gone to church. Everybody went to church back then. Religion played a paramount role in Amálka's culture where the church and state intermingled on many levels, including education.

We left the church and made our way toward the city's thirteenth-century medieval center. Eyes either followed us or ignored us.

Next we walked on, seeing an obelisk constructed in 1817 to honor the visit by Austrian Emperor Francis I and his wife. It's a granite "notebook" of sorts to commemorate the event. The town's coat of arms, the arrival of important dignitaries, and the places they visited are carved into the obelisk. Who knows, maybe one of Amálka's family members or friends stood before this obelisk, too.

• • •

We walked along the cobblestone streets to the birthplace of King Matthias, as legendary in Hungary and Romania as Abraham Lincoln is in the United States.

Matthias was born in a simple two-story with a stucco edifice. Its arched wooden doorway and wrought-iron decorations mark the plain beginnings of this illustrious king. If Amálka got here, it would have been in a deep ochre tint, just as British author Margaret Fletcher described it in her travels. Today the building is white and serves as an institution for visual arts, which seems fitting for Matthias's birthplace, given his interest in all things refined.

Fletcher visited the region in June 1891 and said that a tablet marked Matthias's birthplace. Emperor Francis Joseph bestowed this tablet to the city as a gesture of goodwill. It's there, pure Habsburg style, with little cherubs surrounding a bust of Matthias.

A Romanian plaque in English and Romanian hangs alongside the Francis Joseph gift. It reads: "According to historical tradition this is the house where Matthias Corvinus, the son of the great Voivode of Transylvania and governor of Hungary Iancu of Hunedoara was born. The Romanian Matthias Corvinus is considered the greatest of all Hungarian kings due to his achievements during his reign 1458-1490."

At first I was confused by the need for two plaques, but then I remembered the old saying, "A beautiful baby has many fathers." Matthias had indeed left an indelible mark on the surrounding cultures.

Standing there, contemplating all that we were seeing in this medieval town, the past became the present for a split second. I felt as if Matthias was going to walk out from behind the arched wooden door.

Mr. D said he was called Matthias the Just and that when he

died, peasants cried that justice died with him. He possessed a powerful combination of traits, from artistic sensibilities and the sense of the common man to fearsome anger. He was celebrated throughout Europe and the world and is talked about now— look at me. We could have stayed all afternoon listening to Mr. D's stories, but we moved on to Saint Michael's Cathedral, begun in the fourteenth century and finished in the fifteenth century. Mr. D pointed out the coats of arms of the Germans, the Czechs, and Hungarians. In the 1800s, a 262-foot tower was added to the church.

We were quiet entering, not wanting to disturb anyone communing with God. Mr. D said that the cathedral started as a Catholic church but that in the seventeenth century, Protestants destroyed the decorations and painted over them in white. In the twentieth century, art restorers found the remains of early paintings.

"The church was Catholic, Lutheran, then Unitarian, and now it's a Catholic church again," Mr. D said.

I was getting used to churches with complicated histories and prepared myself for a lot of conflicting motifs. But since it was once a Roman Catholic church, my first instinct was to look for candles to light for loved ones. I was distracted in my quest by the eighteenth-century Baroque wooden pulpit. Artisans had intricately carved saints and popes in the wood along with angels holding trumpets and the Holy Spirit shown as a dove flying overhead. On top, the Archangel Michael is encircled by diminutive angels.

Outside, the weather served up a tourist's dream, sunshine and a periodic breeze. Mr. D resumed with history, advising us to look closely, because we would be hiking past nineteenth-century buildings, including the Museum of Pharmaceutical Sciences, the Continental (the first hotel), and the town hall. We landed on Boulevard Eroilor, face-to-face with two tall, upward-thrusting stone pillars with a bell on top. This Stalinesque monument recorded the names of prominent Romanians. It was created in 1994 as a symbol of ultra-nationalism.

Near the stone monument stood imperial buildings from the nineteenth and early twentieth centuries interspersed with the gray concrete Communist-era structures. I focused on the neoclassical façade of a light blue building with white trim and four atlantes supporting a marble window frame, as well as an ochre Art Nouveau building with a cream façade suspending bell-like ornaments. Those footprints came from Amálka's time.

Mr. D wasn't one to waste time. He moved us along to make sure that we captured the highlights of Cluj. Directly across the street from the Romania Opera House, and in front of the Romanian Orthodox Cathedral, was a modern art statue of Avram Iancu (1824–1872). It had been erected during the era of the nationalistic mayor. The unusual arrangement of stones left me puzzled, but I could understand what the artist had in mind. At the base were two abstract buglers with long trumpets raised to the sky. In the middle was a stone column with Iancu holding a sword in his left hand and reaching toward the sky for the Gods to admire. During the Hungarian fight for liberation in 1848, Iancu and other Transylvanians went to war against the Hungarians. What can I say here? Romanians against Hungarians in retaliation for the oppression that the Hungarians had heaped on Romanians, and the both of them were getting it from the Austrians.

In the end, Iancu became a Romanian hero even though the Austrians went on to conquer both Hungary and Transylvania. History is a messy thing. Somebody's hero, somebody else's foe. This was Amálka's heritage. No culture is exempt from complexities. Amálka was closer to such tumultuous times than I was, and on this quiet and peaceful day in Cluj, I was just a tourist absorbing the scenery.

Looking at all the flags, Phil asked, "Are Hungary and Romania close to war?"

Richard didn't translate this question for Mr. D. Instead, he laughed and said, "Since Hungary and Romania are both in the European Union and the mayor was fired, there's no war."

The camera had again taken over Phil's attention. He was flicking the settings, trying to correct for background light and mumbling something about too much contrast. I'd been in Cluj for only a day and already I was getting a feel for what Amálka's life must have been like, of the history, the architecture, the monuments, and a millennium of strife.

Off to another church. I have an affinity for churches, having attended various ones all my life and Mr. D said this was a special one. This Romanian Orthodox, the state religion, honored the Assumption of the Virgin Mary. The cathedral, by tradition, was built in the shape of a Roman cross like the one on the wooden door at the entrance. This massive structure arose around 1940 with Neo-Byzantine motifs and a dome styled after Istanbul's Hagia Sophia, which Phil had seen on a visit to Turkey some years before.

When Amálka painted in her album, the Romanian Orthodox Cathedral had not been built and there's nothing hinting at Byzantine artistic styles in her keepsake. Given Amálka's sensitivities though, she would have very much liked the Romanian Orthodox Cathedral despite probably being a Roman Catholic. A chandelier in the shape of a silver crown weighing what must be tons was suspended above a rainbow of colors streaking across the floor. Faded frescos decorated the walls to the top.

My legs were ready to give out but even though there were chairs, I didn't dare sit down. In this type of church the congregation stands in the presence of God. Even without a service going on sitting didn't seem appropriate.

I bowed my head as I walked to the exit, thinking of my mother as I do whenever I am in any church anywhere in the world. I said a short prayer for her and made the sign of the cross.

We walked into the street with Mr. D as bandleader, heading straight for the Tailors' Tower. The long section of a high, medieval stone wall, with steps on the inside to help its defenders quickly ascend to the top, is in good condition. At the far end is a squarish stone tower, which must have housed arms and watchmen. This section of wall has survived in its entirety since 1405, when attacks on towns were frequent. A wall once surrounded the entire city with several defense bastions and gates. Back then business associations were then called "guilds," and functioned like trade unions, but with multiple social responsibilities, including the defense of the town. The bastion or gate they were defending was named for them, hence the Tailors' Tower, according to Mr. D.

We pressed on, landing at the Reformed Church on Wolf Street, named for the wolves that used to roam on hard winter nights, Mr. D said, tantalizing us with images of savage beasts ready to devour unsuspecting people outside at night.

One would think that after being in so many churches they'd all start to look the same, but not so here. This one resembled a medieval castle rather than a place of worship. The fifteenth-century Gothic church is easy to find because the statue of Saint George on horseback slaying a dragon overwhelms one. The statue is a copy of the original in Prague.

Mr. D said that Emperor Francis Joseph commissioned two copies in 1904. Kolozsvár got one and it eventually ended up in front of this church; the other copy stands in one of Hungary's most popular spots, the Fisherman's Bastion in the Buda Castle District.

Once inside the church, my eyes focused on the pulpit, this one detailed in marble with a copy of the Ten Commandments. Near the pulpit is a table with a stone inlay. Filling the balcony and rising almost to the ceiling is a pipe organ with three columns of pipes in the center flanked by a set of three others on each side.

A curiosity of this church, for an American like me, was the obituaries that hung on the wall. This brought my grandmother to mind. She used to read the obituaries, religiously. When I asked her about it—because as a kid I couldn't fathom obituaries being of interest—she put the paper in her lap for a moment, looked me squarely in the eye, and said, "I never know when I might see one of my friends." Then she nonchalantly picked up the paper and resumed reading. Grandma's obituaries had nothing on these wood-framed paintings that capture the essentials of someone's life. For example: Károly Nagy (1863–1926) served as a pastor of Brassó, Nagyenyed, and Kolozsvár; theological teacher of Nagyenyed and Kolozsvár; and a bishop. He was obviously someone important to the community of Kolozsvár. I couldn't decipher the text but didn't need to. The picture of a green laurel wreath with a blue ribbon, framing the hand of a prelate holding open the Holy Scripture, told the story of an honored man in death.

I did find it fascinating later on to learn that the script for the word "bishop" was painted in German Gothic type. Does it get any more obscure than this? The answer is yes.

Some of the plaques were in Latin. Their presence was compelling, all the moreso because Latin was the language of the literate and literary from the glory days of Rome to the Renaissance. The melancholy words hung suspended in time on a church wall for all to read:

IN MEMORY OF THE ADMIRABLE AND LARGE-HEARTED
D. STEPHAN PATAK OF SÁROSPATAK.
OF THE FREE ROYAL TOWN OF KOLOZSVÁR.
ONCE A SENATOR AND THE FIFTH JUDGE OF THE
HIGHEST CHURCH COURT
AND DOMESTIC CURATOR OF THE REFORMED COLLEGE OF KOLOZSVÁR.
BORN IN 1711. DIED THE 5TH OF FEBRUARY IN THE
YEAR OF THE LORD 1775.

One of the most interesting motifs, and one that I'd never seen used in obituaries, is the pelican. Legend has it that a mother pelican uses her own blood to nourish her chick. This symbolized the sacrifice of Jesus Christ for humankind.

The dead are remembered so differently everywhere. The colorful obituaries, like our cemeteries, are a loving tribute. But what happened to Amálka?

We walked in search of a little refreshment, passing the university. Mr. D said that the student body was diverse, both culturally and in age. I liked hearing that retired people studied there. But then he spoiled it by telling us about a classically nationalist problem that had occurred at the university. Two young Hungarian professors posted information in Hungarian and were fired for it in 2006. Apparently only the Romanian language could be used.

The nature of any legal action was rarely so simple, I thought. On the other hand, the incident seemed so utterly consistent with the history of the place. If this case resulted in a lawsuit, there would be another and another until finally the people would have to accept their future and forgive the past.

I hadn't expected to trip over this type of cultural dilemma when I bought Amálka's book. Phil's sister has traveled the world and once provided me with some insights about racial groupings when she said, "It's everywhere to different degrees. We're just lucky to live where we live because here it is a melting pot despite our problems."

As we walked and talked, we passed a small store where a friendly saleslady happily accepted our last four lei for some water.

Unbelievably, the Spanish tourists showed up again. Were they on the Amálka tour, too?

It was time to say good-bye to Cluj.

· · ·

DASHING BACK TO ORADEA IN THE VAN, MR. D DOWNSHIFTED into Hungarian history, this time to a tale involving Saint László, son of Géza I, and in the Árpád house of Kings, who built a bishopric in the eleventh century, the seed of a strong town. Before that, Oradea was just a small settlement.

Mr. D picked up with the Tatars, the Mongols, wreaking havoc on Nagyvárad in 1241, and lifted us on a carpet ride through time to the nineteenth and twentieth centuries. When Amálka arrived here at the turn of the twentieth century, Nagyvárad, one of Hungary's largest cities, had forty-seven thousand inhabitants. Baedeker's *Austria* identifies the Archaeological and Historical Museum and a bronze statue of King László as worth seeing. Summing up his presentation, Mr. D provided a short list of natural disasters and momentous historic changes.

1831: Earthquake. Actually the one everyone knows about happened in 1834 about sixty miles north of Oradea, according to Mr. D. I filed that for a time when I want to impress someone with surprising facts about Oradea.

1836: Big fire.

1850: Six cities joined with Várad to form Nagyvárad (*nagy* translating as "big" in Hungarian).

1851: Huge flood.

1900–1945: Nagyvárad—Hungarian, Romanian, Hungarian, and finally Romanian.

It was starting to sink in.

But Oradea has had its good days, too. Amálka recorded good times here.

. . .

WE RETURNED TO OUR HOTEL, THEN QUICKLY RE-EMERGED walking to the restaurant we visited the night before, now our favorite. This time we knew the way and made it before the rain hit. Halfway into our goose, the sky crackled.

"Nagyvárad had a big earthquake, a fire, and a flood and now it will have a huge thunderstorm," Richard said.

The water began to leak through the roof covering the end of the table, forcing our group to move in closer. We ate, laughed, and drank the local brew.

Our luck held when the waiter got us a cab again and the meter wasn't turned on. The night was over, we retired to our rooms. I got ready to go to bed among visions of historical tumult, hallowed churches, and green countryside that once attracted Amálka and her family and friends. The current of history runs through this place. I began to worry about Amálka.

CHAPTER 20

The Black Eagle

ANOTHER FLOOD DELUGED THE BATHROOM FLOOR.

After having dealt with the stubborn faucets the previous day, I had a much easier time taking a shower. Only a small flood this time. I didn't wake Phil up out of a dead sleep and didn't use all the towels, making him much happier than he'd been the day before.

Breakfast was delicious: fried eggs, toast, yogurt, meats, and fruit. Then I discovered the instant cappuccino maker. Coffee purists I know don't like these machines, but I find them quite fun and the coffee tasty.

"Watch the coffee," Phil said, figuring I might bounce off the van's walls. The pastries made a delicious companion and Min and I sampled those we hadn't eaten the day before. He just shook his head at the two of us as she cut pieces for me to taste. He had learned not to pay attention to our antics lest he be unintentionally involved.

After breakfast, we gathered in the lobby with our luggage to make our way to the van, dodging raindrops. They didn't deter us from seeing the city. I wore an inexpensive gold captain's hat

I'd picked up in Paris. Phil shared an umbrella with the Romanian guide. Min had wisely packed an umbrella. As always, Richard was prepared; he had a hood attached to his jacket. We were ready to explore Oradea, which for Hungarians will always be Nagyvárad.

. . .

MUCH HAS CHANGED SINCE AMÁLKA'S TIME. CASE IN POINT, the first site Mr. D pointed out: the First of December Park. Transylvania was annexed to Romania on December 1, 1918, after World War I. Later the Romanian government made this date a national holiday.

We pushed on, stopping for a look at a stone fortress. Mr. D said it had been fortified over the centuries but that didn't keep enemies from attacking. We gazed at the center of the citadel, which was devised to protect royalty while lesser nobles and the wealthy occupied the next ring of defenses. Our Romanian guide asked us to use our imagination to see that the fortress formed a star with five bastions to improve its ability to withstand invaders.

"There was a geothermal spring here that was used for hot water," Richard said, giving us a stray fact that Mr. D thought we should be aware of. Little did he know we were acquainted with the area's geothermal springs, as a result of our hotel showers.

The old fortress's evolution was what we expected. The Austrians used it for military purposes in Amálka's time. Every conqueror used it, including the Communists of the twentieth century. Today the University of Oradea uses the space for various art exhibits and projects.

A few large pieces of artwork remained, lonely, inside the fortress, with walls in need of renovation. Mr. D said that the Baroque-style church in the distance was built on the remains of the original destroyed by the Turks in the seventeenth century. He also pointed out that inside the annulus of the fortress there had been at one time statues of the Hungarian kings, but now the space was empty. We looked around the grounds, desolate, save for a few office workers and a morose dog off leash staring blankly at Phil, as he was taking the dog's portrait.

It was faded glory, a shell of its past, destroyed in a quest for power, a constant of all ages. Phil's mindset was purely analytic. He observed a particularly grim-looking building with modern iron bars in all of the windows. The explanation slowly came. The basement had been a prison, and they found lots of skeletons after 1990. I could have done without knowing that, but this fort had seen a continuous series of conflicts over the ages, including during Amálka's period.

We would not stay much longer because Mr. D wanted to make sure we got to the Greek Orthodox Church. A true tour guide: complete to the last footnote. He took us to an Orthodox church, similar to the one in Cluj. There were no chairs and again my feet were tired. Mr. D took my mind off that right away, though, when he transitioned into the local lore. It turns out that the church priests of the eighteenth century were impoverished like the rest of the population and had to eat beans, which rendered the church "terribly smelly," he said.

Mr. D's story caught us by surprise. I hadn't heard a tale like that since the fifth grade, but I'm always up for a little levity.

We had obviously drifted off into one of history's tributaries and everyone agreed with a wink it was time to move on—in this case, to the van to continue our tour. The water streamed down the windows in little rivulets. In spite of that, the old Town Hall, the Palace of Justice, the Gymnasium, and the Ady statue in front of the prison were clear to us.

Ady's presence was out of place. Endre Ady (1877–1919), a fiery literary force, lived in Nagyvárad, and his writings about the social, intellectual, and political issues of the day could be found in the literary journal *Nyugat*, (*West*, in English), launched on January 1, 1908. That same year Amálka was with her family and friends in Nagyvárad for a harvest. It seemed likely to me that someone within her circle had read his works.

We drove past the Black Eagle Palace, a Secession-style building, without stopping even though I was anxious to see it.

I wasn't in charge and churches came first. The Orthodox Cathedral Assumption of the Lord Mother, or Moon Church, was up next. Phil likes science so he was captivated by the device below the bell tower that shows whether the night sky would deliver a half or full moon.

Trying to stay dry, we walked quickly and finally got to the Black Eagle. Constructed in the first decade of the twentieth century to be a collection of stores and a hotel, it looked like the area's first shopping mall. Patrons could enter the building by one of three passageways. The Black Eagle's predecessor was an upscale inn in 1820 that regularly held masquerade balls.

In 1909, colored glass shimmered on the ceiling throughout the Black Eagle's passageways. The weather challenged the structural integrity of the ceilings and over time the storms won. The only stained glass to survive is an archway window depicting a black eagle. The city has replaced the others with plain glass, which might have been prudent from the beginning, given the meteorology of Transylvania.

"Violent thunderstorms occurred several times during August, also hailstorms of the most devastating character," reported H. Ellen Browning in *A Girl's Wanderings in Hungary*. "These used to begin suddenly. A raging wind would arise; the air would be filled with dust; man and beast would run for their lives to the nearest shelter. Doors and windows were often torn off their hinges before they could be closed; trees and shrubs were uprooted, roofs sometimes blown off bodily, and then came the hail."

Today the black eagle in the remaining stained glass window soars within a bright landscape bordered by the kind of flowering vines that Amálka drew.

Mr. D's voice softened. He said that he had seen the original stained glass ceiling. He gazed wistfully at the eagle, taking us back to a time long ago.

Only those with wealth and vision could have created something sprawling for a city block or two. Its original owners and architects traveled throughout Europe and the United States gathering ideas and inspiration for the project in the early 1900s. Mr. D said that a member of the Adorján family helped finance the Black Eagle Palace.

"Adorján was Jewish," he said. "After the political changes, his family was offered the Black Eagle. His relatives did not want it, but had one request. They asked that there be a plaque for his family on the wall in the building."

I couldn't verify this part of the hotel's story. Later on, I did a quick Internet search for "Dr. Emil Adorján," which produced a Claims Resolution Tribunal document regarding Holocaust Victims Assets Litigation. His grandson was ultimately awarded the assets in his grandfather's Swiss bank account. According to the document, Adorján, the financier of the Black Eagle, was tortured before being deported to Auschwitz.

Mr. D didn't linger on the past. He said that the building today houses a hotel, a cinema, a puppet theater, shops, a bank, a copy center, and cafés. I noticed them, plus several Romanian flags, inside the Black Eagle's walkway. Too many of these flags can be unnerving.

Browning, on the other hand, found the plethora of red, white, and green flags in Hungary in the 1890s, waving, swooping, and swinging in the wind, "enlivening, especially on a sunny, breezy day." That may have been true from her tourist point of view in *A Girl's Wanderings* but I have some confidence that a local non-Magyar would not have agreed with her.

Richard turned my attention from flags to coffee.

"Amálka could have had a coffee here," he said.

Indeed, I was sure anyone who came to Várad would have

wanted to do so. I lifted my head, holding on to my rain hat. With a blink, I could see her walking with her mother past the stores, carrying her keepsake album, the black eagle staring down.

"You should be very happy," Phil said, seeing a twinkle in my eyes.

"I am. We have an idea of what this place used to be. Amálka would be happy we're here, remembering her, the good times she had, and making our own memories."

"I think so, too," he said.

We lingered as long as we could and then visited the Square of the Union, referred to in Hungarian as Saint László Square. The usual Soviet-style buildings lurked in contrast to the detailed early twentieth-century architecture nearby. Mr. D pointed out the statue of Mihai Viteazul (1558–1601), or Michael the Brave. He is best remembered for unifying the three parts of Romania—Transylvania, Moldavia, and Wallachia—for a short time, and the ill-fated alliance he made with the Habsburgs to help win Transylvania from Duke Zsigmond Báthory (1572–1613). The Habsburgs later had him murdered. A lot must have happened between the battle and the murder, but after so many of these stories from Mr. D, I let it slide. What a horrible fate.

We continued driving and I asked about the number of tourists who pass through Oradea. He said about ten thousand to twelve thousand tourists come to Várad each year, but that most of them travel through the city without stopping.

Our discussion was cut short when we arrived at the Roman Catholic Basilica of Nagyvárad. The eighteenth-century basilica held light passing through stained glass windows of Saint László and Saint Erzsébet. It was ever so reverential. A plaster bust of Matthias holding an ax had been mounted on the wall. What woman wouldn't love a warrior/scholar? I did.

Next to the basilica sits the Bishop's Palace, also constructed in the eighteenth century. It's similar in design to Vienna's Belvedere Palace, Mr. D said, adding that this Baroque palace had fifty-two rooms for the number of weeks in a year, and 365 windows for the days of the year. A sealed "blind" window represented a leap year.

Adding to the details of his tale, Mr. D said that the palace was nationalized in the 1940s and used for refugees who "bankrupted" the building. He meant destroyed. In the 1970s, it was renovated and converted into a museum, which now had to be moved since ownership had reverted to the bishopric.

We skipped that museum in favor of the Saint László museum inside the church. We walked up a stone staircase built into the wall, up to a balustrade several levels above the church floor. A vestment made from a gown of Maria Theresa, a portable altar used by Hungarian troops in the nineteenth century, and a wide selection of chalices and other religious objects and numerous relics stand testament to the importance of the church.

Phil mentioned the active trade in relics during the Middle Ages and the controversies surrounding the most sacred of them. He was correct. King Saint László (1046–1095), founder of the Oradea bishopric, lives on as one of the most revered and heroic kings in Hungary. Mr. D said that King Saint László's reliquary was moved to Győr in 1606, when both cities were part of Hungary. In the eighteenth century, the bishopric got back a small piece of his skull. The reliquary, a bust of the king, sits today in the museum.

Before we knew it, noon was upon us. To make our appointment at the Szolnok Art Colony, we would have to rush back to Hungary. We tromped through the rain to the van and sped toward the border with Mr. D along for the ride.

I thought about our time spent in Romania, about everything we had seen—and especially about how isolated it had been during Communism from the rest of the world. Richard said that travel for Romanians during those years was very restricted compared to what it had been for Hungarians. "There had to be a revolution to change that," he explained.

Amálka's book is not a historical treatise. She may not have seen much beyond Central Europe, though her memory book resonates in an unforeseen place in a distant future. Let's call it New York City for now.

I put these thoughts aside while we waited in a line of cars at the checkpoint.

"Passports?" our Hungarian guide said.

We reached into our bags and surrendered them. A brief exchange ensued between the driver and the official. All I understood was "American." This was another one of those moments when it seemed best to keep quiet. The guards' review was quick but not cursory. The door to the van abruptly swung open and a policeman matched us to our passports. He gave an official nod and I got a certain degree of comfort seeing him hand back our passports. Trouble at the border was common enough in 1900, too. Baedeker's *Austria* calls passports in "Servia," or what we know as Serbia, and Romania "indispensable."

"Congratulations. You got us out of Romania," Phil said to the driver.

He gave a mocking smile, then meticulously donned his black glasses and hit the accelerator. We surged forward in the direction of Hungary.

CHAPTER 21

The Art Colony

MOTHER HUNGARY.

That's what I thought as we drove down the asphalt highway that surely paved over much older roads. The clip-clop of horses pulling carts and the gilded carriages of royalty whispered to me through the engine's hum. Out the van's window, the sun broke through the clouds.

We passed rolling fields of sunflowers, corn, and wheat, just as we did on our way to Pécs. Amálka and her family may have seen this, too, on their way from Nagyvárad to Szolnok. I was becoming more familiar with Amálka with each place we visited, and I had a strong feeling that she must have been a daydreamer, too. She looked softly on the scenery, thinking about what lay ahead for the day, about the things she would do, the meals to be eaten, family to care for, and friends to see.

For our burly and friendly Romanian driver, who makes the 310-mile drive from Nagyvárad to Budapest and back nearly every day, this often-trodden path lacked any romance. He looked sculpted into his seat, hands firmly gripping the wheel, at one with his machine.

The Romanian driver told Richard that he would pass István Fogadó, the Inn of Steven, in the rural town of Kisújszállás. He recommended it as a good place to stop for lunch.

We took him up on his suggestion of going to the Inn of Steven. Mr. D, however, decided not to eat lunch. I asked Richard why he kept to himself. We liked him and enjoyed hearing him rattle off legends, local lore, and current news, at twice our capacity to understand. Richard said Mr. D was definitely more comfortable that way, especially since he didn't speak English. We could easily have felt the same way when Mr. D spoke Hungarian with Richard, but we worried about pressing matters, such as not losing our passports, remembering our hotel keys, and hanging on to our cell phones. Mr. D's insularity would have been common in Amálka's time, with over a dozen nationalities in the Austro-Hungarian Monarchy. Given their different languages, it's understandable that these groups tended to cluster together and didn't understand one another.

Aside from this, I also had to remember that our Romanian guide had lived through all twenty-four years of Ceaușescu's regime. During that time he must have learned not to trust anyone, and that included us, however friendly we might be. We would never really enter his personal space despite his inviting demeanor. He took a short walk while we all proceeded into the restaurant.

A steep and thatched roof covers the Inn of Steven. A row of rounded windows in the Hungarian style leaned forward from high above the roof. A rustic twig fence protected a plush green lawn. Min and I paused for the inevitable picture. I dragged Phil in, too. He would have preferred to be behind the camera but I didn't give him a choice.

Several picnic tables under low canopies beckoned us to sit outside, but in the end we opted to be inside, surmising that the strong breeze might ruin our lunch.

Richard left the table for a moment, leaving us with our

Romanian driver, who said he spoke a "little Hungarian, little English—universal." We laughed.

We asked about growth in Romania: Which cities were prospering?

"Transylvania, the Hungarian and German parts, Bucharest, and a few other cities," he said.

"Government—good, bad?" I asked, making small talk.

He just nodded.

The waiter handed us spiral-bound menus in the shape of thin, wooden cutting boards. Pictures of numbered dishes were shown on laminated pages. All we had to do was point.

"That's for us," Phil quipped.

My soup had sour cream on the bottom and pieces of beef and chicken. It was served in a bowl made of bread, like the clam chowder at Fisherman's Wharf in San Francisco. The driver decided on goulash. Phil opted for the beef broth soup since Richard said it was a house specialty and that he was having it, too. Theirs came with a side of bread topped with a thick layer of beef bone marrow. Main courses included turkey, steak, and chicken stuffed with apple and pork. We ate heartily while swatting away flies that had entered through the open front door.

The restaurant began to fill quickly with couples and families, including a party of six. When the last group entered, Richard said, "Now we share the flies. Why should we have them all?"

After lunch, we were off to Szolnok, so often referenced in Amálka's book. This was almost certainly her hometown, the place where she enjoyed many happy events, including a wedding on October 4, 1916. On that day in Szolnok someone wrote a small message, asking Amálka to think of them, and below it several people signed their names.

Twenty-six miles from Szolnok, Richard began telling us about the main art colonies of Hungary: Gödöllő, Szentendre, and Szolnok. The first two are favorite day trips outside Budapest because they have retained their historical flavor despite years of military conflict and political strife. Szolnok is less visited due to its distance, but no less important.

We wended our way past a group of small, neat suburban houses and high-rise buildings on our way to the Szolnok Art Colony. Driving over the Tisza town bridge gave us our first glimpse of the slowly flowing river. We navigated our way east across a smaller bridge over the Zagyva River, which flows into the Tisza from the north.

Finally, the Szolnok Art Colony materialized among tall green trees and shrubs. After parking and stretching our legs, we met György Verebes, the artistic manager, and his assistant, Edit Nagy. They had kindly agreed to discuss Amálka's paintings and to show us around the colony, which dates back to the nineteenth century.

They received us with kindness. Szolnok has a long history of generosity to travelers. British writer John Paget effusively complimented a Szolnok native's generous spirit in his 1839 travel log.

György and Edit launched our tour in the gallery featuring the work of resident artist Tibor Bráda. Bráda, born in 1941, holds the post of associate professor at the Hungarian Academy of Fine Arts and is one of the founders of the Day of Hungarian Painting, an annual event held in October.

Bráda is principally a painter but we got to see his glassworks. One room displayed Bráda's sketches for stained glass. His pastels took center stage in another area. I thought about the multiple talents of Hungarian artists and I wondered what else Amálka did other than painting.

Fine art graced the walls of the Szolnok Art Colony. Bráda was recognized but we were also interested in how other artists found their way into the colony.

György explained the process: A national competition is held annually for the National Association of the Hungarian

Creative Artists. They provide project plans for works they'd like to do at the colony, along with their portfolio. The art colony board of directors makes its recommendation to city officials for their review. The recommendations of the colony and the city are forwarded to the Hungarian Creative Arts Public Foundation, which makes the final decision.

The Szolnok Art Colony is essentially a nonprofit institution that benefits the public. With city funds for basic expenses, colony employees maintain the facility, install exhibits, and collaborate on art festivals featuring theater, dance, and concerts of jazz and classical music. Other art programs are funded by such sources as Hungary's ministry of culture.

The artists retain ownership for work they create at the colony. They often donate their pieces before leaving. These works can end up in the colony's permanent collection, in an exhibition, or other displays.

György stopped for a minute. I looked at Richard and then seized the moment to show György what we had come for: Amálka's art. He scanned the pages to see if he could find any names of artists who had worked at the colony so long ago.

"No," György said.

"Which picture do you like the best?" I asked.

He immediately pointed to the serene scene with the horse pulling a blue farm wagon on an overcast day along a yellowish dirt road. Green trees surge behind the wagon as the driver goes about his chores. The sky yellows in the light of a setting sun, and I can feel a long day on the farm coming to a close. A sinuous vine with red buds encircle the picture, holding the promise of spring. The image acts as a doorway into an earlier agrarian age. I like this one, too. I'd bought Amálka's album in some measure to have it.

"This could have been made here in Szolnok. It's quite nice. Ripened work," he said, bringing the page closer to his eyes. "Now this artist would have been someone with the skill level to become a part of the art colony of Szolnok. Excellent work."

I wish I could make out the microscopic signature but it is just too small for the naked eye.

Another watercolor, a spring bouquet of purple and blue pansies, attracted his attention but he added an important stipulation. "If this was created of the imagination, out of the mind, then this could be a professional artist," he said.

It looked to him to have been copied from another picture, however, because it seemed too complicated to have been done by an unpracticed hand. It is not signed either. György doubted that it was Amálka's work, but "We'll never know for sure," he said.

I looked at this picture drawn in Szolnok on April 12, 1914, in a memory book now being judged by the finest standards in the art world. I concluded that it failed to measure up only because she was young and the moment it captured so private.

Instantly and effortlessly, he organized the rest of the watercolors.

He grouped the horse-and-cart scene, the man rowing among lilies at sunset, and an idyllic Italian villa pressed against the hillside near a brown lakeshore, signed by Márton Fekete, to make one set. To the untrained eye, they all looked special, but György understood a deeper unifying theme.

"Those had to be have been done by men at the time; women didn't typically paint these types of scenes," he said. They don't fit the style of the watercolor scenes that were signed by Amálka. Two of the three in this set were unsigned.

"Are these true to the colors?" he asked, inspecting the copies.

"Yes, that's what attracted me to the book," I said. "The scenes are as vibrant as the copies."

"Watercolor can be time resistant. The quality of the paper is more important," he said.

The remaining two water scenes drew quick commentary.

The Fekete water scene: "a fine copy of a landscape, but it was not made in open air and could not have been created in Szolnok because there are no mountains here," he said. The watercolor of the man rowing at sunset: "Not so good," György quipped. Neither Fekete nor the person who painted the man in the boat would have been admitted to Szolnok's art colony, György said.

Two notes written to Amálka are ornamented with Art Nouveau-style filigreed flowers, icons of the age, with their twisting stems and delicate buds curving toward the sky, lazily guiding the reader's eye. György noted that these pictures were definitely drawn by the person who had written her the note.

Four meticulous pencil sketches of flowers and branches shaded to show contrast were "well detailed and well done—but not of an artist," he said. Even though they lacked Amálka's signature, György surmised that she drew them.

If they didn't rise to the level of art, they certainly were beyond my abilities. They looked so delicate and precise, betraying how long they took to produce and full of hope for what would be written within them.

György grouped together the remaining eight drawings, four signed by Amálka. Two unsigned watercolors, one of a lavender iris with yellow accents, the other, a still life of two golden peaches and a bunch of purple grapes nestled among green leaves, looked like copies to him. Of the two, the iris didn't look like it was Amálka's work, but as György stared at the fruit, he felt that it had come from her hand. How old was the hand that drew the peaches and grapes in 1908?

I asked him to prioritize Amálka's work in order of quality. The oversized red poppy with the white daisy and blue corn poppies and a single strand of yellow wheat came first, Amálka's signature nearly lost among the vines. The pair of bluebirds sitting on a branch surrounded by forget-me-nots follow, but here a much stronger Amálka signed and underlined her name in a swirl, reflecting all the power of newfound love. Last was the unsigned picture of three maroon chrysanthemums on their forest green vines, reaching down the side of a page, eagerly awaiting a good wish to be penned by a willing hand.

The pattern of the painter's strokes made him think it was Amálka's work. Slowly turning the page from one side to another, he said, "The motion . . . the drawing is nice. I like it a lot."

György also liked the blooming roses. Amálka obviously prepared pages to be signed at some event. The page with a salmon-colored rose and bud set against a pale azure background has the scribbled signatures of happy people on the occasion of Kucika's wedding in Szolnok on October 4, 1916. Was Amálka betrothed? It looked like a bridesmaid's gift to a dear friend.

The dark pink rose and a strawberry bud set against a celery green background rising above the nakedness of a white page, however, may have been an expectation unrealized. It had been readied but remained barren. No signature, no good time to record, no love. Just a rose, alone.

György was doing his job, being an art critic. He thought the dark pink rose was a copy. It lacks the imagination of the first. It could have been a case of the first one brought to life by the wedding its signers had experienced, while the second one wilted in unfulfilled anticipation.

The last drawing, a swirl of pink cyclamen, garnered only a nod that it was indeed Amálka's work because she'd signed it. Maybe György didn't have much to say because it was done by the young Amálka. He could tell by the artwork, but I could tell by the signature on the stem. She signed the diminutive Amálka in 1907 but her full name Amália in 1908. Girls do grow up fast. It was only a year but it might have been a very important year.

"Was Amálka's work strong enough for the art colony?" I asked.

"No, she would not have a chance," he said.

Even though this was the answer I expected, I had become Amálka's promoter and it hurt a little to hear his appraisal. But her drawings were just what they were supposed to be, a framework for collecting memories. They were not in and of themselves supposed to be the message but expressions of her time. Every flower attracted the little bee in me. Without her art, these memories might have disappeared, too. But they had survived long enough to bloom again.

"The theory of Amálka as a local teacher is the most likely version, which is what art historians said of her work," said Richard, who had taken the copies to the historians before our arrival. "At that time, there weren't many other professions where painting ability was required. Most likely she was from a relatively well-off civil family. She wouldn't have been the daughter of an aristocrat because remember I was able to identify one of the people who signed the book and he was a railway man, which would have made him a commoner."

György nodded and said, "A teacher of children—A teacher of that period would have had to teach many subjects, including art and history. The teachers were multidisciplinary and multi-faceted."

"It's like a one-room schoolhouse," Phil said.

György agreed, saying, "The father of my grandmother could play the piano, write poems, and paint. It's on a similar level. My grandfather, it was 1926, prepared a genealogy of his family history and it was in beautiful handwriting. He had learned how to do this in school; he knew how to write well."

I had to agree. Educated people at the turn of the twentieth century had fine penmanship, as did the contributors to Amálka's album. This was especially true in the acrostic created using each letter of Amálka's name in script to start a sentence.

Before we left György's flat, he handed me two postcards. The front showed a painting from a series and the back had a biography about him, thankfully in English. György was carrying on the tradition of his great-grandfather. He is an artist, pianist, composer, and scene designer for the theater.

Multidisciplinary talents are steeped like the finest of dark teas in this country, and often necessary for survival.

"Now let me show you some other flats," said György.

Our first stop was a painter's flat. A door in the center led to a large studio space with twenty-foot-high ceilings. The flat faced north and got no direct sunlight.

"We never had this at my school," said Min, staring out at the wide open space.

"What is that area for?" she asked, pointing to a short set of stairs leading to a loft area.

"The paintings can dry upstairs. It's warmer and less dusty than here," György said, as we looked around at the artist's plein air work.

It was time to move on to György's own flat. Outside stood an artificial tower built with stones from an old castle. We took in the peaceful scene, trees standing like umbrellas on a hot day, towering over the colony's simple stone and wooden building.

György swung open the door of his studio. On one wall was an expansive hand-sewn cloth with an abstract representation of a globe. On another wall was an oil painting of oversized clasped hands, part of his current Mudra series.

"Why hands?" I asked.

"Hands and faces are the most characteristic [features] that can be used to step above personality. They show a state of mind of the humanity found in each of us," György said. "The hands in this picture make a mountain. They show the solidity that can be found in human beings."

We noticed a painting leaning against a table. György walked toward it and swept his thumb through the air to show us the strokes he had used to create the portrait of an old man against a black background. He had done it without a brush, a very refined version of finger painting in oils. György said this type of painting can take two days to a few weeks.

Min was aware of the technique but Phil and I were not.

Two other paintings in need of small restoration work came from a set of ten portraits by ten people who lived on one street. The series is called, logically, Good Neighbors.

György decided we should also visit the flat of a sculptor. This artist employs wax to create a form of the ultimate image, which he then uses to make a mold. We walked out slowly, not disturbing anything.

As we left, I had gotten one rung closer to Amálka and learned something about the contemporary art scene in Szolnok. But the real bonus was meeting György. The contrasting dark and light hues of his paintings and the realization that Amálka had left a place for another entry to be made in her keepsake came together in my mind. In a wild moment, I wondered if Amálka would mind if I signed my name.

• • •

RETURNING TO BUDAPEST, WE THANKED MR. D FOR THE GIFT OF his history. His twinkling blue eyes made it hard to say goodbye.

SZOLNOK ART COLONY

Austrian painter August von Pettenkofen began visiting Szolnok because of the vista provided by the Tisza River and the plains. Hungarian painters Pál Böhm, László Mednyánszky, and Artúr Tölgyessy were also attracted to the area and helped establish the foundations for the Szolnok Art Colony.

When Hungarian painters suggested that an art colony should be formed at Szolnok, giving them studios, the government agreed. The trend toward public education, which included instruction in art, at the end of that century, influenced the decision. The colony opened in 1902 with a dozen founders. In its early years, the colony was noted for plein air and Impressionist-style painters. Its golden period aligns roughly with the happy days of Hungary itself. Amálka used her little book to collect memories from 1906 to 1919, right through the art colony's most productive times.

In the period between the world wars, the colony continued its commitment to Hungarian art, adding new artists through time. The building was heavily damaged during World War II, limiting its activities after that. From the 1960s through the 1980s, Hungarian artists would cluster there like birds perching on a favored tree. They stayed a while, and when the wind shifted they were off, freeing their perch for others. When the colony hit its hundredth anniversary in 2002, the studios were remodeled and updated for the needs of twenty-first-century artists.

Typically an artist who is accepted into the Szolnok Art Colony stays for one year and can extend it for a second. The stay usually runs from October to September. The colony has ten flats, three used by resident artists who have lived there for forty years.

The Colony has an artist exchange program with a "brother city" in Bavaria, Reutlingen, Germany. This enables one Szolnok artist to work in Reutlingen for a six-month visit while a Reutlingen artist travels to Szolnok for six months. A flat is reserved for each of the exchange artists.

1839 TRAVEL LOG

John Paget in *Hungary and Transylvania* wrote about Szolnok: "No sooner did he learn from our conversation that we had taken the trouble to examine the riches and beauties of his native land, and found much to admire and respect, both in the country and institutions, that he scarce knew how to express his joy. . . He would not allow us to leave the town till he had filled the carriage with the choicest peaches, melons, and plums, from his own garden; not to mention a large loaf of Szolnok bread, which he pronounced, and I believe he was right too, to be the very best in Hungary. It is true, all this might be nothing but the effect of good nature: and yet, reader, had you seen the real kindness with which it was done, the interest the good man took in our journey, the sentiments he expressed in favour of our native land; had you received all this attention from an individual you never saw before, and whom in all human probability you would never see again; and had you felt that it was to your country rather than to yourself you owed it—you must be differently constructed from me if you did not find yourself a happier man than when you entered Szolnok."

Part III

CHAPTER 22

New York City

OUR LAST NIGHT IN BUDAPEST ENDED WITH THE BOAT RIDE ON the Danube. Phil did not get seasick. As Richard said, you can't get seasick on the Danube. Maybe it was the champagne and the good company, which included Phil's friend from work and her husband, who just happened to be in Budapest at the same time and were staying at the same hotel.

Amálka was sprinkling fairy dust on our night cruise. Little pearls of light glowed from the base of Buda Castle and reflected in the water like spotlights. Amálka's memories seemed to be shining at me from the darkness.

The next day we gathered ourselves, four overloaded bags, and set out for the airport.

. . .

SITTING ON A COUCH AT HOME IN NEW YORK CITY A COUPLE OF days later, I said, "I wish I had known about these places years ago."

"Everyone's like that," Phil responded. "Someone either teaches you or you learn it yourself. In this case, Amálka has led you to some of the treasures in Central Europe. It's part of your education from Amálka."

He continued.

"She's your teacher. It's the old Buddhist saying, 'When the student is ready, the teacher appears.' "

I perked up.

"That's true," I said. "Did you know Anjou King Charles Robert was crowned three times? It only stuck the last time when they used the real crown, not a substitute. That's when it was legal and that's when he became king."

Phil looked up.

"By the time the crown got to Francis Joseph, it got even crazier. Remember Andrássy?" I said. "He was sentenced to death by the Austrians for his role in the Hungarian Revolution in 1848, only to find himself placing the Hungarian crown on Francis Joseph's head in 1867. It was 'forgive and forget' because they ultimately made Andrássy the foreign minister of the Monarchy."

"Must have been a very clever politician," he said.

"Had to be to survive those times," I replied. "Charles, the Emperor's grandnephew, was the last Habsburg to have the crown actually placed on his head. And after that the Monarchy was over."

Phil got up to get a cup of coffee and kissed me on the cheek.

If he was getting coffee, he must have wanted history. How could coffee be a priority?

"That crown is inordinately precious," I said a little louder, as he brewed another pot. "No amount of money could ever replace it," I added, swallowing hard. I didn't know if the gulp was for Amálka's life, the crown, the conflagration in European history, or all three.

"Oh, and remember when we were in Transylvania and the Ceauşescu regime came up?" I asked Phil. "I found something about Timişoara in Amálka's time."

I paused. He sat down with his coffee cup.

"Baedeker's *Austria* said Temesvár had a theater, a savings bank, a cathedral and churches, a museum, hotels, a tramway, a post and telegraph office, and an arsenal nearby. It was definitely one of the largest cities in the Hungarian kingdom and known for its industry and trade," I said. "It was like a 'Southern Manchester.' That's what Bovill had called it."

Phil gave me a strange look. I forgot that he wasn't acquainted with this adventurous traveler at the turn of the twentieth century.

"This is all just part of the cultural environment that Amálka had to have experienced," he said. "Beauty amid conflict lies in so many places that she must have visited. In due course, conflict overwhelmed everything in the region, and almost certainly in her life."

I nodded.

. . .

A MONTH AFTER WE RETURNED FROM EUROPE, WE FOUND ourselves sitting in a San Francisco hotel room on a business trip. Phil ordered room service and as he poured tea for me, I said, "Look at your cup. You've got to admit it's nowhere near as nice as Zsolnay."

"It's a hotel. Zsolnay is a little upscale for room service," he quipped.

. . .

ONCE BACK IN NEW YORK AGAIN, WE WERE TRADING E-MAILS with Richard. It was August 2007. I had forgotten to tell him about our Amálka moment from San Francisco in favor of a Yankees game that Phil was going to see in the Bronx. Richard replied that baseball is not well-understood or closely followed in Hungary. This would come as a terrible shock to rabid New York fans. In Amálka's time, football got its start, and here I mean soccer. Apparently the Hungarians could give the British a run for their money in soccer back then. But American baseball was a long way off.

In turn, Richard described the extreme heat wave that hit Budapest, 108 degrees in the shade, and 133 in the sunshine. But he was managing, staying inside as much as possible.

Ofen, Buda's German name, means "oven."

They called it Ofen because historically—as D. T. Ansted wrote in *A Short Trip* the city has "a hot stifling atmosphere, which is derived partly from position and partly from a multitude of hot springs bursting forth from the hill sides."

In *Researches on the Danube and the Adriatic*, A. A. Paton agreed, complaining that, "The worst feature of the climate of Pest is in an east wind, which in the summer, is hot and suffocating."

It was hot in New York, too, but we had air-conditioning; and we intended to see family in Seattle, which was experiencing a rare dry spell.

When I returned to New York City, I remained immersed in Hungarian history, to which Richard e-mailed, "You like challenges, don't you? To get deeply involved in the Hungarian history is a real challenge, even for most Hungarians."

. . .

THAT SUMMER PHIL AND I TRAVELED TO BEIJING, THE SOUTH Gobi, and Taiwan. Prior to leaving, I mentioned to Richard that we'd pick something up for his daughter. He replied, "Dorina is a very lucky child, she hasn't been born, but already has a godmother."

I slowly closed my laptop.

On the plane, while the rest of the people were sleeping, I was reading about multiple invasions over the centuries. Even the flight attendants glanced over, obviously wondering what had me so engaged in the middle of the night. It all seemed reasonable to me. After all, we were traveling to the land of one of Hungary's nemeses, Genghis Khan, and on to the South Gobi. I could understand that Hungary came close to being wiped off the face of the earth in 1241. Modern Hungarians were lucky to be there at all, especially because in war after war, enemies massacred the population and plundered the country.

Somewhere between Ulan Bator and the Flaming Cliffs of the Gobi, I found what I was looking for.

"I don't think that any other baby in Hungary will have camel shoes from Mongolia," Richard wrote to us in an e-mail a month before the birth of his daughter.

. . .

IN EARLY FALL, WE HEARD FROM RICHARD. "DORINA IS LATE, she hasn't arrived, keeping everybody at the end of their nerves."

I shared this news with Phil.

"I have a suspicion she'll get here soon enough," he said, with a wink.

. . .

ON SEPTEMBER 22, PHIL'S EASY PREDICTION CAME TRUE. SIX days past Julia's due date, Dorina decided it was time to arrive. "I am a happy father," Richard wrote.

We were happy for him, too. My life, this trip, Amálka, the baby, past and future, twisting roads.

CHAPTER 23

The Hungarian Language

Often on hot summer nights we all sat together in the vine-covered
veranda at the back of the house. The parents spoke German fairly
well, the daughters hardly at all, and yet they contrived to give us
little exercises in Hungarian, generally consisting of a list of simple
words, which we were expected to be able to commit to memory
and repeat at the next lesson. Fő, head; kéz, hand; láb, foot; nap,
sun; hold, moon—how hard they were to learn, how easy to forget!

THE PAINTER AND WRITER ADRIAN STOKES WROTE THIS IN
Hungary in the first decade of the twentieth century, but they
captured my experience in the first decade of the twenty-first
century as I sought to learn Hungarian.

I chuckled thinking that Richard's baby and I had something
in common right away—neither of us knew how to speak
Hungarian. But even if I had a head start, this tiny, gurgling tot
would quickly gain on me.

Just as I prepared to jump into the language waters, Phil
cautioned me about signing on too fast. As I continued reading

about Hungarian, I could see his point.

Germanic, Slavic, and Romance languages are not related to Hungarian. Hungarian is part of the Finno-Ugric subgroup of the Uralic language family. Other languages grouped with Hungarian include Finnish, Estonian, and the exotic Lappish and Mordvin. What's Mordvin? The Mordvins are a people found in Russia.

Phil politely said, "Learning Hungarian looks like three full-time jobs to me: reading, writing, and speaking."

If I was going to learn the language, he made me promise to seek private lessons and not a structured course at a university that would be filled with people already exposed to Hungarian. I agreed and got a few names. I was on my way.

· · ·

MY TEACHER, KIND AND MEASURED, WENT OVER THE ALPHABET clearly and concisely, again and again, until I could say the forty-four letters correctly. My mouth emitted sounds like dz (ds) and zs (zhey). Palatal consonants were also a revelation, requiring me to move my tongue up to the roof of my mouth as if I was searching for peanut butter. The tongue sticks a little there and then releases. The gy sounds like "du" in the word during, but with a little y sort of twang. I had to hear it a lot—"dy, dy, dy, dy, dy," my teacher said one day when I pronounced it as a "j"— before I got it. I can hear her voice in my head every time I see a word with those particular letters. The two sounds for the letter a, two for e, four for o, and four for u, took time to learn how to pronounce correctly.

Within the first few lessons, I realized that adding Hungarian language studies was a little like going to Szolnok and expecting to enroll in the art colony. The forty-four letter alphabet, and a verb "to be" which is used in some cases and not in others— everything was so different from English, especially the sound of the language. Hungarian is actually a very melodic language because of its vowel harmony rules.

"Hungarian, like Italian, is a powerful language, without harshness, whose gliding gentle entonations have a marvelous euphony," evoked travel writer Victor Tissot in *Unknown Hungary.* "It sounded like the warbling murmur of a little streamlet in the moss, or the breeze stirring the foliage. . . . Original, brilliant, florid, full of colouring, and of movement, it is par excellence the language of imagination, of poetry and feeling."

Actually, when Richard talked about adding things to the end of a Hungarian word to say something else, he was referring to the language's agglutinative nature, in which suffixes are attached to words to add to their meaning, and how these endings must also adhere to vowel harmony rules.

I remembered Irénke signed one of the harvest entries in Amálka's book. Irénke is a nickname for Irén. That's Hungarian for Irene. Irénke wouldn't have added the ka ending we might expect in English because it doesn't sound right. The endings must produce a word pleasant to the Hungarian ear. For learners, this vowel harmony can be especially nettlesome.

Vowel harmony is not illogical, just different for an English speaker. Think about Amálka. She and her friends enjoyed painting. The word for picture is *festmény* (fesht-mainy). To break the word down, *fest* is to paint and *mény* is a suffix that makes a noun out of a verb. If I wanted to say "her painting," I'd need to add e to the ending, thus *festménye*. On the other hand, if I talked about several of her paintings, I'd need to add another ending, this time the letter i, hence *festményei*. However, if I wanted to say just paintings, it would be a different ending, k, thus *festmények*.

Another tricky area for me: Hungarian word order. To Americans, Hungarian word order appears to be in reverse order, and for Hungarians, Americans have it backwards. For example, Linda Fischer, 150 Elm Street, New York City, born on

June 5, 1953, would read in Hungarian as: *Fischer Linda, New York City, Elm utca (street) 150., született (born) 1953. június (June) 5-én (on)*. As you see, Hungarian uses ordinal ranking. The words stack in the order of importance. The big ones come first. Fischer is my family name and would precede my first name Linda. Looking at the address, the city comes before the street. How many Elm Streets are there in how many cities? If someone actually wanted to find me, they'd want to know the city before the street. The date construction works on a similar premise. Start with the year. Hungarians give you the most important things first. It is logical in many ways. But learning a language often means unlearning some old habits. In this case, it would be many habits, but I'd have to start somewhere. Amálka, how would I keep all this straight?

I was practicing pronouncing every letter in a word, always emphasizing the first syllable and trying to get the intonation right, which depended on my intent.

• • •

By lesson number nine, overwhelmed but unwilling to quit, I took solace in a story about Franz Liszt giving up on Hungarian after five lessons. The word that killed him was *tántoríthatatlanság*, which means "unshakability." Try to pronounce it: tan-tor-eet-haw-tawt-lawn-shug. Other words can be equally challenging: *időjárásjelentés* (ee-dew-ya-rush-ye-len-tashe); *repülőút* (rap-ew-lew-oot) *különszolgáltatás* (kew-luwn-sole-gawl-taught-aush). They mean "weather report," "plane ride," and "special service," respectively. With Amálka's native tongue, one speaks every syllable in a Hungarian word, none skipped.

At its most extreme, the pronunciation of a Hungarian word might be hairy if it has several endings: *kiművelhetetlenségeskedé-seitekre*, (ki-mewh-vel-het-et-len-shage-esh-ke-day-she-it-tek-re).

This means "to counteract your uneducatedness." I have seen many writers cite long words like this in their books about Hungary to underscore the complexity of the language, but the funny thing is, Hungarians actually dislike long words. They use a hyphen to clarify compound words that are longer than six syllables. An example would be *képzőművészet-szeretet*, "love of fine arts." I breathed a sigh of relief. Even if bizarre constructions with many endings can be made, it doesn't mean anyone would actually use them in everyday conversation.

Like Americans, Hungarians have long words just for amusement. I learned supercalifragilisticexpialidocious as a child, and my husband is fond of antidisestablishmentarianism. The word *megszentségteleníthetetlenségeskedéseitekért* means something like "for the condition of not being able to be desanctified," which will never find its way into any of my casual conversations. I wonder which ridiculously long word Amálka committed to memory? Every kid has one.

For foreigners, buried landmines abound in the pronunciation of Hungarian words. I don't even know them all, though I have figured out how not to embarrass myself in a few places. Accents, also known as diacritics, are potentially hazardous. If I was sloppy and didn't pronounce them properly, I could easily say something completely wrong, causing someone like Amálka to wince.

H. Ellen Browning of *A Girl's Wanderings in Hungary* had a hard time getting diacritics right, too. When she said "*Csokolom a kezet nagyságos kissasszony!*" ("I kiss your hand, honorable damsel!"), she really meant to spell "*Csókolom a kezét nagyságos kissasszony!*" In either case though, she would have been understood.

"Did I not speak German beautifully and French to perfection?" Browning wrote, in a near-desperate tone.

As to my Hungarian conversation . . . my very partial knowledge of accent was always bringing me into the most embarrassing situations. It appears to me as though there is no language under the sun—unless it be Chinese—in which a foreigner finds so many pitfalls of pronunciation as Hungarian. The same word with a different accent on the vowel sound means half-a-dozen things, and when you fondly imagine to be making a complimentary remark, or stating some simple every-day action, you suddenly discover from your auditors that you have been perhaps swearing most horribly, or (what is even more embarrassing) descending into gross obscenity!

Browning wasn't kidding. *Egészségedre* (eg-ace-shage-ed-re) means "to your health." By the way, *egészségedre* is the informal versus formal word being used in this case, another nuance of the language. If I ignored the diacritics and mispronounced the letters ség as segg in *egészségedre*, I could end up saying—my apologies for the vulgarity—"to your whole ass," all the while happily making a toast and clinking glasses with friends. This really worries me about learning Hungarian. How many knots are tied in thousands of knots in no time flat?

If I were trying to order dessert, which is *édesség*, I should be careful not to say *édes segg*, or I would be telling the waiter he has a sweet ass. I'm sure Phil wouldn't appreciate this.

The verb "to introduce," *bemutat*, can present its own complexity. If I wanted to introduce Phil, I better be saying *Bemutatom a férjemet* ("I would like to introduce my husband"), not *Bemutatok a férjemnek* ("I would give the middle finger to my husband").

This brings me to sausage. The word for sausage is *kolbász*, that is unless I didn't say *kol* loudly enough and someone heard only the latter part without the accent. Then I was back to an obscenity.

Another problem emerges because a word can have one meaning as a noun and a totally different meaning as a verb. *Fej* can mean "head" or "to milk a cow," and *vár* means "castle" or "to wait." Sounds innocuous, right? *Hal* can mean "fish" or "to die."

Telling a waiter *Halat szeretnék* ("I would like fish") is fine, but if I said *Halni szeretnék* ("I would like to die"), the server may end up calling an ambulance for me.

A blunder like this would have been particularly embarrassing to say at the dinner table in Amálka's time.

It's also easy to exhibit bad form by inadvertently being rude to someone's mother and referring to her as *anyád* instead of *édesanyád*. My saying *anyád* would be like swearing "Your mother!" in English. This would have gone over poorly in the conservative society of Amálka's rural Hungary at the turn of the twentieth century.

Minor sins can be committed, too. Failing to enunciate each letter l in *viszonthallásra* (ve-sont-hul-lash-ra) turns it from "Good-bye" to "Dying again." If you're like me, this kind of faux pas feels a little like dying . . . of embarrassment.

Pairing words improperly can raise eyebrows. In Hungarian you never say nice wine, *szép bor*, but rather good wine, or *jó bor*. You may get a good-natured laugh but it's a gaffe nevertheless.

I am consoled to know the word *bor*, which incidentally looks nothing like the word wine. That's largely the case with Hungarian, even if some words may resemble English: *étterem* is "restaurant," *állomás* is "station," *gyógyszer* is "medicine," *gyógyszertár* is "pharmacy," *étlap* is "menu," *szálloda* is "hotel," *megálló* is "stop," *leves* is "soup," *lakás* is "apartment," and *sör* is "beer." I'm terrified of speaking Hungarian in public, just like H. Ellen Browning, who described her perpetual series of embarrassments as "so painfully awkward" in *A Girl's Wanderings*.

English travelers and artists Margaret Fletcher and her girlfriend Rose LeQuesne simply threw their hands up during the last part of their visit in Hungary in 1892 and cried, "we can no more" after having "terrible conflicts with the difficulties of language."

I didn't feel so bad after reading their recollections in *Sketches of Life and Character in Hungary*, though I would have loved to know what Amálka thought of foreigners trying to learn Hungarian. It would have been amusing to see her reaction, but she had to have been a kind soul. It runs in the blood. My teacher is that way, too, ever gently pulling me out of my shell with the tools of the trade: books, written exercises, and even a folk saying about Szolnok.

These experiences made me admire those in Amálka's time who did speak the language, including Emperor Francis Joseph. Apparently, no emperor or king since the battle at Mohács in the sixteenth century had made the effort to learn it.

His wife, Elizabeth, mastered the Hungarian language with the help of an old Hungarian professor. "I wrote till my fingers ached," Elizabeth reportedly said, according to biographer Clara Tschudi's *Elizabeth: Empress of Austria and Queen of Hungary* (1901).

Elizabeth benefited from Hungarian works being read to her as servants brushed and styled her long hair. I'm not royalty, and all I hear around me in the melting pot that is New York City are fractured English sentences as people rush about their daily jobs. Everyone is in a hurry, but Hungarian takes time—and a lot of it.

• • •

AMID ALL OF MY EFFORTS TO LEARN HUNGARIAN, RICHARD and I found some levity. I sent him a picture of my dachshund dressed as a zebra for Halloween, and he showed me a picture of his newborn daughter. Then we turned to Amálka. Was there anything else we could discover about her? I zeroed in on Szolnok, the place mentioned most in the book and likely her hometown. Richard agreed to send me any materials he could obtain from or about the town.

Continuing my research for sources on Szolnok and Hungarian history in general, I tripped across the American Hungarian Library in New York City on the Internet. The first time Phil and I went there they were closed. We went again and found ourselves standing in a compact library with a long dark wood table, books neatly arranged in glass cases, standing at attention lining the walls. Anikó, the librarian, mentioned that the collection housed the classics and contemporary tomes.

During our visit, Phil looked through one of the books. When we were ready to leave, he handed it to me so I could see the cover: *The Illustrated History of Hungary*. We borrowed the book.

•   •   •

AT HOME, I DEVOURED *THE ILLUSTRATED HISTORY* WITH ITS digestible descriptions and images like the gallant Andrássy in full military regalia, red and bronze, hand on a sword, fist on the table, and a stare of purpose emanating from his ancestors. I found a copy on Amazon and purchased it, the only copy available at that time. When it arrived, I read the inscriptions in the front of the book. Friends of the previous owner, another Linda, had offered her best wishes. It was like Amálka's little book, too. What was it about these books that they ended up with me?

On the lower right-hand side of the page, it read: "In case there is anything you still don't know about Hungarian history, which I doubt, you can look it up." The author had left another good wish at the end of the sentence with a happy face.

CHAPTER 24

The Hungarian Culture

My Hungarian teacher must have known that I needed a break when she suggested a cultural outing.

"I don't know if you get these, but there's an event at the Hungarian Cultural Center," she said, holding up a red-and-black postcard announcing the book launch for *Fire and Knowledge* by Péter Nádas. "I'm going and you might want to think about it, too."

I took her up on the offer and that night found myself mingling with Hungarians, all of whom seemed to know someone in the crowd. Seeing me, my teacher waved. We took our seats. The audience was hushed before Nádas began.

Through a translator, he told the audience that European history is a very heavy story—of genocide—and that it was difficult for him to extricate himself from that past. Every five minutes he thought about it.

That mindset struck me as profoundly different from the forward-looking approach that many Americans take to history. The study of our nation's past is only one element in preparing for the future. But the ancient animosities I witnessed while visiting Central Europe surely prove the gravity of his words. The closest thing I could think of to the repeated brutal conquests of those lands was the attack on the World Trade Center and the Pentagon on September 11, 2001, which Americans may not have fully internalized yet. We will have to see if we become like the Hungarians, unable to forget certain parts of history.

Amálka may have had a similar worldview, but cultures are kaleidoscopes, brilliant in the present and the past. These colors in conflict bring a new view of objects we thought were simple. Her book beamed with hope, emanating from the same place that Nádas was talking about. I bought his book and called it a night, reminding myself of the good that can come from troubled regions. Here I'm including the whole of Central Europe. I'll bet there are many Amálkas out there.

· · ·

AROUND THIS TIME, I MADE IT A HABIT TO VISIT THE LIBRARY to see Anikó. She continued to help me identify books that might contain the obscure facts I was hunting for, especially books about Szolnok. After we had gotten to know one another, she intimated that she was born in Szolnok and had lived in a village ten minutes away from it. Her life, my life, Szolnok, kismet.

CHAPTER 25

New Year New Options

NEW YORK CITY RANG IN 2008 WITH ONE MILLION PEOPLE crowding into Times Square. Budapest welcomed the new year with a thirty-inch blanket of snow. We wished Richard and his family good cheer, and he asked if we might be coming back to Hungary to see Novska, the city we hadn't seen the prior summer. Phil and I talked about it and agreed to travel to Hungary again, this time on my way to see Novska and Zagreb in Croatia, Vienna, and, of course, Szolnok. Other places once governed by the former Austro-Hungarian Monarchy were a possibility, too.

In addition to the trip, Phil and I talked about Amálka's real identity. From the beginning, we'd all known that the little book had remembrances about two weddings and an engagement.

"Maybe some detail in any of those entries would be enough to figure out who she was," I said. "There's one way to find out: hire a genealogist in Szolnok to go through the town's archives, using whatever information we have."

"We've come this far with Amálka . . . ," Phil said. "See what Richard says."

After reviewing my long and detailed e-mail, Richard declared he was open to everything. He offered to go himself to the archives in Szolnok.

Our best shot was to find the official record of the Kucika's wedding in Szolnok on October 4, 1916.

"We are ninety-five percent sure it happened in Szolnok, which means I can find it," Richard said during a call in late January.

"Oh, one more thing," he added. "On one of the pages, the one where Amálka went ice skating, she signed it herself. It would be worth showing her signature to an expert in graphology. There are many graphologists here. If the graphologist can tell us Amálka's potential age, that would be a big help."

The clue had been right in front of us. Her simple signature was like a key, unlocking the process that could help us trace the young girl who had once enjoyed ice skating in 1908. We hired a female and male graphologist to obtain independent opinions.

Her signature had faded through time and was barely visible on the page. But this faint remnant of Amálka shone under close inspection. A little twenty-first-century computer magnification made it perfectly clear.

Richard and I swapped e-mails: I sent the signature off to him and he returned the preliminary summer agenda with stops in Vienna, the Istria Peninsula, Croatia, and Hungary, covering a total of eighteen hundred miles in fifteen days. I wasn't the first traveler to be excited about a tour of a few thousand miles. Artist F. D. Millet and a few other friends gamely canoed down the Danube in the 1890s. It took them nearly three months to make their way through Germany, Austria, Hungary, Serbia, Bulgaria, Romania, and Russia, racking up 1,775 miles by the time they reached the Black Sea.

Nor were they the region's only fearless travelers at the time. Socialite Lion Phillimore recounts the experiences she and her husband had while camping through the Carpathians in Transylvania a few years before World War I. It was primitive and brutal. At one point, she was nearly beaten when she grabbed her papers from the hand of a local who was drunk. We had the same spirit of adventure even if Richard was going to drive and we would be sleeping in hotels.

The trek was going to give us an opportunity to see the Istria Peninsula on the Adriatic Coast, vital during Amálka's time as Hungary's access to the sea. In some places the Monarchy's architecture was preserved, providing another chance to get a feel for how it might have looked one hundred years earlier.

"People who lived in Novska surely visited Rijeka," Richard said, referring to the Hungarian port named Fiume during Amálka's time. "I know there is no mention of it in the journal, but still I think someone who traveled so much would not have missed it."

We reviewed the schedule while Richard got ready for his trip back in time to Szolnok. In the meantime, we pursued another angle about Amálka's period in New York City.

My Hungarian teacher pointed out that the Budapest Festival Orchestra was in town and would be performing works by Strauss and Bartók at Lincoln Center. Béla Bartók (1881–1945) is famous in his homeland and around the world. In the early 1900s, Bartók and his colleague Zoltán Kodály (1882–1967), another accomplished Hungarian composer, toured villages in Transylvania and the surrounding countryside, recording the Magyar folk songs on phonograph records.

Bartók's only opera, *Bluebeard's Castle*, was heavily influenced by Hungarian folk songs and French opera. I got tickets. Most women would appreciate the story: a man subject to his fate and a woman desperately trying to understand him. This is revealed with a series of doors the woman was destined to open. When she opens the last door, she is swallowed up in blackness. The play could have been written for Amálka. She was advised to think wisely before she selected someone to love.

• • •

THE RESULTS FROM THE TWO HANDWRITING EXPERTS CAME IN right around Valentine's Day. Both graphologists provided similar opinions about Amálka's personality. Amálka was about twelve to fourteen years old in 1907. This would make her date of birth between 1893 and 1895, arriving just in time for the preparations for the Millennium celebration.

The female graphologist said:

- Amálka has a kind personality
- She enjoys what she is actually doing
- Emotion oriented
- Instinct oriented
- Listens to her intuition
- She likes forms
- She has her own world of imagination
- Her imagination works very well
- She attaches too much importance to externals/form
- She is a teenager, twelve to fourteen years old

Here's what the male graphologist said:

- The manuscript's form is school age type, definitely controlled
- She has a lively, dynamic and ambitious personality
- Strong and balanced character
- Good decision maker, self-conscious, but still sensitive
- Not very interested in details
- She has good logic
- Very instinctive and emotion dominated in her social relationships
- Care-taking and faithful
- She has a positive, imaginative ego
- Possession gives her security
- Self-consciousness is important
- Her value judgment hesitates between her milieu and the greater society.

- She attaches more importance to externals/form
- Very determined
- She is hardly susceptible to influence
- Creative and flexible
- She thinks her life is too controlled
- Her intensive and instinctive subconscious ego can't find connection to the conscious ego
- She is around fourteen years old

"It is amazing to see how Amálka's personality emerges in front of us," Richard said. "I can order a third opinion. Still, it is quite thrilling to see somebody who died decades ago reborn."

We didn't need a third graphologist to confirm that Amálka was young, energetic, artistic, and hopeful.

Almost immediately after the report came in, Richard took off for the archives in Szolnok.

"Please don't expect an immediate report about the Szolnok research because I come back on February nineteenth at night but on February twenty-first we go to ski in Austria," he said. "We will be back on February twenty-fourth."

I waited on pins and needles.

BARTÓK

Béla Bartók and Zoltán Kodály are remembered for preserving and perpetuating ethnic music from Transylvania and its environs. These rhythms beat as the signature of gypsies, people "free as the birds of the air, paying no taxes, acknowledging no laws, and making the whole world their own," wrote Scottish novelist Emily Gerard in her book *Land Beyond the Forest*.

CHAPTER 26

Searching the Archives in Szolnok

"I AM BACK FROM SZOLNOK!" RICHARD ANNOUNCED IN AN e-mail.

I read faster.

"I found the link between Amálka and Novska," he said.

I froze: After reviewing eight thousand names from all the birthdates between 1890 and 1897, he found 120 girls with the name Amálka. "But there is only one who, at least partly, fits our profile," he wrote.

I gasped.

"There is a good chance that I found her but the story is more complicated," Richard said. "As we go to Austria, I have no time to give a full report, but will be back with all the details next week."

Oh my god! We got her!

Later that evening, I breathlessly told Phil that we'd had a major breakthrough.

As promised, the report from Richard on the "Jász-Nagykun-Szolnok County Archive" showed up in my inbox as soon as he got back from Austria. Until I read Richard's report, I didn't realize that the archives were not open to everyone. As a journalist and a member of the Association of Hungarian Journalists, Richard obtained permission to view the archives after filling out and signing several forms. He must have felt he was signing his life away for his American friends. Phil found good humor in this.

Richard described how the archives work. Each time he wanted anything, the elderly librarian gave him a paper to fill out with details, years, dates, names, and book titles—he said it felt like the old Communist bureaucracy. The gentleman worked very hard, Richard said.

Once he filled out everything, Richard would pass the paper to the librarian, who would shuffle slowly away and, after a short while, come back with two heavy books. Richard would sign a document saying that he'd received the books, then proceed to inspect them in the reading room. When Richard was finished, he'd pass them back to the librarian, fill out additional paperwork, and go through the process again. It went on this way for two days. Ultimately, Richard got what he needed, thanks to the librarian, who was "very helpful." Other people doing genealogy work there gave him advice, too.

The graphologists had said that Amálka was probably born in the early to mid-1890s, right around the time the Register of Births, Marriages and Deaths was created as an institution in Hungary. Before that, churches were the main source of records, much as it was in many other countries, including the United States.

Privacy laws in Hungary allow searches only for births that occurred over ninety years earlier. By the time I found Amálka's keepsake in the antique shop in 2005, 110 to 112 years had passed. Richard searched 1893, 1894, and 1895 as Amálka's possible birth years. A side note: Between 1891 and 1892, about 40 percent of Hungarian children under five years of age died, and for a time between 1891 and 1895, children under five represented the majority of deaths in the country. Infectious diseases were the primary cause. Amálka's story survived beyond all this.

Hungarian law also prohibited searching records of marriages that had taken place within the last sixty years and deaths within the last thirty years. Again, sufficient time had passed, allowing us to find Kucika's marriage, which occurred on October 4, 1916. Richard found a wedding on that day that matched the name of the groom and other family members. Kucika, it turned out, was a nickname used by the bride, Fruzsina Orbán. The groom, János Németh, worked as a railway stoker. János signed his nickname "Jancsi" in the entry about Kucika's wedding.

The bride and groom had similar socioeconomic and religious backgrounds, both were born in Szolnok—she in 1893 and he in 1892—and both baptized in the Roman Catholic faith. Their parents worked in agriculture as day-wage laborers. Right there, we knew that neither bride nor groom was directly related to Amálka. The intellectual tone and text of her memory book didn't fit with the agricultural background of Kucika's and János's parents. The difference in social status was too wide.

But the class difference between the wedding couple and Amálka wasn't unusual. In urban cities like Szolnok at the turn of the twentieth century, an emerging middle and mercantile class mixed with most socioeconomic groups below those of the royals and aristocrats. Amálka and her family would have attended Fruzsina and János's wedding.

Anna also attended this wedding, and presumably it was the same Anna who had joined Amálka and her friends at harvest in Nagyvárad nearly a decade earlier. Now she was at Kucika's wedding, saying, "Think of your sad Anna." It read like a snippet from a personal diary. She didn't sign her last name, which surely meant that Amálka knew her. This passage made me feel as though I'd invaded a personal space.

The engagement of Gizuska on November 28, 1909, was the next possible link to Amálka. We didn't have a town listed but we thought it might be Szolnok. The Jász-Nagykun-Szolnok County Independent Newspaper for November and December 1909 was available on microfilm. It was a long shot because weddings, not engagements, typically were mentioned in the paper. And, indeed, we had no luck finding it.

We had one last chance: the wedding of Valéria and József on May 11, 1907. Again, no town was listed but we tried Szolnok. Richard tracked down their official marriage record.

The groom, József Kiss, born in Novska on January 18, 1878, was the son of Etelka Horváth and Tamás Kiss. Amálka was connected to Novska, which is about two hundred miles from Szolnok. Her mother had signed the album in 1906 in Novska and so did D. Vajnai that same year. In 1914, someone whose name we couldn't make out also signed it in Novska, sharing the words of Petrarch with Amálka.

The bride, Valéria Kárász, born in Szolnok on October 8, 1882, was the daughter of Klára Szigethy and Péter Kárász. Lenke Kárász had signed Amálka's memory book, too.

The witnesses for the Roman Catholic couple were Gyula Földvári from Püspökladány and Ottó Tolnai from Szolnok. Tolnai signed the entry for the wedding. Földvári's wife signed the entry, too.

"According to the book, Amálka spent time in Novska in 1906 and was present at the wedding in 1907, so presumably she had a close relationship with either the Kiss or the Kárász family," Richard wrote.

The last document to check for was Amálka's birth record. The two weddings were Roman Catholic, but just in case Amálka was Jewish, Richard searched both the Jewish and Catholic records from 1890 to 1896 in Szolnok.

He checked Valéria's birth year of 1882, too, but it said little beyond the marriage record.

The records showed that about eleven hundred Catholic and one hundred Jewish babies were born in Szolnok each year from

1890 to 1896. Each year, fifteen to twenty girls were named Amália, the basis for the nickname Amálka. Her first name wasn't very popular during those years.

By cross-referencing the names in Amálka's memory book with the parents and godparents on church birth records up to 1895 and state records from 1896 forward, Richard found one match: Amália Endrei.

Amálka. You came from a living book and bridged the worlds of the ethereal and the sentient. You brought to life your parents, godparents, and friends, everyone enjoying weddings and engagements, special times. The aphorisms written to you were like the roses in the book, in full bloom every time you see them. Richard said Amálka and I had a karmic connection. Karma doesn't know size. Karma doesn't know fame. Karma doesn't know time. But karma binds through all, and every life is bound by it.

Amália Endrei, born in Szolnok on January 1, 1891, was the third child of György Endrei, an engine driver at the Railway of the Monarchy, and Piroska Kárász. Her godparents were József Radnai and Jolán Borovits.

The link between Amálka's and Valéria's family was the last name Kárász.

Valéria's maiden name, Kárász. Her father, a Kárász. Amálka's mother, a Kárász. Amálka and Valéria must have been cousins.

The agricultural professions, the succulent fruit in her watercolors, the train jobs, and the aphorism relating to trains—everything started to gel.

"It was a very interesting feeling to sit in the archive and think of the past," he said. "Even handling the books and the papers, you can't really imagine touching 140-year-old paper, which is dusty and dirty and you want to cough," he said. "It was unbelievable."

"There it is," I said quietly, as Phil and I relaxed on the couch. "Valéria's maiden name was Kárász, her father was Péter Kárász and her aunt, Amálka's mother, was Piroska Kárász."

Leaning back, Phil put his cup down, looked at me, and said, "I knew she could be found."

As for Richard, he had culled through thousands of records of a century past and still was able to see straight. When Richard called he said, "These two days were enough!"

The results were good enough for me. I felt that we had found the right Amálka and had pulled back the curtain, shining light on part of her family tree.

"It's personal and touching even without knowing anyone in Amálka's book," Richard said. "As I have already gotten to know some of the family members, what happened, marriages, engagements, I'm much closer to it. I think we are in her book now."

Richard, we have always been in her book.

WEDDING

Travel writer W. B. Forster Bovill attended a working-class wedding in the Transylvania hills in 1908. Writing in *Hungary and the Hungarians*, he said, "No hitches, nothing forgotten, all merry and bright, and service over we sat down to a most excellent spread in the best room the girl's mother could provide. . . . After dinner, fiddlers three were dragged in, and dancing commenced. It is the custom for everybody present to dance with the newly married peasant girl, and when your spell is over to place a thank-offering of money in a plate. . . . Quite a large sum of money was collected. The quantity of useful wedding presents amazed me."

CHAPTER 27

Winter Time

THE SZOLNOK ARCHIVE FINDINGS WERE A HUGE LIFT. BUT MY bubble soon popped. By lesson fifteen, on February 28, 2008, to be precise, I slumped in the chair, set the pen free, and sighed.

"Don't get discouraged," my Hungarian teacher said. "It's a lot to absorb and you're doing fine."

I plowed on, spending weeks trying to comprehend and remember the different verb conjugations—just in present tense. I could barely speak a word but I was beginning to recognize verbs in sentences and questions. A light flickered at the end of the tunnel.

All this because of Amálka, I thought, shaking my head. I finally knew a few genealogical details about her. We had a name, a birth date, and a location. But in early March, when Richard and I finally caught up with each other on the phone, he lobbed the hand grenade that had been in the last paragraph on the final page of his report, the one I'd tried to avoid reading. In his conclusion, he identified the weak link. In order to absolutely prove that we had the right Amálka, we would need to establish the concrete relationship between Amálka and Valéria as first cousins. That would require creating a family tree for the Péter Kárász and György Endrei families.

While this was not completely necessary to do—Phil thought we had the right person, too—I was driven by curiosity and by what else we might find. All I hoped to get was confirmation of Amálka's family tree. So much destruction had occurred in her century it seemed unlikely that we would get very reliable data for much else.

Having hung up his research hat, Richard suggested that I strongly consider hiring a genealogist in Budapest for this work. If the identification from the Szolnok records was right, the genealogist would be able to prove that Valéria's father and Amálka's mother were brother and sister. It wasn't practical to find out whether Amálka and Valéria were second or third cousins because of the increased difficulty and associated costs of doing so.

It would be next to impossible to find out whether Amálka was related to the groom, since he was from Novska, Croatia. I suggested to Richard that we go back to the Internet to see what, if anything, could be found now that we had the last names of Amálka and her parents. This might be helpful in proving her identity, especially if her last name wasn't that common.

My Google search in America turned up nothing. Hungarian Google produced numerous results but none specifically fit our needs. The multiple hits for "Endrei Amália" simply had been a matter of people having the same name.

We definitely weren't going to track down the thirty people named Endrei who lived in Szolnok, the two hundred and fifty in Budapest, or the nineteen in Pécs without knowing far beyond what we had already found.

This reminded me of a situation I'd encountered in Sicily. The staff at a hotel knew that my husband and I were going to be searching for my grandfather's records in his hometown of Leonforte. I heard a knock at the door. It was the bellman, all teeth. That's it. He managed to get across that his last name was the same as my maiden name. We stood there stunned in our cultural dissonance, friendly but frozen, each silently waiting for the other one to speak. Phil jumped up to smooth over an awkward moment with his Italian sign language—gestures indicating big, small, high, low, left, and right; locals get him, but I don't, though it's gotten us out of many jams.

This taught me an important lesson: to be very wary of anything I said about the details of our travels.

I was led right back to a fundamental question. Even if Amálka's book was accidentally discarded, the lack of care for it would have led to rebuke in most families.

"When my grandmother died," Richard said, "we had to empty the flat, and I took out all the personal stuff I wanted to keep and sold the rest to an antique shop. An album like this might have found its way to the antique shop if all the people with a personal relationship to Amálka had died. Otherwise, it's just too personal. We Hungarians would never drop it away."

Before we hung up, I agreed to think about getting a genealogist to search for additional information about Amálka. I talked to Phil about this.

"We both know it's just not feasible to dig up her living relatives," Phil said. "We don't know the language though you've been working at it. If anything, what we can do reliably is to try to find the genealogy because every step of the way has taught us something. But let's consider what this process means."

CHAPTER 28

Life Goes On

I pondered whether to engage a genealogist.

I was visiting Anikó at the library on Wednesday afternoons. When I stepped through the door into the library time slowed down. I looked through the books, borrowed some, returned some, and spoke with Anikó about my difficulties learning Hungarian. She couldn't help laughing when I pronounced something completely wrong and I couldn't either.

. . .

Easter rolled around and Richard and I continued to trade e-mails. In one of them I learned something about how Easter traditionally has been celebrated in Hungary.

They had the same tall tale of the Easter bunny, but they also participate in an unusual ritual dating from before Christianity. Easter's the watering, or sprinkling, season in Hungary. This fertility ritual takes a variety of forms, depending on the social class of the participants.

At the turn of the twentieth century among the peasant class, a young man used a bucket of water to "sprinkle"—more like douse—a young maiden. She could get him to stop by giving him painted eggs and bribing him with a kiss. In the refined version, a young suitor visited a girl and sprinkled perfume on her to express his interest in her. Amálka would have had the better treatment as a member of a higher class. Richard surmised that with over a half-dozen women in his life, he needed a bottle of perfume to get his work done.

Phil and I informed Richard we would skip the perfume but not the genealogist. We had come this far, why stop here.

By early spring the genealogist was in full swing and our trip back to Hungary was nearly organized. The plan, start in Austria, jump to Slovenia and Croatia, then head through Hungary back to Austria.

CHAPTER 29

The Genealogist

A BELL RANG ON MY COMPUTER. I LOOKED AT AN E-MAIL FROM Richard with the genealogist's findings. The genealogist started with the marriage of Amálka's parents, György Endrei and Piroska Kárász. Their nuptials took place on July 20, 1886, the groom twenty-six years old, Piroska twenty-three. The bride was the daughter of Dénes Kárász, a miller, and Erzsébet Majsai, according to records in the Jász-Nagykun-Szolnok County Archive. Information about the groom was yet to be discovered.

ERZSÉBET MAJSAI — DÉNES KÁRÁSZ

(MARRIAGE: ?)

↓

PIROSKA KÁRÁSZ — GYÖRGY ENDREI

(BORN: ~1863)   (BORN: ~1860)

(MARRIAGE: JULY 20, 1886)

↓

AMÁLIA ENDREI

(BORN: JANUARY 01, 1891 IN SZOLNOK)

The genealogist tried to document the wedding of Valéria's parents, Péter Kárász and Klára Szigethy, and also looked for Valéria's birth record in the Szolnok archives. Both were missing. He turned to Valéria's marriage record in the Roman Catholic Church register, from which he obtained further details. Valéria had been born in Berettyóújfalu, about seventy miles east of Szolnok, and her husband in Cegléd, about twenty miles west of Szolnok. The genealogist also confirmed that Richard had gotten the correct names for Valéria's parents.

KLÁRA SZIGETHY — PÉTER KÁRÁSZ

(BORN IN ?)   (BORN IN ?)

↓

VALÉRIA KÁRÁSZ

(BORN: OCTOBER 08, 1882 IN BERETTYÓÚJFALU)

All that remained to confirm Amálka and Valéria's relationship were the names of Valéria's paternal grandparents. For this we would need the Roman Catholic registers of Berettyóújfalu. The genealogist, hot on the trail, waited for the record book in use by someone else.

In the interim, I asked Richard if the genealogist could tell us when and how Amálka and her parents had died. The answer to that proved complicated. The only way to gather this information would be to check all the death records in Szolnok over the last sixty years. But if they died somewhere else, the entire effort would be for naught. We decided to wait on those questions. The genealogist had more work to do.

A week later, another e-mail with data about the genealogist's findings dropped with a thud into my inbox.

The record books from 1873 to 1893, the exact period we needed, were missing. Most likely they had been destroyed in a church fire or simply disappeared in the turbulent period that was to follow.

How could it be that the information supremely valuable only to a few soul searchers like me was fated to be lost in the annals of a few old books?

The genealogist called the parish priest at the Berettyóújfalu Roman Catholic Church to ask whether he had any duplicates. The priest confirmed that the records we sought were gone and said that there were no copies. But the genealogist knew that Roman Catholic registers duplicated records beginning in the nineteenth century, and that the Berettyóújfalu records would have to be held in the county archives in Hajdúböszörmény. The genealogist set off to the Hajdú-Bihar County Archive, Hajdúböszörmény Unit. The records weren't there either, which led him to believe that the original records had been wiped out before duplicates could be made.

Richard and I agreed that the genealogist should check the Szolnok archives for Amálka's death record. We'd have to wait until the beginning of June for his final report to see whether Amálka died in Szolnok.

Around this time, Richard began to end his e-mails with a Hungarian sentence, which I was to translate and send back in the next e-mail. His wife Julia wrote me a letter in Hungarian, telling me how their daughter loved to play and wave to people. I'd like to say that I read her letter as if it had been written in English. I really would like to say that. However, the Hungarian sentence isn't like English, from left to right. Sometimes it's right to left; other times it's a jumble of words that you have to know how to assemble into a sentence by the context. Her e-mail took me at least an hour, maybe two, to translate and fully understand. Then I spent a few hours creating a response in Hungarian.

When Julia replied, I got kudos for writing the note, but one sentence had completely baffled her: Csukott válaszok de még több rajtacsípni. I was trying to say, "We are close to answers but there is still more to find out," referring to Amálka. But what I actually wrote translated to, "Closed answers but even more to catch them in the act."

I laughed so hard. Clearly, I had a long way to go with Hungarian—and Amálka.

CHAPTER 30

Closing in On Things

THE VERDICT WAS IN: AMÁLKA EITHER HADN'T DIED IN Szolnok, or she passed away there at an old age and the information was restricted by Hungarian privacy laws.

When I read all of the details of the final report, I realized that the genealogist also looked in a variety of other places to find Amálka's heritage. On the off chance that Valéria was Protestant or an Israelite, the genealogist checked the registers of Berettyóújfalu for her birth record. Nothing Jewish.

Searching the state registers of Szolnok in the archives, the genealogist came across the death record of Amálka's sister, Katalin Endrei, who had died on October 14, 1918, a month before World War I ended. How did she die? Was she one of the millions of victims worldwide of the Spanish influenza, killing the troops fighting in World War I? Could her death have been another reason why the messages to Amálka so intensely focused on her happiness?

The genealogist also found the death record for Amálka's father in the Szolnok archives. György Endrei, the son of Magda Endrei and an unknown father, was a rail-engine driver who died at fifty-one of a heart attack on April 2, 1911.

In addition, he uncovered the death record of Péter Kárász, Valéria's father, and the names of his parents, Gyula Kárász and Rozália Füzes. This retired railroad watcher passed away at age seventy-five on January 1, 1921.

RozÁLIA FÜZES — GYULA KÁRÁSZ
(MARRIAGE DATE: ?)
↓
PÉTER KÁRÁSZ — KLÁRA SZIGETHY
(1846 – JANUARY 22, 1921)   (BORN: ?)
↓
VALÉRIA KÁRÁSZ
(BORN: OCTOBER 08, 1882 IN BERETTYÓÚJFALU)

• • •

ERZSÉBET MAJSAI — DÉNES KÁRÁSZ
(MARRIAGE: JULY 20, 1886)
↓
PIROSKA KÁRÁSZ — GYÖRGY ENDREI
(BORN: ~1863)   (~1860 – APRIL 02, 1911)
↓
AMÁLIA ENDREI
(BORN: JANUARY 01, 1891 IN SZOLNOK)

The research established that Piroska and Péter could not have been siblings because they didn't share the same parents, unless an error was made when the record was created. Therefore Amálka and Valéria were not first cousins. Yet one of the witnesses listed in the Szolnok archives exactly matched a name signed in Amálka's album on the day of the nuptials of Valéria and Józsi. What were the odds of that?

I reached for the next best possibility: If Gyula and Dénes had the same parents, they could have been brothers, making

Amálka and Valéria second cousins. But to prove it, we would need additional genealogical work showing that the Amálka we found in the Szolnok archives was the owner of the memory book. But at this point, it seemed excessive given that we had identified the structure of the family and the place Amálka held in it.

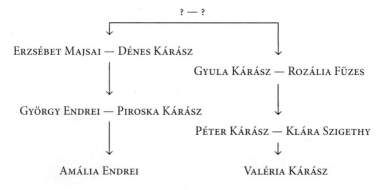

• • •

SUMMER HAD ARRIVED AND VIENNA, LIKE A MAGNET, PULLED us toward horse-drawn carriages and chocolates deluxe.

PART IV

CHAPTER 31

Vienna in a New Light

THE AUSTRO-HUNGARIAN MONARCHY REVEALS ITSELF IN Vienna's architecture. This time I was determined to get into a few of the historic buildings that we had seen.

We brought along a little help. We had not one but two guides because Richard hired an official Austrian guide, Hans. At this point we agreed with nineteenth-century author Charles McArmor's comment in *The New Handbook of Vienna* that "unless the tourist can speak the language, an intelligent interpreter is almost indispensable" in Vienna.

Our first stop was the Hofburg, a collection of government buildings. Bureaucrats occupy the former Habsburg castle dating from the thirteenth century. We took in the sights, passing the Demel confectionery bakery with K. U. K. on the awning. Because of the map room at the New York Public Library, we knew it meant that the bakery had been given the imperial seal of approval. We went in for a quick coffee and cake, and before I left, I bought some of Demel's candied violets so favored by Empress Elizabeth.

Richard and Hans led the way to the Capuchin Crypt,

located right in the historic heart of Vienna. The Imperial Vault, outfitted with railings, good ventilation, and adequate lighting, allowed for a steady flow of guidebook-clutching tourists. We were all doing our best to be respectful of the environment, but I'm not sure that gawking at all the coffins offered the dead an adequate degree of deference. Truthfully, the whole place struck me as fairly macabre, even if Emperor Francis Joseph, Empress Elizabeth, and their son Rudolf were safely tucked away in dark, cold bronze coffins in one room.

The coffin of Francis Joseph is perched on a white granite block with a brass casting of the old man's face. He looks across on his wife and son. I found it particularly odd to be standing in front of Empress Elizabeth's coffin. She hated people gaping at her and regularly used a fan to cover her face. No one knows what Sisi looked like in her later years because she wouldn't let anyone take her picture.

Now, I felt she would have bristled, even in a coffin, at being an object on a tour. Still, I asked Phil to take a picture of the triumvirate, since Francis Joseph called the shots in Hungary when Amálka lived. She would have recognized the royal couple. Their images surely hung on many a household wall.

We sought out the museum devoted to Sisi, joining throngs of other tourists fixated on the fans and parasols and even the luxury train car that Elizabeth used in her many travels across Europe. Sisi was obsessive about her looks and weight, which the museum highlights, but she was also focused on education her entire life. Phil pointed out that she had plenty of time do that, unlike the rest of the working folks, including Amálka and her family in rural Szolnok.

We quickly traversed from antique to modern. The Hundertwasser-Krawina House in Vienna entertained us with multiple floors painted in bright blue, yellow, and white. The house is covered in plants. Vines are everywhere and, depending on the season, the foliage takes on different colors. Its roof is topped by a minaret. The only downside to that excursion came when we couldn't get a waiter's attention at an adjacent café.

Not to worry, said our Viennese guide. There would be plenty of places to stop en route to Sisi's hunting lodge, Hermesvilla, on the outskirts of Vienna. Ever vigilant to save us money, Hans had decided that we should take a few buses to get there. When we discovered that the last bus we needed was out of service, Hans finally relented and we took a cab.

Hermesvilla sits in a heavily wooded area, and as we passed through it I noticed a lone deer resting in the distance. The park and its deer and other animals appealed to the nature-loving Sisi.

By now we were familiar with the lavish Habsburg life and Sisi's mercurial nature. Hermesvilla is full of statues, inlaid wood, and stained glass windows. For me, one insight into Sisi's life came in her bedroom decorated in the fashion of *A Midsummer Night's Dream*. The bed is small with gold Rococo ornamentation and bright red bedding. Its immense headboard is emblazoned with an imperial eagle in black and carved on one side is a scene from Shakespeare's play, complete with an ass tail protruding from one side. I suppose that was meant to be amusing, but I would have had nightmares sleeping in it.

· · ·

OUR ADVENTURES, BOTH LIGHTHEARTED AND SOLEMN, PICKED up on day three outside Vienna. Seegrotte is now Europe's largest underground lake, but in Amálka's time it was a gypsum mine. During World War II, Germans transformed the mine operation into a factory for their first fighter jets, which were built by workers conscripted from concentration camps. It cast a pall over the place.

Passing through a small door, we walked down a long, dark tunnel. Electric lights illuminated wooden fortifications at various intervals. An eerie heaviness exudes from the quiet of those rock walls. Old tools strewn about in the primitive work areas spoke to long, exhausting hours of hard labor.

This grim history was juxtaposed against Disneyesque touches, like the gold-painted Viking-style boat floating in an underground alcove near our official tourist craft. They were left over from a movie shot on site. Surprisingly, I enjoyed the ride. The blue-green water glistened in the artificial light as music serenaded us on our short tour through the caves.

The tone lightened considerably when we reached the ancient town of Baden, renowned for its thermal spas, attracting royalty and the leading lights of Europe for centuries. A few of the early notables included Roman Emperor Probus, who used his army to develop the shores of the Danube.

Taking a big skip forward, Ludwig van Beethoven spent time in Baden in the eighteenth century, as did Emperor Francis Joseph in the nineteenth century, luxuriating in the romance of stately villas and ubiquitous greenery.

The city has some stately imperial buildings but I was interested in the spas. In the late nineteenth century, Baden's mineral waters were highly prized for their supposed curative powers against a host of human maladies, including rheumatism and various skin problems. No time to wade into the water here but the knowledge that it was less than an hour's train ride from Vienna convinced us that we would have to return.

Our guides pulled us away from Baden to visit Heiligenkreuz. This abbey has been in operation without interruption since its founding in the twelfth century. Today it is a Roman Catholic theological college that prepares men for the priesthood, serving as a place for monks to commune with God and work various trades in order to preserve the abbey for future generations.

The abbey's imposing church, filled with stained glass and detailed marble-and-wood carvings of religious icons, has ceilings grasping at heaven. The monastery's two-story buildings overlook a lush, green courtyard. I, for one, could feel a holy presence. Rudolf wanted to be buried in the Heiligenkreuz cemetery. His mistress, Mary Vetsera, (1871–1899) did end up there, but Rudolf lays in the sterile Imperial Vault. She got the better of it, buried in the serene countryside. Even in death, these scandalous lovers had so much privilege. Amálka, I'm certain, had far less.

With lunch approaching, our Viennese guide insisted that we eat at the abbey restaurant. He said the food was fresh, delicious, and reasonably priced. We happily agreed. As we walked to the table, our guide regaled us with stories about Leopold III, Margrave of Austria, who provided the land for the abbey. It grew from a dozen monks to nearly seventy monks today.

"The abbey has a direct tie to the Vatican," Hans proclaimed.

I wondered if he hadn't said this to make us feel devout.

The birds sang and in the middle of the restaurant was an old stone fountain surrounded by round lunch tables with red and white umbrellas. We sat down and the waiter came over with menus.

Most of us ordered some form of game, but Phil liked fish so he selected the trout. Amálka must have eaten a lot of fish, plentiful in the region's lakes and rivers, especially the Tisza in Hungary.

Our drinks came and we learned about the abbey and its residents. Hans described the ways the monastery supported itself over the centuries, through farming, winemaking, and a variety of other occupations. But I was soon too distracted to listen to him.

"Look, look at the fountain," I said, spotting a man wearing a chef's toque and apron, and holding a pole with a huge net. "Oh my God, he's trying to catch the fish to cook."

"Yes, they are catching Phil's trout for lunch," Richard replied.

"I told you the monastery had to be self-sufficient," our

Viennese guide said, lifting his glass filled with the award-winning local Blauburgunder wine.

The cook, shaking his head, pushed the huge net around in the fountain water as daintily as possible, but each time came up empty. I bolted to the fountain. This was too good to miss. Man versus trout.

I briskly walked back to my chair, satisfied that nature was ahead, and implored Phil, "Go and see what's happening."

He got up and discreetly walked to the fountain, tilting his head and turning his shoulders inward, as if the whole affair was as mortifying as having a piece of spinach stuck between his front teeth at a business dinner. I doubled over in laughter.

He sheepishly came back to the table and announced, "If he doesn't catch the fish soon, I'm going to change the order."

A pudgy older man jogged from the kitchen to the fountain carrying a square piece of wood, which he dropped into the water. The man with the cook's hat continued shaking his head.

"That's it," Phil said firmly. "I should change the order."

We all laughed uncontrollably as other restaurant patrons gathered around the fountain to watch the impromptu show.

"I don't think I'll have fish," Phil insisted to the waiter.

"No, your fish is inside," he said, scurrying away.

Given the intensity of the work at the fountain, I doubted that they had any fish inside. But God knows—we were at the abbey. Maybe the Lord was delivering loaves and fishes all over again.

The man with the board abruptly whipped it out of the fountain and disappeared. A much younger third man, obviously amused, sprinted toward the fountain, carrying another piece of wood. He maneuvered it into the water, telling the man with the net to do something. I assumed it was to follow the fish around again.

No luck.

They tried again. No luck.

But the young man persisted, urging the cook and the fellow with the board to keep at it. This is the only time I felt that I understood German. I'm almost certain he was saying, "Don't give up! Try again!"

Finally, on the fifth try, the cook proudly lifted the net to shoulder level for all to see the flopping gray meal.

Everyone applauded.

Normally, fish is served whole with the bones and head intact, but at Phil's request, the trout was deboned, although the cook did leave the head to decorate the plate.

By meal's end, the laughter and amusement had died down and Phil was describing how light and delicious the fish had been.

"Nothing beats this lunch at Heiligenkreuz," he said, a big grin, dimples and all.

. . .

GOOD THING WE HAD A LAUGH AT HEILIGENKREUZ. WE descended into the solemnity of Mayerling, the former hunting lodge that had been the site of the deaths of Rudolf and Mary. It was a tragic event that everyone in the Hungarian kingdom would have known about. An early account had Vetsera poisoning Rudolf and then herself, but the truth emerged with the bodies. Rudolf allegedly shot Vetsera and then turned the gun on himself. His notions about a peaceful coexistence between the ethnic groups in order for the empire to survive faded with the bullet. His father, Emperor Francis Joseph, managed the empire, and his son's views were not often aligned with his.

Mayerling has a peacefulness about it, as though all the tears shed there had washed away its crimes. Nature was in charge, not the royals. Green hills with majestic trees rolled on and on in the distance. Birds chirped and the water from a little creek near the convent path rippled with life. The quiet speaks of deep sadness.

The Viennese guide said that if this erudite and capable young prince, not his father, had been in charge, the empire might have had a chance to adapt to the challenges of a new century. Rudolf may have had forward-thinking political ideas. Nevertheless, good ideas might not have been enough to withstand a tide of violence.

Exiting Mayerling, we passed through a little museum with pictures of Rudolf and his family alongside a few remaining furnishings from the lodge, a poignant reminder of the lost potential.

Like Mayerling, Laxenburg, our next stop, would certainly have been off limits to Amálka as it was the summer residence of the royal family. But the lore of this home and gardens surely would have sprung to life in a young girl's mind. One could have only dreamed about them because they were completely beyond the means of all but a few.

"Visitors for whom money is no object should drive to Laxenburg in an open carriage," recommended travel writer Charles McArmor in *The New Handbook of Vienna* in the late nineteenth century. Back then it cost the considerable sum of twelve florin, or five dollars.

Today, Laxenburg houses various business and educational institutions, including the International Institute for Applied Systems Analysis. That group carries out research on the environment and natural resources, population and society, and energy and technology. It seems quite fitting for a scientific organization to be located at Laxenburg, given that Rudolf was deeply interested in the sciences.

We focused on exploring the outdoors, just as the Habsburgs did in their time. Laxenburg had "some charming ornamental waters, and an old ivy covered feudal castle, The Franzenburg," according to A. De Burgh in *Elizabeth, Empress of Austria: A Memoir*. Laxenburg was also known for its diverse bird species in the nineteenth century, from mallards in the pond to lesser spotted eagles and buzzards.

It was a clear day and we set off for a short walk. The Habsburgs and Amálka. She didn't have many options and I bet the Habsburgs didn't really either, in spite of their great wealth. Some reigned, some were good subjects, but the times dictated how people lived.

THE IMPERIAL VAULT

In 1900 the public could visit the Imperial Vault on All Saint's Day and All Soul's Day, the first and second of November, and also daily from Easter to All Saint's Day from 9 a.m. to 12 p.m. Baedeker's *Austria* is thorough.

The vault was built in the seventeenth century by Empress Anna as the final resting place for Austrian and German rulers from the House of Habsburg. By the time Elizabeth, Empress of Austria and beloved Queen of Hungary, was being laid to rest in 1898, its narrow interior had space for just one coffin besides hers.

"But infinite is its grasp of weal and woe, and in the darkness of its dismal vaults has been quenched the light of the life-dreams of many a scion of the historic House of Habsburg," wrote A. De Burgh in *Elizabeth, Empress of Austria: A Memoir*.

RUDOLF

A sensitive and intelligent child, the young Crown Prince Rudolf of Austria was subjected to a harsh military education until his mother, Empress Elizabeth, threatened to leave Francis Joseph unless the boy was sent elsewhere to receive a liberal education. Beyond that, however, historical accounts indicate that Empress Elizabeth's role was limited in his life. However, this intervention was valuable, allowing Rudolf to pursue ornithological research, and science and technology in general. As a young man, he had liberal political ideas, some of which were modern, that did not sit well with the powers in Austria. He had insights about the future, including a United States of Europe. Rudolf's ideals rattled the status quo, represented by his father, and he was marginalized by the emperor.

Rudolf married Princess Stéphanie of Belgium (1864–1945). Although their marriage started out harmoniously, over time he descended into alcohol and prostitutes. Occasionally he spoke of suicide. Rudolf shot his mistress Mary Vetsera and then himself at Mayerling, according to various sources.

CHAPTER 32

Heading to the Outskirts of a Former Empire

THE SLOVENES, CROATS, SERBS, AND OTHER NATIONALITIES struggled ferociously for their independence, including for the right to speak their own languages, during the Austro-Hungarian period. The people of these nations don't like to be reminded of their past under the monarchs of Austria-Hungary. Nevertheless that is the history and Amálka led me here to see the remains of the Austro-Hungarian Monarchy and the countries that had emerged from it.

After Austria, we sought out Austria-Hungary's old border on the Adriatic Sea. On our way, we stopped at Ljubljana, the capital of Slovenia, formerly a federal republic of Yugoslavia. Slovenia became a nation on June 25, 1991, carrying with it its ancient Roman history.

The Roman settlement Emona, now Ljubljana, is a modern city of about 280,000 people having grown from about 40,000 people at the turn of the twentieth century. Much of the old city remains, including the sixteenth-century castle and moat, and its late-nineteenth century architecture. Andreja, our guide in Ljubljana, was career focused, educated, and optimistic, with a cheery personality that brought this clean and green city to life under the warm summer sun. She took us to the busy riverside promenade where the streets were kept tidy by the city's maintenance crew men in white shirts, black ties, and black pants. We followed her through narrow, winding streets lined with weathered row houses in various shades of pastel.

Prešeren Square got its name from the national poet, France Prešeren (1800–1849) who is looking in the direction of Julia Primic, another edifice in time. However, their relationship is independent of their presence, permanently bound to the square but impermanently attached in love. She did not love him as he did her.

She gazed down on me, leaning half way out of her window, drawing me into her eternal moment.

I absorbed the square's dramatic architecture spanning from the seventeenth through the twentieth centuries. My eyes seized upon the Hauptmann House, a survivor of the 1895 earthquake, renovated in blue, green, and red tiles in the Viennese Secessionist style. Across the square is the striking Centromerkur, longstanding since the turn of the twentieth century. Its translucent Art Nouveau fan awning invites customers.

Near the seventeenth-century Franciscan Church of the Annunciation and close to the Triple Bridge over the Ljubljanica River, I could almost hear the hoofs of horses clacking on its cobblestones and see little puffs of dust kicking up behind them. The polished brass buckles and buttons of the imperial officers shone in the sun as they rode from the center of the square toward Castle Hill.

This vision of the Habsburg military evaporated as soon as I read a plaque in the castle memorializing one of its most notable political prisoners: Lajos Batthány (1806–1849). He was the Hungarian prime minister who fought for Hungary's freedom from the Habsburgs from 1848 until 1849.

I could feel the imperial reach from Vienna. Amálka may

have lived in a diverse culture, but it was overshadowed by the Habsburgs, who so often ruled with tight grip. Dictators and Communist governments in Europe over the last century also had imposed their will on the people, but their architecture wasn't half as good.

We zipped from Ljubljana to Škofja Loka, a quaint village that Abraham, Bishop of Freising, received as a gift from German Emperor Oton II in the tenth century. A whole town as a present? Now that's a gift.

Škofja Loka is a classic walled medieval town and a castle on a hill. A stone bridge constructed on a Roman arch straddles the medieval moat. We stopped, surveying the pale green tree-lined river stretching into the distance. A vegetable garden was planted in the miniscule backyard of a home alongside the moat. The hike through nature to the museum at Škofja Loka Castle reminded me of the pressed leaf that fell from Amálka's book the first time I opened it, and how we take tokens of our moments and press them with our own memories.

We pushed on northwest to Radovljica, another preserved medieval town whose central square has Renaissance and Baroque touches and features a beekeeping museum commemorating the country's apicultural history. I noticed an art shop. I picked up a deep blue porcelain bowl even though Phil was shaking his head to remind me that our suitcases were already overloaded. I looked at the artist's dog, a black labrador, lying in the sun. I liked the bowl. I liked the dog. The dog wasn't for sale so I bought the bowl.

Lake Bled, a little farther north, was the day's final destination. I'd never heard of the place before, but Andreja assured me that we'd never forget this bucolic lake gifted with charm, history and romance.

Deep aqua waters, a small pilgrim's church on an island, an eleventh-century castle teetering four hundred feet on a sheer cliff, and the snow-capped Julian Alps peaking in the hands of a prayer—Lake Bled is as fantastic as it is real. I almost expected to see a princess waiving from a castle balcony. Every girl in the Empire, including Amálka, must have dreamt of a god creating a glacier and a lake to follow and a spirited island with the twinkle of a church and a mystical bell. She could be married there or just find love.

I wanted to believe that Amálka had traveled here, maybe on one of the train lines in the area, to rest for a time at this acclaimed health resort. But visitors to a spa don't typically spend a lot of time picking apples at harvest. Lake Bled was well-enough known among the aristocracy since Elisabeth, daughter of the deceased Austro-Hungarian Crown Prince Rudolf, honeymooned here in 1902.

We took a ride to the island in a small boat operated by a man using giant oars, like some misplaced Venetian gondolier. Motorboats are prohibited on Lake Bled. I scanned the shore-line, spotting a few hotels in the distance, including one partially hidden behind trees. It had been a royal villa, later converted to a residence for Yugoslavian dictator Marshal Josep Broz Tito (1892–1980), president of Yugoslavia from 1953 until his death. Tito entertained world leaders amid the natural wonders of Lake Bled from his Communist-era palace with its bland exterior and blunt lines. Today it is a hotel.

From the Habsburgs to Tito, some things never change, I thought.

My musings were interrupted by the sight of families swimming along the shore and lovers drifting in boats of every sort, wooden or inflatable. A woman quietly nursed her infant son on the island dock before hopping into a kayak.

Things had changed—a lot. Communism was out, so was Tito. New leaders are in and the lake and the church are owned by the state, the people. Everyone can enjoy them, including the busloads of tourists.

But that's not to say things are free. We had to pay fifty euros to the oarsman so the four of us could ride in his gondola-like boat with a cloth roof to the island in the middle of Lake Bled. We had to dig in our pockets for three euros to make a wish and ring the bell three times in the Church of Mary, the Queen.

The beauty of the lake is enhanced by the mystery of the bell. In an ancient time, bandits killed a young man, and his wife grieved mightily. In his honor, she gathered all her gold and silver to pay for the casting of a bell to hang in the chapel on the island. But fate was cruel and the boat carrying the honorary bell was swamped in a storm, sinking the bell and killing the boatman. It is said that when the wind is calm and the nights are clear, one can hear the bell ringing at the bottom of the lake. After this terrible event, sadness overwhelmed the poor woman and she withdrew to a convent in Rome. The Pope, moved by the story, sent a new bell to the church. The Blessed Virgin grants wishes to those who ring the bell.

Andreja had a simpler version: If you ring the bell three times, you get your wish. Amálka's memory book was full of good wishes. I pulled hard on the bell's rope for her.

For all the beauty of the lake, the delight of that day at Lake Bled was the Kremšnita, or Bled Cream Cake. Andreja ordered four pieces in spite of Phil's objections. In the end, he finished his first. I asked Andreja to send me a typical recipe for cream cakes in the region.

· · ·

MY TRAVELS IN FORMER HABSBURG TERRITORY WEREN'T OVER. I found myself in Piran, a medieval fishing port with red orange tile roofs, a blue ocean, and the time to enjoy the warm sun at an easy pace. It dates back to the first century BC. It is in Slovenia now but has a distinctly Italian history. The Venetians beat back the German Emperor Frederick Barbarossa in 1177 and it stayed under the auspices of Venice for several centuries until 1813, when it was subsumed into Austria. I could have stayed for centuries. Skips and single-mast sailboats lined the pier and shimmered in the bright sunlight. Offshore, a few large yachts floated languidly like large, folded euro notes in the sea. Maybe the Habsburgs heirs had given up their castles for, shall we say, more liquid investments.

Standing in the broad marble city square is a statue of Italian composer Guiseppe Tartini (1692–1770), a native Istrian. I got into the Venetian spirit and tried on a carnival mask that I found in a shop on the square not too far from a fifteenth-century Venetian house.

The pace of the town is slow, but we had much to see. We started with the Church of Saint George built over the late-sixteenth and early seventeenth centuries. The bell tower, its most notable feature, invited us to circle up its winding staircase to the top for a 360-degree view of the harbor and town.

Victor Tissot, author of *Unknown Hungary*, summed up Piran in 1881, then a city in Italy: "[T]he smallest details of the landscape and of life are pictures here; under an Italian sky, everything takes an original and individual character, delighting both the poet and the artist."

We sauntered back into town along serpentine streets with high walls overlooking crosses on the churches that sat inevitably at the end of Piran's many paths. For medieval people, life was bound and controlled by the church and civil authorities who were usually extensions of the church.

We were leaving fifteenth-century Venice and going back to third-century Rome as we moved from Piran on to the port city of Pula in Croatia. Pula isn't far down the Istria, just a thousand years or so. Although Pula had happy people, lots of ice cream, and intrepid tourists willing to brave the hot summer sun, it is the ruins from its Roman era that I remember most clearly. John Paget thought Pula, called Pola in his time, was too familiar to bother putting in his book, but I don't think Americans today would agree.

If someone had told me a Roman coliseum survived in Pula, I would have needed more proof. But sure enough, in this shipping port that served as the Austro-Hungarian Monarchy's naval headquarters, sits a giant oval arena whose massive stones display the engineering genius of third-century Romans.

The bleachers have been reconfigured for modern concerts. But no music played as we shuffled across the floor of what once was the stage for bloody combats between gladiators and animals, and those unfortunate enough to be prisoners. Men were marched through Pula's streets and thrown to the lions or bears. I wondered how many inches down one had to dig in that soil to reach their blood.

Victor Tissot, writing in *Unknown Hungary*, had the same bloody impression of this arena that once held fifteen thousand spectators.

> This Roman amphitheatre, with its giant architecture, made as if to last for ever, dwarfs all. Thorns and thistles and a harvest of parasitical plants now fill the basin hollowed by the hand of man for mock sea-fights; in these naval fights two or three thousand slaves butchered each other to distract for a little the ennui of their masters.

Not too far from the Temple of Augustus is the triumphal arch erected by the Sergii family in the first century. It had a railing around it in 1900. But now it's open and people freely wander through it. We did, too.

It turned out that we were following Tissot's path down the Istrian peninsula toward Opatija, Croatia, known as Abbázia, Austria-Hungary, at the turn of the twentieth century. About sixteen thousand visitors a year flocked to this summer resort, which had a year round population of only twenty-three hundred people. I was one of 337,000 visitors to come through in 2008 and delighted to be there.

One need only view the landscape of old villas and palaces facing the Adriatic—many revitalized, others merely rehabilitated and some in desperate need of repair— to see the opulence that the aristocracy and the celebrated enjoyed if only for a short time.

"And then the wars disrupted everything: changing the guests and caterers, dispersing the idyll like a ring of smoke from the pursed lips of soldiers," wrote Amir Muzur in *Opatija Abbazia A Stroll Through Space and Time* (2007).

Opatija's historic structures stand tall. No question, they built them to last, and it's these buildings that anchor the area along the sparkling Adriatic. The description of Abbázia in Baedeker's *Austria* as being "in a splendidly sheltered situation with beautiful grounds of evergreen laurel" rings true in many ways.

I thought it would be simple to find the hotel. The town has only one main thoroughfare, which is named for Marshal Tito. But it was dusk. Driving up and down the street slowly looking for Marsǎla Tita 138, we surveyed virtually every other hotel but ours. How do you miss a pink hotel?

Our hunt had led us back into the hills on a small, winding, distinctly untouristy road, into the old part of town. Worn buildings and villas as well as intractable roads prompted Richard to reset the GPS. He reversed course and drove through a series of tight S curves, barely missing buildings and barriers on his way back to find Marsǎla Tita 138. We ultimately found the hotel amid throngs of people that had emerged like nocturnal animals for the night scene. Phil and I hopped out, working our way through the crowd. We were New Yorkers. This was nothing. The hotel desk clerk greeted us warmly, as he heard about our driving experience, as though other guests routinely have this adventure.

The hotel charmed us with its fairy tale pink Art Nouveau renovation and scalloped awning over the front door, flowers on all five delicate levels. We could have been in the 1890s, with one important exception: air-conditioning. It was withering, over 95 degrees outside, and entering the hotel was a distinct relief. Our room was spacious and gracefully furnished, providing a restful night after a long day.

The next morning I took off on foot to see what I could find while Phil took care of some work. Armed with a pocket guide to Opatija written by the mayor of the town (apparently he and his father are the local historians), I set off along Marshal Tito Waterfront, which has plenty to keep a curious New Yorker occupied for some time.

Casinos are sprinkled around town but this is not the Las Vegas strip. The Opatija Riviera, as it's called here, appeared to be occupied by mostly older couples and young families. I didn't see any limousines, Hummers, or Ferraris. The "beach" is free. The beach in front of the hotel was rendered a concrete enclosure open to the sea—not a rocky shoreline—and surrounded by colorful umbrellas and lounge chairs available on a first-come, first-served basis for a small fee. Under Communism, I'm betting that party members got the best lodgings.

The most accurate way to sum up that era came from a hotel employee. "Tito had everything. We had nothing, but we had everything." This was just one of the witticisms that the people expressed during Tito's tenure, he said. The employee gave me another one: "We are Tito's. Tito is ours."

The way I heard it was that the Communists would say, "What's mine is mine and what's yours is negotiable."

An unintended result of Communism's fall in 1989 was that the beaches became widely available to tourists like us. Most everyone on the beach looked reasonably middle class, not a homeless person in sight. The beach is free to anyone who can get there and doesn't mind putting their mat on concrete slabs when all the chairs are taken. The hotels, apartments, and villas are not free. The prices are dictated by the demand for various quality rooms.

From what I could see, the hotels looked well kept, with furniture dating from the 1960s to the 1980s in a few of the lobbies. Richard called it "Soviet Realism." The state owns some of these hotels and is upgrading them over time.

I meandered into a few small hotels on par with the larger four- and five-star ones. In 2008 I counted three five-star hotels in town—Hotel Mozart, the Ambassador, and the Milenij. All have had very large renovation programs. The receptionist at our hotel proudly informed us that one of the owners of Hotel Mozart, Croatian tennis player Ivan Ljubičić, won the Davis Cup.

Opatija is a mixture of new and old. The older hotels are cheaper, but need work. In one of them, the 1950s-style plastic bubble phone, sans the phone, completed the image. For a Hungarian, plastic bubble phones are not rare; they can be seen here and there in the country. In America, you've got to dig up an old movie to see one.

To the experienced eye, a Habsburg ballroom inside one of the hotels had been tarnished by the city's old electrical system. Think Francis Joseph and Joseph Stalin meeting in a dissonant dance today. Being a modern hotel requires beyond a can of paint. The locals are aware that change is here and that it seems the vanguard.

"Okay, we must be private," said one hotel employee regarding the privatization of such state-owned assets. "It's good. They buy the hotel and it gets renovated. The state has no money, so it's a good thing (the new owners) help to make it beautiful. But now it's still okay," she said, meaning that the common people were sharing in the benefits. "But I'm suspicious."

Of particular concern is the number of people buying up coastal land and cutting off access to the beach. It's starting to happen, she said, adding, "That's not nice."

Then she pulled out a map and made a copy for me so that I could see how many islands there are off the Croatian coastline.

I noticed an odd break in the coastline on the map. She said, without batting an eye, as if she knew the man personally, "Tito decided Bosnia needed a bit of coast so he gave the country twenty-four kilometers of coastline."

She was close. It is actually twenty kilometers, or about twelve miles, nestled between the Croatian coastline on both sides.

I wanted to stay and continue to talk, but she had a job to do. I gathered up my new map and said a good-bye.

From another person working at a different hotel, I learned that property ownership is not always clear because of a tradition of oral contracting, overlaid by seventy years of socialism. This can complicate today's land and building purchases. When he called the Austro-Hungarians good administrators and said that they had tighter property records than what came later, I thought it spoke volumes about the past. Then he added, "So were the Romans."

Property rights are central to modern economies and it's all got to get straightened out at some point in Croatia. But no one I spoke to wanted to lose the old Opatija.

When I got back, Phil remained busy with work so I went to the beach. Richard joined me. Resting on sun chairs on a hot July day as we faced the shimmering Adriatic Sea, Richard turned to me and said, "If you want to think it over you can, but if you'd like, we should make it official that you are my daughter's godmother."

I was stunned for a second and then smiled broadly. "I'm sure it's a yes, but let me talk to Phil first."

The sun glistened on the waves. Richard picked up his sunglasses and started reading again. I rested my head against the sun chair and closed my eyes, soaking up the sun and Amálka's spirit. Breathing slowly, I felt her essence warming us all, even Phil in the hotel working. He was here because of her, too. When we were wandering in the area of the antique shop, neither one of us ever dreamt that Amálka's little book would be a web enveloping so much time, so much space, and so many dear people. Amálka's roses were lingering. Having passed through a century, they were now our charge. As they bloomed again so life became a little brighter. The past seeded the present and we were to watch over one.

The waves came and went as noisy beachgoers moved chairs and chatted. My thoughts stayed. I held on to them. Amálka and the venerable buildings of Opatija were looking down on me.

· · ·

PHIL AND I BEGAN DINNER ON OUR LAST NIGHT IN OPATIJA with the sun setting over a sea darkened by nature's nightly forces. We were at the Kvarner. This is the city's oldest hotel. It was nine in the evening, barely two tables taken. The air warm, the evening languid.

The band cranked up with an international set of music dominated by local interpretations of "Back to Massachusetts" and "There Goes My Reason for Living," pulling in the crowd. We braved the dance floor along with a few other couples and some kids. Back at the table, we rested in our chair, holding hands, talking quietly. Unannounced, the band struck up a Viennese waltz and the old Opatija unfolded beneath the starfilled sky. The music was a magic elixir, unlocking the past. Couples glided onto the dance floor as if it was their national anthem, and in a few minutes they all danced in sync.

Looking at them, I didn't see their tank tops and shorts or capri pants, but long coattails and gowns twirling on the terrace built in the time of the Habsburgs. The people were spinning around the dance floor as Opatija was spinning into a future that carried a new set of worries. But these worries would be left to the next generation. I don't know exactly when I'll be back to Opatija but when I return, I imagine that they'll be there dancing at every sunset.

. . .

When we saw Richard the next morning, we promptly said we'd be honored to be Dorina's godparents. It was early in the day so before we left Opatija, we took a side trip to Rijeka, the old Hungarian port in Amálka's time. It was another ancient city in the region and its history recalled another name from the long-gone Holy Roman Empire: Charlemagne. I do remember him from world history. He conquered Rijeka at the end of the eighth century.

Hungarians controlled Rijeka in the late nineteenth century. The place wore its industrial legacy like a thin coat of ash that gathered over time. The old sugar refinery is featured on the tourist map. In front of me was a bustling old seaport with a commercial and industrial flavor mixed with Roman remains and façades featuring angels, grapes, and gods, so characteristic of the Habsburg style. The Habsburgs left a legacy of beauty throughout the old Empire. But in Rijeka much of it appeared in need of restoration.

. . .

We shot on to Zagreb, the capital of Croatia, on our way to Hungary. We needed to get to Szolnok.

In Zagreb, the Habsburg imprint seems fainter than we had seen in other cities. The one exception to this is the university renowned for its Romanesque style dating to the turn of the twentieth century.

Overall, Zagreb is a modern city with many interesting tourist spots, including a park filled with busts of its distinguished patrons.

I experienced an example of the intertwined history of Hungarians and Croats as I looked at a bust of poet and warrior in a bust of Count Miklós Zrínyi. Actually, I already knew there are two Miklós Zrínyis, but to be truthful, I didn't know exactly which one we were seeing at the time. I paid attention to what our Hungarian and Croatian guides were saying. Both knew the story of the Zrínyi family, but each one put a slightly different emphasis on it.

Given how interwoven the Zrínyi families are with Hungary and Croatia, it's only fair for both countries to claim the men.

In the city square, a statue of the Croatian *ban* Josip Jelačić (1801–1859) drew a curious stare from Richard. (A ban was the title used in southeast Europe for a regional ruler.) This wasn't unusual since Jelačić sided with the Austrians against the Hungarians. The Hungarians were ambivalent about giving the Croats equality, liberty, and fraternity. The French and American revolutions emboldened the Croats against the Hungarians in pursuit of their own rights.

Zagreb offers well beyond one statue. The city brims with treasures, among them the thirteenth-century Lotrščak Tower, Saint Mark's Church, and the Mirogoj Cemetery—an expansive stone city with ivy-covered walls, vaulting domes, and paved pathways for dead to roam. But Zagreb was not in Amálka's memory book and we needed to press on to a place that was, Novska.

When we said we were going there, our guide in Zagreb looked at us strangely, since Novska is not a tourist stop. There really was no way to connect the points, and I didn't have time enough to get into it with our Croatian guide.

LJUBLJANA

Slovenia is squeezed between Austria on the north, Croatia on the south, Hungary on the east, and Italy on the west. If you notice the odd sliver of Italy's coastline at Trieste, the one that looks like it logically should be part of Slovenia, you've just discovered an important source of contention between the Austrians and the city's Italians, who were a majority there at the end of the nineteenth century. The Austrians ultimately lost Trieste at the end of World War I in the dismantling of the old Austro-Hungarian Monarchy.

Ljubljana was settled by Emperor Augustus in 34 BC, who called it Emona, preserving a name from an even earlier period. When the Roman Empire collapsed in the fifth century, Europe was conquered sequentially by the Huns, the Magyars, the Turks, and others. After the defeat of the king of Bohemia by a Habsburg in the thirteenth century, the Habsburgs first occupied Ljubljana. They lost it for a while but got it back again by inheritance. In the beginning of the nineteenth century, Napoleon Bonaparte (1769–1821) conquered Ljubljana, making it the capital of the Illyrian provinces of France. These provinces today include Slovenia's eastern coastline on the Adriatic Sea.

This city became part of the kingdom of the Serbs, Croats, and Slovenes, later Yugoslavia, following the collapse of Austria-Hungary at the end of World War I. It took another world war and fighting for the Slovenians to get their independence in the twenty-first century.

PULA

We paid a small fee to enter the coliseum in Pula. Amálka would have gone to a municipal building to hire a guide with a key to the place. The same guide could have taken her to the amphitheater, the Temple of Augustus, frozen in a small square, and a museum of Roman antiquities.

As I stood in front of the temple with its Corinthian columns, I pondered what the Habsburgs thought when they were building their mansions in the shadow of the ancient Roman Empire. It would have been fun to hear Caesar Augustus debate Francis Joseph about who was the greatest. For the sheer force of the man, I'd put my money on Caesar Augustus.

Victor Tissot of *Unknown Hungary* said, "We contemplate with wonder these noble and imposing ruins, and we ask ourselves whether, when other men shall have invented other laws, and shall adore other Gods, the travellers of future times will in like manner come to seek for ancient cities once flourishing on the shore of the Rhone and the Rhine, and to search the banks of the Seine for the site of the grand Opera and the ruins of the Louvre, the Arc-de-Triomphe and the Pantheon. Athens, Sparta, and proud Tyre have all disappeared . . . What is it to be eternal? To be born, is it is not to begin to die—for men as well as for civilizations and cities?"

RIJEKA

John Paget arrived in Rijeka when it was part of the Austrian Empire in the 1830s, and he found it to be a pleasant Italian city with a decent harbor, a theater, and a paper mill. By the 1900s, when the British painters Adrian and Marianne Stokes passed through, it had become part of the Austro-Hungarian Monarchy, and they didn't have much to say except that the city looked like many other southern European seaports with steamer ships, crowds, hotels, and outdoor cafés.

The remains of a Roman triumphal arch built in honor of Emperor Claudius in the third century impressed me but not the Stokes.

Amálka would have liked the Cathedral of Saint Vitus with its façade that mimics the Pantheon in Rome. If she had a Baedeker's *Austria* in her hand, she would have read that the cathedral is similar in style to the Santa Maria della Salute in Venice.

Another holy site in Rijeka is Pilgrimage Church, or Madonna del Mare, now known as Our Lady of Trsat. The painting of the Madonna inside the church is attributed to Saint Luke, and during Amálka's time people would have made pilgrimages to the city, as they do today.

Adrian Stokes, however, thought there might be another reason that Hungarians came to Rijeka, then known as Fiume. "Many pious Hungarians come to Fiume, the object of their pilgrimage being, I suspect, not this holy mount; but, rather, to worship by the last expanse of open sea remaining to the Magyar race," he wrote in *Hungary*.

Sea over saint. He got it right.

COUNT MIKLÓS ZRÍNYÍ

M iklós Zrínyi's fight to the death defending the castle of Szigetvár in Hungary against Suleiman the Magnificent in 1566 made him a Hungarian hero even though he was a head of an important family in Croatia. Zrínyi was a Croatian and Hungarian noble with extensive land holdings in both areas.

His great grandson of the same name, Miklós Zrínyi, (1620–1664) was a soldier, a poet and—a hero, too. His warrior fame reached its zenith at the Battle at Esseg in 1664 defeating the Turks. He was honored by the pope and the major kings of Europe. The emperor offered to make him a prince but he declined. Zrínyi's literary fame was achieved with the epic poem *Obsidio Szigetiana* written to commemorate the glory of the earlier Miklós at the battle of Szigetvár.

CHAPTER 33

Novska

LONG FIELDS OF CORN STALKS, SUNFLOWERS, AND FARM HOUSES lined the road to Novska, a city in Slavonia, a mere three miles from the Bosnian border. I'd been confused about whether Slavonia was another country among the old Yugoslavian puzzle pieces, like Slovenia and Serbia.

Slavonia is actually in northeastern Croatia, so it's a geographic region, not a country. Croatia, Slovenia, and Serbia do have at least one common denominator that was relevant to Amálka's time: They all were part of Austria-Hungary, as were the former Yugoslavia republics of Montenegro, Macedonia, and Bosnia-Herzegovina.

To help give me some perspective on this Slavonian city located between the Drava and Sava rivers, Richard had done some research on the area and came across the Government Office for Hungarian Minorities Abroad. This led him to the Federation of Hungarian Associations and eventually the Friendship Croatian-Magyar Association Novska. I thought it was a stroke of genius.

Richard programmed the address for the association into

the GPS, hoping we might be able to catch the person at home, since no one had answered the phone when he called. Having a destination keyed into GPS relieved us of the burden of detailed map reading, although we did keep an eye on it to make sure we hadn't made a mistake that would lead us on a country road to nowhere or to areas strewn with old land mines.

I began reading about the town in a local guidebook, which mentioned that some houses, buildings, and churches, including Saint Luke and Saint Joseph, were damaged during the "Fatherland" War from 1991 to 1995.

Mention of that war shot me back to Amálka's time, when Croatia, Slovenia, Bosnia-Herzegovina, and Serbia were all part of the Kingdom of the Serbs, Croats, and Slovenes. The struggle for dominance among these peoples had led to decades of conflicts with nationalistic movements and widespread atrocities. The latest war was no different. Non-Serbs wanted their independence.

As we chugged into Novska, I was confronted with a Soviet-style apartment building pitted with fist-size holes that Phil thought were made by 50-caliber machine guns. I didn't see a clear pattern to the holes, but fifteen years had passed and the people were engaged in repairing the place.

Novska is a small city, immaculately clean, with small houses lining the main road, which eventually runs through the modern city center. We turned off the road looking for the house listed for the association.

Splotches of red, purple, and white flowers hung over the balconies of buildings, adding cheer to the pockmarked, pastel concrete walls.

Nineteen fifties–style television antennas poked out from corrugated-steel roofs. Ice cream stores and outdoor cafés lay like flakes on the road as I tried to adjust to the juxtaposition of bullet-riddled houses, new construction, reconstruction, and tractors rumbling their way to the fields.

"I've seen whole burned-out houses in Croatia, and they have been fixed. Damage from the war on the Dalmatia coast, most of those had been fixed, too," Richard said.

Seeing my pale face, he asked flatly, "Have you ever been so close to where there was a war zone?"

"No," I replied, observing a few children in the distance playing serenely and chickens walking casually on the side of a road.

"Here it is," Richard said, stopping across from the house listed for the association. "You know it's a Croatian person who heads the association," he added.

The gate was locked. Our potential guide from the association wasn't at home. Richard tried the phone number again. No answer. Then we did the only logical thing two tourists and a guide could do—we drove back to town to look for the tourist office.

We parked in front of the town hall and got out to walk around. At the building's entrance we noticed a poster of Ante Gotovina, a controversial general in the recent Croatian war. Obviously, war sentiments were fresh. Later, I found more information online about museum nights, government conferences, and other civil matters. The city's Web page offered the following notation: "Protecting the memory of the history of the fatherland. Members of the association of widows of the fighters of the Croatian War of Independence actively participate in events connected with the hostilities, as well as in activities organized by other associations connected with the War of Independence."

We were drawn to a large photo in the lobby of what the town looked like some time ago. It wasn't dated but given the condition of the road, the modest homes, and what looked like telegraph poles, it could easily have been taken in Amálka's time.

Some of those same-style houses—simple and sturdy, mimicking the empire's taste for permanence—were standing on the town's main street, albeit with some bullet holes and broken windows.

Scaffolding surrounded buildings in renovation where soft hues of yellow, orange, and red peaked out from behind the metal. Several men were hammering on a damaged roof. This was the picture of a modest agricultural town, improving its situation. Phil's words resonated with me: Life is easy to destroy in a nanosecond, hard to repair in a decade.

The three of us left the town hall in search of someone who could direct us to the tourist office. Phil and I would be relatively useless: me with English, Spanish, and a neophyte's knowledge of Hungarian; him with English and the traveler's sign language.

Richard continued to be our ray of hope. If the first Croatian woman we bumped into had known the direction of the tourist office, Richard might have been able to figure out what she was saying since he spoke Russian, a Slavic language that is similar to Croatian. But she was lost, too. Instead we had to rely on another stranger who knew tidbits of English from her schooling decades before. She pointed to a small street off the main road. We were back to the traveler's sign language—Phil felt right at home. The men led the way.

We strolled along a side street. We didn't have to be Hungarian to see that whatever Hungarian influence that had once been there, had now vanished. This became especially apparent when we stepped into a small shop and the shopkeeper looked at Richard curiously when he asked if she spoke Hungarian. Most likely Novska's Hungarians moved or were simply assimilated into Croat society. One hundred years had passed, but the question remained: what happened to Amálka's family? Are they now Croats?

As I approached the post office, my heart quickened. I was facing a distressed remnant of the empire in imperial yellow. The post office, a monument of its time, would find itself surprised to be anchored by a small memory book with the first entry dated 1906, Novska, from Amálka's mother to her daughter. And now POSTA T. T. NOVSKA and 1906 protruded from the façade of the post office, right over my head. I disregarded the beat-up air conditioners hanging out of the windows, and the clumsy concrete patching on the façade and bullet holes; I was back in 1906, before any of the violence, when Novska's post office was the talk of the town.

After a moment of reflection, I said, loudly, "Let's go in."

If the outside retained its original style, the inside was dull and utilitarian, lacking any romance. No shiny counters or neatly uniformed workers from the Habsburg days, just twenty-first century postal workers and stacks of materials for purchase. Friendly and patient women manned the counter. I scanned for a postcard to send to America. I had to settle for some stamps to put on other postcards in my bag. I wanted to linger.

I was standing in the shoes of Amálka's mother. Amálka's mother holds her daughter's hand on a sunny day just like this one as they walk down a little slope, heading to a relative's home. Amálka pulls to break free and runs ahead into the fields. She leans down to pick a few flowers. Her mother trails behind with a basket of food. I was lost in my daydreams staring up at the façade.

We moved on from the post office since we wanted to get to the information center. Across the street near an abandoned, covered market, a sign read: TURISTICKA ZAJEDNICA GRADA NOVSKE. The Novska Tourist Office. At the door, I noticed a poster showing pictures of the local schools, the police building, the train station, a lake, the post office, with which I was now familiar, and Saint Luke's Church. The church was originally built in 1773, torn down in 1902, and a new one built in its place.

The tourist office wasn't open either. In hindsight, who would have expected two unannounced Americans and a Hungarian stomping through Central Europe on an off-the-beaten-path journey that included Novska, a city that is barely mentioned in guidebooks? We went to the center of town, where we confronted the bust of Luka Ilić Oriovcanin (1817–1878), a priest who founded the Reader's Association of Novska and is buried in Novska. One of his interests was numismatics and he is said to have had an extensive coin collection.

We also came across the bust for art historian and preservationist Gjuro Szabo (1875–1943). This Novska native produced several volumes on painting and photography, and was also in charge of art preservation in Croatia and Slavonia. His artistic interests would have likely appealed to Amálka for its refinements.

Our walk continued and we ended up at the city park and another memorial for about one hundred local victims of the most recent Serb-Croat War. Long poles commemorate the dead. Our guide in Zagreb had said that about fifteen thousand to twenty thousand died in the war, but no one knows for sure because bodies continue to be uncovered in various places.

Phil and I walked past houses with blown windows and shards of glass sticking to the frame. They looked abandoned, but Phil said people were living in them.

He stopped taking pictures when it drew a few frowns from the locals. We had a cool drink, absorbing the atmosphere of Novska before heading to the car.

"It's time to go," I said, sliding into the car and closing the door on this sojourn on the wisp of Amálka's trail.

NOVSKA

Novska's history is similar to that of other Central European towns controlled by feudal lords beginning in the middle of the eleventh century. Novska was a farming and commercial town known as Bjelavina in the early fourteenth century. The nobles weren't able to withstand the Turkish invasion in the sixteenth century. Once the Turks succeeded in overcoming the Novska region's forts, most of the people were driven out, except for those who adopted the Turkish lifestyle or Christians who fought as mercenaries for the Turks. As in Transylvania, the Turks were forced out at the end of the seventeenth century. Croats and others then settled the territory, which now makes up Novska and its environs.

Roman Catholic Church records from the mid-eighteenth century indicate that the Novska parish had 336 people living in fifty houses. When the area's economy expanded dramatically in the eighteenth century, the town gained new roads, a military regiment, and a community school. By the nineteenth century the area got a rail connection.

Novska wasn't far from Agram, otherwise known as Zagreb, where books and other literary material, the lifeblood of any culture, were flourishing. These written works were finding their way into the provinces and villages, including Novska. "Like the Magyars, the Croatians are very jealous of German influence, and the publication of books and papers in that language is in every way discouraged," traveler Nina Mazuchelli wrote in *Magyarland*.

CHAPTER 34

More Traveling

"Here we are," Phil said, cracking open the map to figure out where we were. "It looks like we're heading to the Bosnian border," he remarked casually. Richard hit the brakes and pulled over.

"Even though it's not a war zone anymore, we better not be headed to Bosnia or Serbia," he said, checking the map, which was in Hungarian, and pointing out Slavonia's location relative to Bosnia.

We'd been driving in the wrong direction. It was a reasonable enough mistake. We would have done better if we had access to the map of Bosnia drawn by the Austrian Military-Geographical Institute of Vienna in 1884–1885. Baedeker's *Austria* called it the best map of the region in 1900. We hadn't known to ask for it when we were at the New York Public Library.

With our compass reset, we were soon driving past little farming villages, abandoned barns with bullet holes, newly mowed hay fields and an old woman wearing a babushka tending to her vegetable garden.

It dawned on me that we had another emergency, this one involving the postal system. Of course, the postcards had to be mailed in Croatia because the stamps I'd bought in Novska would be useless in Hungary. We had a new mission: find a mailbox. They were yellow in Amálka's time, too. Sure enough we saw one as we cruised through Garešnica, another town with Habsburg-era buildings interspersed with drab Soviet-style structures. We stopped and Phil strode over to mail the postcards, heading straight for a large, yellow plastic container beside the road. Richard looked amused; Phil was heading to the trash bin.

Richard politely corrected him, pointing to the real mailbox nailed to the front of a building about thirty feet away. I grabbed the camera and ran out to photograph Phil mailing the postcards. Amálka would have used the Royal Hungarian Mail. It wasn't the Pony Express but pokey old horses lumbering along. But Amálka's horse-and-wagon version of snail mail was very likely reliable because the Habsburgs were noted for their efficient administration.

The yellow mailbox in this distant little outpost was a milestone of sorts for us because it represented the beginning of our return. We had visited every place mentioned in the memory book. I insisted on having my picture taken by the little mailbox, too.

Leaving Garešnica for Pécs, Richard said we should stop in Villány, a wine-producing region with nineteenth-century houses and wine cellars frequented by Hungarian tourists. Since it's out of the way, Villány doesn't always fall on tours. But it's a local favorite, and we wanted to see it. But then, we wanted to see everything. Who said there are only twenty-four hours in a touring day?

We had expected Villány to be a Napa Valley East, with endless miles of vineyards overrun by crowds of tourists and upscale hotels. Instead there are rows of small houses with pitched roofs.

Chalk white walls and doors colorfully painted in green, orange, or red, flanked by old wooden barrels overflowing with flowers. The houses have wine-tasting rooms and subterranean wine cellars, containing a limited quantity of each vineyard's production. Villány is the antithesis of Napa Valley's ultramodern, vineyard-endowed estates. It offers an earthy nineteenth century alternative with its half sunken wine cellars and empty pathways. It is as inviting now as it was in the nineteenth century.

"Villány is an interesting locality," wrote British writer D. T. Ansted in *A Short Trip*. "On the slopes of the hill is grown a well-known and excellent red wine, and all around the cultivation is high, and the scenery picturesque."

We had a tasting at the Gere winery and also ordered fresh vegetables with Hungarian meats, a meal that Amálka could have had if she traveled here. Gere is in a joint venture with an Austrian winery to revive traditional Austro-Hungarian wine-making in the region, starting with a 2006 pinot noir. The best parts of the empire are being put back together.

"The characteristic qualities of the Hungarian wines are their strength and fire," John Paget wrote in *Hungary and Transylvania*. "Vienna consumes also a considerable quantity of Hungarian wine."

Imitating Phil, I swirled the glass to see the streaks and rich red color. He said it needed a little time to develop its bouquet, but as I drew the glass to my lips, smelling its fine aroma, I was satisfied. Moreover, it pleased me to know that this very wine would have been served to the Hungarian or Austrian court.

We had to reach Pécs before nightfall, so we left before we really wanted, arriving in the early evening. The following day we agreed to a quick visit to the Zsolnay store before heading to Budapest. In the gift store, I opted for a token from the factory. Looking at its luminous green veneer, I was sad to hear that the factory has had marketing challenges and management changes recently.

Herend is another fine Hungarian porcelain company that has had its ups and downs over the past century and a half, but is more mechanized than Zsolnay. I observed this firsthand after Richard suggested a side trip to Herend near Lake Balaton, rather than proceeding directly to Budapest.

When I entered the company museum, Herend's pattern selection was broader than Zsolnay's. One exhibit featured numerous brightly colored whimsical porcelain gnomes, in fairy tale settings of oversized mushrooms and tree trunks.

"Time hasn't stopped here," Richard said, contrasting Herend with the rustic Zsolnay factory.

His comment was ironic because we had driven nearly two thousand miles following Amálka's memory book precisely to find places where time had stopped.

Not far from Herend is Tihany, the only city on the little peninsula jutting into Lake Balaton. It is a favorite for water sports and medieval history.

Walking around, we came across a bronze nymph shouting into the distance. To help things along there's a sign, TIHANER ECHO and VISSZHANG. *Tihaner Echo* is German for "Tihany echo" and *visszhang* is Hungarian for "echo." We didn't hear any echoes but we still had fun trying. From Tihany, we got on the expressway to Budapest.

• • •

THE NEXT DAY WE VISITED GÖDÖLLŐ, NINETEEN MILES EAST OF Budapest. Royal Palace of Gödöllő and its grounds consist of renovated halls, a theater, and various rooms in addition to the sixty-four-acre Upper Park. The Hungarians have systematically attempted to restore the estate since 1989, but the indignities of the past will be difficult to erase. The final blow to Gödöllő came in 1989 and 1990, when the Soviets retreated and left the place in ruins. The estate's Baroque church remained relatively unharmed, as far as I could tell. People in Amálka's time would have been able to attend services there, with the royals participating from a separate area above the common people.

The remaining rooms at Gödöllő Palace were reconstructed to demonstrate what they would have looked like during Elizabeth's time, including some original pieces that had been preserved in Hungarian museums and replicas of others.

The horses and stables at Gödöllő are long gone, so we went to an equestrian park in nearby Domonyvölgy (Domony Valley). The Magyar spirit is tied to horses, and Amálka would have been comfortable with them in a way most Americans are not.

"The horse forms not only an object of speculation and commerce with the Magyar population: it is at the same time one of the greatest delights of every class. . . . In riding, driving and racing, the Magyar has not his equal. It is no figure of speech to say that he looks as if he were a part of his horse," wrote travel writer William Pitt Byrne in *Pictures of Hungarian Life*.

At the park, a nineteenth-century wooden farm wagon served as our transportation. I climbed onto the bench with the driver for a better view. The horses, sweating in the heat, jerked us along past meadows and dozens of quietly grazing horses. A dusty dirt road led into the forest. Warm air pushed against my face and leaves glistened in the sunlight. The ride was bumpy but exhilarating, suspending time as the horses sped on.

• • •

Ki a Tisza vizét issza, vágyik annak szíve vissza.
Whoever drinks water from the Tisza River
Will long to return, his heart all aquiver.

THESE ARE THE FIRST LINES OF A HUNGARIAN FOLK SONG, which my Hungarian teacher taught me when she knew I had an interest in Szolnok. Apparently they were true. We were back.

Szolnok is a county seat in Hungary and a large regional

center. It was always a practical town with its industries and railway hub, never the center of court of life. But the thermal baths and the old evangelist church with a statue of King Saint Stephen pointing to epitaphs at his feet recall an earlier time. The epitaphs were written to his son, the heir, who had the misfortune to die young in a hunting accident.

BEAR IN MIND THAT EVERYONE AT BIRTH IS IN THE SAME CONDITION.
ONLY HUMILITY CAN RAISE YOU;
ONLY PRIDE AND HATEFULNESS CAN DRAG YOU DOWN.

IF YOU WALK WITH THE WISE, YOU SHALL BE WISE YOURSELF.

BE GRACIOUS TO ALL WHO APPEAR BEFORE YOU,
FOR DEEDS OF KINDNESS LEAD TO THE GREATEST HAPPINESS.

Most Americans have never heard of this city settled by Hungarian tribes around the tenth century. But Szolnok, so close in pronunciation to Zounok, the governor for whom the town was named, was on the map of almost every invading army through the centuries. But none of the destruction that had been inflicted on Szolnok was evident as we drove.

We landed at a good hotel near a thermal bath. The staff was friendly and cheerfully pointed us to a restaurant with a most amusing menu, if one knows Hungarian. In addition to listing its delicacies, it had items from the local newspapers at the turn of the twentieth century, including the Nagykun-Szolnok Megyei Lapok (Nagykun-Szolnok County Papers). This was one of the sources that Richard had searched in the Szolnok archives to learn about Amálka.

On our menus we read about naked ladies jumping into the Tisza and not caring if they shocked people. Who would have expected skinny-dipping in 1904? A chicken heist and a madcap pursuit of a cow loose in town made it into the paper in 1887.

Chickens and cows were newsworthy items back then.

We were in our zone. This restaurant, decorated with a three-pronged wooden pitchfork, a wooden wagon wheel, and various other farm tools hanging on the wall, was reminiscent of our favorite eatery in Oradea. Both restaurants had fine food and the same heavy wooden tables and chairs.

. . .

LIKE THE HOTEL IN ORADEA, THE BATHROOM IN THE GARDEN Hotel had a tub that presented me with an interesting faucet dilemma. I called Phil.

"It's easy," he said, referring to how one turned it on. "I see how it works."

The oversized white tub had a snake coil attached to the handheld shower. It was hanging over the water faucets for hot and cold.

I walked out to get some toiletries.

"Oh, my God!" he screamed.

I tore into the bathroom from our spacious living room, dropping everything I had in my hands.

"It got out of control," Phil said, looking at the water that had sprayed the walls, the vanity, the toilet, part of the ceiling, and the towels. He was stuck with a hand towel again, just as he had been in Oradea, but this time it wasn't my fault.

. . .

IN 1900, SZOLNOK WAS FLOURISHING WITH TWENTY-ONE thousand people. It lies at the intersection of the Tisza and Zagyva rivers, but beyond that geography, Baedeker's *Austria* highlights only a few war memorials. We weren't sure though if they survived, so I ended up consulting a book about Szolnok published in 1975 with a Communist orientation, and the second edition of Baedeker's *Hungary* from 2000. I identified fifteen possible locations for us to visit. Several no longer existed but a few remained. Richard lent a hand, cleaning up the list and organizing our schedule.

We got off to an auspicious start, passing a roundabout at the bridge three times before ending up at a gargantuan limestone statue of General János Damjanich (1804–1849) under a stone arch alongside a busy highway. We were by ourselves at the site commemorating the Battle of Szolnok on March 5, 1849 with the general who had destroyed an enemy brigade in Szolnok that year. One of the inscriptions on the statue read:

WHERE THE MOST PATRIOTS' BLOOD
COVERS MARTIAL FIELDS
THAT IS WHERE PEOPLE'S FREEDOM
SPROUTS THE MOST BEAUTIFUL FLOWERS.

As the moment captured me in all of its dreadfulness and honor, I realized that I was not alone in history or its respects. Loew, translating János Arany's "Beggar Song" in *Selected Lyrics and Ballads by John Arany* (originally published in 1914), was with us.

I fought on many fields, and bore our flag
At Versecz, Szolnok, Vacz and Isaszeg;
My right arm I have lost, and though a crutch
I bear, it helps—one foot is gone—not much.
These rags are all I saved that awful day—
Give me of what God gave to you, I pray.

I paid my respects to this general who sacrificed his life for his country in the war of independence. He looms large there, just as he must have in battles during his short life of forty-five years.

We sauntered along the bridge only to find a lone fisherman who could have easily been the model for the watercolor in Amálka's album. The Tisza was like a mirror, reflecting the trees on the far bank.

Walking along, we stopped at a Turkish well, whose construction was marked by a plaque that read:

TISZA CHEMICAL FACTORIES MARCH 15
SOCIALIST BRIGADE
AND THE GREAT PLAIN
SILICON DIOXIDE INDUSTRY
STONE CARVING BRIGADE
JUNE 1977

Most tourists wouldn't find this interesting but it says something about living under Communism. The workers donated their time to build a monument in the style of their historical enemy, and it doesn't even work.

We got in the car to find the Tabáni Tájház, "the house of a man who works with animal skins," a tanner. There's only one left and it exists just to show visitors what the old farmhouses built near the Zagyva River used to look like. The house is located in the area that used to be known as "Gypsy town." Today the Gypsy encampment has been replaced by homes with Suzukis and Volvos parked out front.

Although we had the street number of Tabáni Tájház, we couldn't find it. An old woman in a plain house dress, with patterns likes the ones my grandmother used to wear, stood at the end of a driveway. Richard rolled down the window and asked for directions. She didn't know, though she said she was born in 1920. Noticing that we were Americans, she said that a close relative of hers had children in the United States. Through her wrinkled face she wished us good luck in finding Tabáni Tájház. As we drove away, I wondered if I was looking at an Amálka.

Next we asked a young woman for the location. She didn't know either, but somehow we finally fell upon Tabáni Tájház. It wasn't open. We poked our heads over the fence, sneaking a look at a flat-bottom boat under an awning in the yard. A ladder next to the house led to the upstairs. The boat didn't look like much, but in the peaceful waters of the Tisza not much else was needed.

On the way to Kossuth Square we took a reverential drive by the Szolnok archives where Richard had labored so long, poring through voluminous records. A woman was leaving the large, bright imperial yellow building, and a man was locking the door behind her. We couldn't go into the archives without proper authorization, which we didn't have, but Richard might not have gotten into the archives at all during Communist times.

After driving farther, we ended up near Kossuth Square known as just Market Square from 1863 to 1892. The square is the center of Szolnok and is framed by tall, yellow classical buildings and the Damjanich Museum built in 1860 and formerly a hotel, according to a plaque on the building. Fountains shot up in the air and children ran through the water to beat the heat.

We wouldn't have an entry problem at the Damjanich Museum since we were there during their open hours and it wasn't a Monday, when everything in the world seems to be closed in Europe during the summer.

The museum's exhibit contained a replica of a sewing shop, vintage 1900s. It gave me a good idea of what Amálka might have worn: a simple maroon top that buttoned down the front and a matching long skirt, appropriate for small-town living at the turn of the twentieth century. Maybe she even wore a bonnet with a big bow tied to the left, glowing in the prime of her youth, an innocent energy with a little memory book.

Moving on, a museum employee unlocked a door to reveal several rooms re-creating life in the Tisza region in about 1900.

One room showed a street scene with a woman in a long coral gown with a white veil covering her face arm-in-arm with her man near a tobacco shop. A few additional steps brought me to a dining room and a drawing room with a cimbalom, a hammer dulcimer played even today. Next, a kitchen with clunky pots, then a refined bedroom with armoires carved with care.

For all of our travels we never deeply got into the real psyche of the people. But we had an opportunity to do so at the museum's exhibit about public health and hygiene in the 1950s and 1960s in rural Hungary. It taught that cleanliness and public health go together. It also displayed the superstitious nature of the people. They poured water down a sickle to wash a baby to ward off hexes. Primitive treatments like coal mixed with water were used as antidotes to illness and abnormal behavior. These were brought on by curses. I checked my hands as I left the floor.

We crossed paths with the Szolnok Art Colony again at a different exhibit featuring works of the colony's founders and notable visitors. Before we left, we quickly toured an exhibit on Bertalan Székely (1835–1910), one of the most notable patriotic painters of the nineteenth century.

By now we were famished and for lunch strode to the oldest hotel in town, existing during Amálka's time. As I approached the Tisza Hotel, I noticed that it was connected to thermal baths. Amálka had to have been there. The women on the building's façade evoked the ideal of the day, narrow-waisted modern physiques and strong but slender arms. They were nymphs, not farm goddesses.

Even though the hotel was much smaller than the hotels I had seen in Opatija, its interior evoked the same grandeur in need of restoration. The Tisza Hotel was built in the early twentieth century, holding a ballroom much smaller than the Kvarner's, but enhanced with crystal chandeliers, a balcony, and dark wood furniture. In a blink I could see Austria-Hungary at its height.

Richard touched a worn wooden door frame and said, "Socialism. Lack of money."

Walking to the outdoor patio area, I imagined how the place would look with enough money. This always raises the questions, who will pay for it, and who will come? These questions dog many European cities, including Leonforte, Sicily, the birthplace of my grandfather. Leonforte's Branciforte Palace was being used for apartments. It's the only practical thing to do. Practicality is something people knew in Amálka's time, too, when the poor far outnumbered the rich.

The patio of the Tisza Hotel held a garden complete with a Grecian woman holding a water jar. Draped over her arm was an early twentieth-century electrical cord. Beside a set of French doors was a fuse box with five large fuses sticking out of it like the bottoms of light bulbs. The concrete dance floor was simple but showed the same potential as we had seen in Opatija on a warm night.

We sat down and engaged in a lively political conversation with plenty of time for our laid-back waiter to bring the meal. It wasn't long before we started relaxing and enjoying the lazy afternoon. We had lunch under the shade of trees, after which we took a short walk past a former synagogue, now an art gallery, and some other notable sites, including a church built in the eighteenth century.

We hung up our walking shoes until later that night.

. . .

THE TISZA GLISTENS AT DUSK. THE MATRIX WE'D FORMED OF Amálka's world was nearly complete. We stumbled across the missing piece by chance, on our way back to the car after dinner. Backlit by the setting sun, a stone archangel holds a dying soldier and the two are gripping a sword. The soldier's body is covered with gashes, his clasp shows that he knows no surrender. He is on his knees, staring at the angel, his muscles chiseled in rigor mortis for all the future generations who were supposed to learn but didn't. The trees grew dense and green against a fading blue sky. At the base of the statue it read:

IN MEMORY OF OUR HEROIC SONS WHO FELL IN BATTLE

IN THE GREAT WAR,

1914-1918

On another side of the statue was an excerpt from "The Appeal" by Mihály Vörösmarty.

IT CAN NOT BE THAT NOBLE HEARTS

HAVE SHED THEIR BLOOD IN VAIN!

AND TRUE SOULS NUMBERLESS CRUSHED

BENEATH THEIR CRUEL PAIN.

Amálka's life flashed before me. She lived with death as much as life.

. . .

WE WRAPPED UP OUR TIME IN SZOLNOK AND HUSTLED BACK toward Budapest to have dinner with Richard's family. When we arrived at our final destination about twelve miles outside of the city, Richard's wife, Julia, and her parents were putting the finishing touches on a feast of homemade apricot-filled rolls and goulash, boiling on a wood-burning stove as flames licked the bottom of the pot.

In the midst of all the activity, Julia had prepared a cooking class for me—a person who can barely navigate around a kitchen on a good day—on making native goulash. It brought back memories of my days as a kitchen appliance whiz when I appeared on television demonstrating the newest gizmos for cooking. I honed my cooking skills back then by identifying the on and off switches on various metallic creations for the kitchen counter. I cook with a plug and am proud of it.

What Julia had in store was authentic Hungarian cooking: little cups of vegetables, meat, and potatoes along with the right utensils and pots to use. The stew bubbled away in the cauldron with a fragrant steam piping out as her father stirred the mixture. Phil's attention was drawn to the two men pitching hay onto a wagon as a horse pulling the cart slowly meandered down a gently sloping hill. The neighbor's puppy, Martin, barked for attention. Richard and Julia's daughter, Dorina, with four small teeth, two on the top, two on the bottom, was trying to walk, standing up and plopping down in the grass.

This was farm country, Amálka's country, and the sight of the horse and wagon brought to mind the miniature painting of the workhorse pulling a blue wagon beneath rich green boughs. In that moment, not all that much had changed, and the goulash was ready, too. We ate slowly, knowing that the end of the meal was the end of the trip.

• • •

RICHARD WHISKED US OFF TO VIENNA FOR OUR FLIGHT THE next day. Boarding the plane, we could declare—mission accomplished. We had traveled back in time with Amálka, recollecting the days of the Austro-Hungarian Monarchy. As the pilot hit the afterburners, it struck me that I had amassed a small village of people around the world. Amálka would have liked that.

HEREND

The Herend factory is located in the town of Herend. The company was founded in the early nineteenth century just like Zsolnay. After Queen Victoria ordered a tea set in a butterfly and flower pattern in the 1850s, other wealthy customers lined up to buy Herend's hand-painted porcelain. Emperor Francis Joseph bought his wife Elizabeth a dazzling red tea set in an Oriental motif to use at Gödöllő, their residence in Hungary. Among Herend's other notable customers were King Carol I of Romania, King Milan of Serbia, Tsar Alexander II of Russia, and Countess Gladys Vanderbilt-Széchenyi.

The company has suffered the same fate as the region—recessions, depression, wars, and other reversals, even closing for a time in 1896, five years after Amálka was born. After many revivals, Herend began thriving once again in the 1980s as a separate entity, not a corporation owned by the state.

TIHANY

The abbey at Tihany has been around since 1055. Its charter was written in Latin interspersed with Hungarian words. It's very likely that Amálka would have come to Tihany given that it is so close to Pécs. When she did, she would have heard that King András I (about 1015–1060) is buried in a crypt, and that there is a big library on the premises. We missed the library but did see the crypt.

Its stone columns are like medieval knights watching over their fallen king, buried under a stone slab decorated with the carving of a sword. Light leaks in from the outside through a small window. András I is perpetuated in time.

The Benedictine monks lived better than their king.

"The views from the window over the lake are fine; the kitchen was large, and seemed well supplied; and among the cooks were the prettiest peasant girls we had seen in the whole country round," John Paget said of his visit to the abbey in *Hungary and Transylvania*.

Another travel writer, Johann Georg Kohl, who ventured to Tihany about the same time as John Paget, said he "passed a few very agreeable days" in lodgings provided by the Benedictines. He was especially entertained by a particularly garrulous "subordinate officer of the Abbott," who was charged with showing him "the curiosities" of Tihany, he wrote in *Austria, Prague, Hungary, Bohemia, and the Danube, Galicia, Styria, Moravia, Buckovina, and the Military Frontier.* The officer prattled on—about the fossils on the lake's shores and of the monks who survived the Turkish invasion by hiding in caves—as he led Kohl to Tihany's echo. Back then one could stand at a certain spot, shout something, and reliably get it back within a minute.

"My companion amused himself by repeating at least ten times the Hungarian style and title of my native city, [']*Bremia Nemet kiralny szabad varos! [Bremen the Germany royal free city!],*['']" wrote Kohl. The correct spelling in Hungarian is, *Bréma német királyi szabad város.*

The priests at Tihany must have been good fun because when William Pitt Byrne went there in the 1860s, they all playfully yelled silly things in Hungarian and English at the echo spot.

"Who's your hatter? Tickled their fancy immensely; and they, as well as we, were in fits of laughter at the frantic endeavors of these sportive but elderly monks to pronounce after us 'How are you off for soap?' and to obtain the Echo's answer to this and other similarly flippant queries," Byrne wrote in *Pictures of Hungarian Life.*

CHAPTER 35

Finding Amálka

My explorations of Central Europe's past and present struck a flame, flashing Amálka's memory book and everyone who wrote in it with a quick sparkle of life in Szolnok's stodgy archives. The people signing her book picked apples, celebrated weddings and harvests, ice skated in the winter, and commiserated at the loss of love. The fiddler of the house, the student, the railroad engineer, the doctor, all these people were there, in Szolnok, Pécs, Nagyvárad, and Novska. They wrote poetry and drew art. They had names: Márton Fekete, Lenke Kárász, Miklós Lindner, Fruzsina Orbán, and, Nagymama (Grandma).

But a single name, P., collected them all.

LOVE COMPENSATES FOR EVERYTHING;
BUT THERE IS NO RECOMPENSE FOR LOVE.

Stepping back into her troubled times,

MEMORY IS BUT THE SEDIMENT LEFT BEHIND BY RUSHING TIME.

They remembered their time in Pécs in 1907 and now I had memories, too.

Valéria and János married on May 11, 1907. I didn't need to know everything about the people behind the randomly scribbled names to have their happiness resonate again or see the treasure that Amálka was.

Amálka's memory book is universal, a heritage from her and everyone in her family. When everyone had gone, she and her book of memories passed into history just like the Habsburgs. Amálka wasn't a Habsburg but there are many footprints in history and hers is one. Her keepsake album carried her story to America. She was another Hungarian immigrant in a long line of talented people coming to our shores with their energy and their stories.

I could hear the Croatian cannons at Lotrščak Tower in Zagreb firing at noon to reset all the local clocks.

The conflicts have been brutal from century to century, and now, too, in the twenty-first century. But hope lives on. Our Croatian guide had proudly announced to our group that she had many Serb friends. So for you, most faithful reader, I now say,

MAY FORTUNE SCATTER ROSE PETALS IN YOUR PATH,...
WHERE OTHERS FIND MERE SHELLS CAST OUT BY THE SEA
THERE MAY YOU FIND PRECIOUS PEARLS.

My Hungarian is improving ever so slowly, too. I can even translate a stanza or two of poetry.

Here's the way an American might read one of Mindszenty's poems written to a person identified only as "B. A.":

To remember or to forget
There is no choice
Better to trust the heart
Follow it home.

Richard and Julia's daughter, our godchild, may someday have a memory book. When hers appears, I'll be back looking for a short, snappy poem to scribble. I'll sign it "L. F.," just as a challenge for future readers.

The power of memory books resides in their magic brew and the one I found knit all of our lives together like the swirls and patterns on the yellow walls of the Baroque architecture standing throughout Europe.

One chilly Sunday afternoon in November, I sat listening to Ádám György at Carnegie Hall, his fingertips rushing across the keyboard. The notes carried me back to a time and a place no longer foreign where the twigs of truisms grew on every branch:

ONLY WITH INNOCENT TEARS IN YOUR EYES

CAN YOU SAY "DEAR GOD I AM HAPPY."

I swept my hand over my cheek and lowered my head. Phil turned to me and reached for my hand.

CHAPTER 36

Postscript

MY JOURNEY TO FIND AMÁLKA IS OVER BUT NOT MY CONNECTION to Hungary. Phil and I continue to attend cultural events and, any time we can, we make our way to Budapest. The American Hungarian Library is filled with classics and worthy of a curious reader.

We finally did locate an authentic Hungarian restaurant in New York City. Andre's Café, on Second Avenue, between Eighty-fourth and Eighty-fifth Street, on the Upper East Side, is a narrowly spaced eatery, with scenes of Hungary hanging on the wall. As soon as I walked in the door, I was confronted with the sight of delicious pastries and cakes for sale. This popular establishment serves up authentic Hungarian dishes on a dozen wooden tables sequestered in the back.

Eating at Andre's felt as if we are sitting in a café in Liszt Square in Budapest, noshing on chicken paprikash and nokedli (pasta), stuffed cabbage and sour cream, and apricot- and nut-filled crepes, with the people around us chatting in Hungarian.

Not far from Andre's Café was the Hungarian Meat Market, whose salami and fresh goose liver, multigrain breads, and pickles were favorites of mine until it closed due to a fire. Hungarian delicacies exist in other parts of New York City. The Spotted Pig, on Eleventh Street in Greenwich Village, has a dish featuring delicacies from the mangalica pig. These portly Hungarian pigs can get as chunky as 1,100 pounds, a record for this species. This "lard-type" pig originated in the region around the Carpathian Mountains in the nineteenth century.

This *kicsi Magyarország New Yorkban* (little Hungary in New York) is nowhere near as recognizable as Chinatown or Little Italy. Its heyday was after the Hungarian Revolution in 1956, when refugees settled in Yorkville, the Upper East Side. From Seventy-fifth to Eighty-third Street, there were at least four restaurants, but over time they were assimilated into that vast melting pot that is New York City. This helps explain why we had such a hard time finding an authentic Hungarian restaurant in New York.

Nowadays more is out there. Brooklyn has Café Dada, a French-Hungarian place and Korzo Haus is whipping up Slovakian and Hungarian dishes in both Manhattan and Brooklyn. In a nod to the multicultural Austro-Hungarian Monarchy, Doma Na Rohu offers Central European fare from its site in the West Village in New York City.

. . .

PHIL AND I TRAVELED TO HUNGARY FOR DORINA'S BAPTISM. It was in Hungarian, and though I recognized a few words, Richard translated for both Phil and me. We said "Igen" ("Yes"), when asked.

. . .

A BOOKSELLER IN WALES WHO HAD SUPPLIED ME WITH SO MANY fine volumes on Central Europe e-mails me whenever she has something she believes I will like. The last purchase took a while because she was away in Croatia. I sent an e-mail, saying that in addition to buying the book, I'd come to Wales to meet her someday.

She replied, "Better still, come and stay in our Austro-Hungarian villa in Rijeka."

In all my correspondence with her over the years, I had never thought to ask what her personal connection was to Austria-Hungary.

. . .

ANIKÓ MOVED TO ARIZONA AND SHE AND I REMAIN CLOSE.

. . .

MY HUNGARIAN TEACHERS, AND I'VE HAD A FEW, HAVE ALL faithfully endeavored to teach me. I keep working at it.

. . .

AS I FINISHED THIS BOOK, I CONTACTED BRIGITTA AND FOUND that she had begun a career to match her talents. She is now working at the United Nations as a team assistant for the Peacekeeping Operations for Africa, covering its great lakes area in the Congo, Central African Republic, and a couple of other countries. As she was telling me about her life, she said, "Before I forget, when I heard from you, I contacted the Hungarian Consulate to see if they might help with your book but they told me to call the Hungarian Cultural Center. I'll do that for you." And she did, sending me an e-mail with ideas and contacts.

. . .

DORINA IS NOW SIX. RICHARD AND I STAY IN TOUCH. JUST before we hung up on our last call, he caught himself laughing. "I wanted to tell you this. I asked Dorina where she wanted to go. I thought she was going to say the zoo or the swimming pool. Dorina paused and then said, "I would like to visit Aunt Linda in New York City."

ADDENDUMS

The Morgan Library

ANY EXPOSURE TO BIBLIOTECA CORVINA, THE FABLED library of King Matthias, brightens in the mind. Richard promised to let us know about any upcoming exhibition of the king's illuminated manuscripts in Budapest. Some manuscripts can be seen at: http://portal.unesco.org/ci/en/ev.php-URL_ID=14904&URL_DO=DO_TOPIC&URL_SECTION=201.html.

But the pictures online do not give the works their due justice. The Morgan Library in New York City has illuminated manuscripts that once were held in Matthias's Royal Library of Buda. I said to Phil that I was going to call them to see if they would let me study the motifs and color palettes in one of them to see how they could have influenced—if at all—Amálka's generation and the painted pages of her memory book. I went online and gathered the history of the manuscripts. Manuscripts 496 and 497 were both illuminated for Matthias in the fifteenth century by Italians and later rebound by the Morgan. In 2009, MS 496 was being prepared to go on loan to Barcelona, Spain; and as for MS 497, the curator wanted a specific reason for my

requesting the original. First I consulted PDFs with biblio-
graphic information, and then pursued other books about the
Matthias manuscripts.

．　．　．

Two years later the Morgan granted me the privilege
of actually seeing manuscript 497.

The night before my appointment at the Morgan, I set my
alarm and looked through my clothes. I selected a pair of
conservative black plants, a soft mauve blouse and low heels.
Then I put high-quality copies of the pages from Amálka's book
in my bag.

I angled for the side entrance to the library, past security, up
the elevator, and into a small room, where I was asked to put my
things in the locker and wash my hands at the sink.

When I was done, a staff person opened another door to a
room with microfilm machines.

The librarian approached me as I entered the room.

"You can sit here. I'd recommend you start with the micro-
films for MS 497 so you can get a good idea of what you want to
see in the actual manuscript."

After what seemed like just a short time, I looked at my
watch and realized I had spent a few hours viewing and copying
several pages from the microfilm. I called the librarian over.

"I'm ready for the manuscript," I said.

"Here are some papers to read while I get it," she said.

I picked up the sheet with a number of bullets outlining
what to keep in mind when viewing an illuminated manuscript.

Wash hands. I'd already done that. I moved my books and
bag away from where the librarian would be putting the manuscript down. The list advised against touching the illuminations
and prohibited taking pictures of them. Somewhere on the list it
said that I could obtain color slides or pictures.

The librarian returned carrying a large book with a burgundy leather cover. I thought that one could have walked by that as easily as Amálka's book in the antique store.

As she laid the manuscript in a book support, I noticed its gilded edging.

"You can use these velvet snakes to hold the corners of the page down, but don't put them on the illumination," she said, walking away.

I opened the book.

The left-hand leaf of the manuscript shone with a medallion of gold, surrounded by twelve smaller ones, encircling text announcing the contents of the book. The paint of the Latin text in small medallions alternated rhythmically between gold and blue. Between the small gold medallions the artist painted red and yellow fruit, pink and blue ornaments resembling flowers, and gold balls.

My eyes veered back and forth between the illuminated leaves and the color images on loose copies of the pages from Amálka's book, laying to the right.

The right-hand leaf of the manuscript displayed evenly spaced block text within a floral border. The beginning letter of the Latin text was a giant golden C within a bed of flowers. Long, lithe tails on the Qs leaned to the right, as if propelled by a light breeze; and looped tails on the Gs looked regal. Surrounding the text were flowers, fruits, animals, and angels.

Page after page, past and divinely present, the text and floral illuminations elevated me to Matthias's time. I was in his library, a quiet and respectful visitor. The book's motifs, age spots, and paint from images that bled into the other pages were suddenly the backdrop for art in later centuries.

I turned the pages slowly. Matthias's book spoke to me of beauty, and even more so of styles and motifs that would bloom in Amálka's clusters of forget-me-nots, swirls of cyclamens and pink roses, scenes of a young girl's life with the artistic shadows of the past.

In my mind, the art and artistry that Matthias and his medieval predecessors brought into Hungarian culture had indeed spread through the centuries. Surely, the pink and blue flowers and subtle curves of the vines around Amálka's text do not represent a conscious attempt to follow any ancient style. They stand in their own right, suggesting a modern version of borders, motifs, and color palettes found in Hungarian art through the ages.

"Five more minutes," the librarian said.

I focused on the small illuminated letters on the pages, thinking about Amálka's book in the antique store and Matthias's books all over the world. Even if only a few of these gems exist, they are flag bearers of an era, an apparition. His faint figure, shoulder-length hair and penetrating eyes, with one hand on his waist, the other extended toward me, sent chills down my arm. I saw the scholar, the warrior, living on through time.

The librarian walked over to me and said, "It's time now." Then she lovingly closed the manuscript.

•　•　•

That night, Phil said, "You just had the experience of a lifetime."

I closed my eyes, seeing the gold paint in Matthias's books on the illuminations and the Latin script, passing again into antiquity.

MATTHIAS'S LIBRARY

Matthias's passion was manuscripts, hand-copied and illuminated by some of Europe's finest artists. The library, Biblioteca Corviniana, was a personal collection and competing technologies were not allowed—Matthias didn't support the arrival of the first printing press in Hungary, which caused mechanical printing to lag in many other places in Europe.

Matthias favored manuscripts on history, theology, philosophy, military, and science. His wife, Queen Beatrice, liked the classics, too, especially the tragedies, which seemed to fit her temperament. "When not creating a scene, shedding bitter tears, or plotting, she probably had her nose deep in a book," wrote Marcus Tanner in *The Raven King Matthias Corvinus and the Fate of His Lost Library* (2008).

The library expanded quickly in the last five years of the king's life, when his reign was at its zenith following his 1485 conquest of Vienna. Most scholars believe that there were about two thousand to twenty-five hundred books in his library. J. Pierpont Morgan's preserved a few of these for us.

SUPPLEMENT 2

Poetry Snippets

HERE ARE A FEW PIECES THAT I LIKE. IT IS A BIT OF A TRAVEL story, more a collage than a collection.

> *O, beauteous scenes that into my mind throng.*
> *Ah, me! By fate's most merciless decree,*
> *These beauteous things I ne'er in life shall see.*[1]
>
> MIHÁLY BABITS, "FAR, FAR AWAY"

> *On fair shores where the Tisza flows,*
> *I seek and follow my sweet rose;*
> *Tisza, Tisza, tell me, where*
> *Shall I seek my rose so fair?*[2]
>
> KÁROLY KISFALUDY, "ON TISZA'S SHORE"

---

1. Loew, *Modern Magyar Lyrics*, 23.
2. Loew, *Magyar Poetry*, 284.

To regions remote I have wandered astray,
Like a leaf by the whirling winds drifted away.[3]

KÁROLY KISFALUDY, "THE WANDERER'S SONG"

Where else, throughout the World's extent,
Wilt thou for refuge fly?
Though Fortune's hand should bless or strike,
Thou here must live and die.[4]

MIHÁLY VÖRÖSMARTY, "THE APPEAL"

"Oe'r the meadows, to the forest,
Little birdlet flew:
Green his pinions, bright his flying,
Beautiful to view.
And he calls me—"Come, go with me,
"I'll go with thee too." [5]

—HUNGARIAN POPULAR SONG, "THE LITTLE BIRD"

Birds must seek a leafy dwelling;
Traveller's parch'd, a cool spring's welling;[6]

JÁNOS ARANY, "HOME"

A stork was taking her flight over Pest
and Buda and settled upon a tower.
"How magnificent these two cities are!" she
exclaimed, looking around her in every direction;

3. Butler, *Hungarian Poems*, 26.
4. Ibid., 10.
5. Bowring, *Poetry of the Magyars*, 231.
6. Butler, *Hungarian Poems*, 23.

*"what a number of storks' nests its chimneys would
hold!"*

"Every man to his own taste!"

*Some travelers, returning home, can give a voluble
account of the hotels in which they fared well and
cheaply; others, where the women were most beautiful
or amiable, or the game tables best filled."*

"Every man to his own taste!" [7]

ANDRÁS FÁY, "THE STORK"

*Here upon the hill-top seated,
I can cast my eyes around ;
While the trees with sigh repeated,
Shake their leaf-loads to the ground.* [8]

SÁNDOR PETŐFI, "THE AUTUMN"

*These are the autumn days. The sunrise is less
    bright:
Far from their nests the birds have taken flight;
Happy is he who flies with friends held dear;
But sorrowful am I left lonely here —
    All lonely here!* [9]

KÁLMÁN TÓTH, "AUTUMN DAYS"

7. Ibid., 78.
8. Ibid., 27.
9. Loew, *Magyar Poetry*, 182.

"Ever absent, ever near;
Still I see thee, still I hear;
Yet I cannot reach thee, dear!" [10]

FERENC KAZINCZY, "SEPARATION"

The winter comes, cold days we feel,
The wind is bleak, the snowflakes fall,
Frost-flowers upon the panes conceal
A fair day-dream to paint for all.
Untouched by wind or frost am I;
My heart, my room are warm and dry. [11]

KÁROLY SZÁSZ, "THE WINTER"

It's cold and hazy, all alone
I   sit at home, a weary grown.
Upon the hearth
The embers die,
I look intent
And ghosts espy. [12]

KÁROLY SZÁSZ, "WINTER TWILIGHT"

In an exchange from the opera *Bánk Bán*, the peasant Tiborc laments the suffering of the poor at the hands of their rulers. I grant you that this is nominally a story about the thirteenth century, but József Katona's drama, made into an opera by Ferenc Erkel, clearly struck a nerve when it was performed in Szolnok in 1912. The power of the opera resided in its themes, the bonds of power and corruption, guiding a king to tragedy.

10. Bowring, *Poetry of the Magyars*, 68.
11. Loew, *Magyar Poetry*, 174.
12. Ibid., 226.

TIBORC: They turn our rich land into their hunting ground, which for us is out of bounds; and if a sick wife or a child with the pox had a craving, and we take down a squab to please them, we'll be tied to the stake in no time.

AND he who pockets hundreds of thousands will judge the one who steals pennies out of desperate need.

BÁNK: How true, how true![13]

. . .

Tell me, old stream, how oft they bosom strong
Is cleft by storms and ships that glide along?

How deep and wide these rifts! On heart of man
Inflict such wounds no grief or passion can,

Yet, when the ship is gone the storm is o'er,
The stream rolls smoothly, showing rifts no more

But when the human heart is cleft, no calm
Can heal the wound or bring it aught of balm.[14]

—ALEXANDER PETŐFI, "ON THE DANUBE"

I am but matter that decays;
    The time will deal its fatal thrust;
And when my course is run, I will
    A handful be of earthly dust.

13. Katona, *Bánk Bán*, 120.
14. Loew, *Magyar Poetry*, 178–179.

But while a spark of life I have,
  While thought my being agitates,
I live for what is beautiful,
  I live for that which elevates.[15]

EMIL ÁBRÁNYI, "I AM"

SPRING, gentle Spring, the rose's breast unfolding,
Sinks in light dews upon the emerald meadows,
Waking to life what wintry cold had frozen,
Calling to joy, and budding into being,
                    Countless creations.[16]

DÁNIEL BERZSENYI, "SPRING"

All the bright world's charm seem brighter,
  All the frowns of grief are gone;
Darkening thoughts have pass'd away,
  All is new delight and day.[17]

SÁNDOR KISFALUDY, "MÁS A VILÁG' ÁBRÁZATTYA"

"EMPTY yet and green, that corn-ear tosses high its lofty
    brow;
See it ripe and full and golden, bend in meek submission
    now.
Such is boyhood in its folly—shallow, proud, and inso-
    lent;—
Such is manhood in its wisdom—modest, and in calmness
    bent."[18]

FERENC VERSEGHY, "TRUE WISDOM"

15. Ibid., 101.
16. Bowring, *Poetry of the Magyars,* 124.
17. Ibid., 87.
18. Ibid., 200.

The air has softer grown and sweet and clear,..
Our good old friend the stork again is here.
He is at work upon his ancient nest,
Where his expected brood shall soon find rest.

Back, back! be not deceived, for truth you took
Delusive sun's rays and the babbling brook!
Back! back! This is not yet the spring that came,
Our life is frozen, held in winter's frame.

Fly, fly away! when in the southern isles
You chance to meet some of our land's exiles.
Tell them of our beloved country's grief,
And that we're scattered like an open sheaf.[19]

MIHÁLY TOMPA, "THE STORK"

A girl, out of her teens, the fire doth nurse, by far
She is the brightest of the stars,—the morning star.
She heats an iron for her new, just finished dress,
To-morrow is a feast,—complete's her happiness.[20]

JÁNOS ARANY, "FAMILY CIRCLE"

O, cities great, and people grand and strong,[21]

MIHÁLY BABITS, "FAR, FAR AWAY"

19. Loew, *Magyar Poetry*, 445–446.
20. Loew, *Selected Lyrics*, 17.
21. Loew, *Modern Magyar Lyrics*, 23.

The music screams; hot, perfumed, blissful,
youthful exhalations spiral and swoop.
And youths, young girls with wreaths of roses
look in terror at a dark couple.

"Who are they?" And we enter in sad silence,
our death-faces covered over with black veil,
and quietly scatter our withered
wreaths in this cheerful hall.

The music dies down in this cheerful hall,
Winter wind roars and out go the lights.
We begin to dance, and the happy couples,
Crying and shivering now, separate and flee.[22]

ENDRE ADY, "WITH LEDA AT THE BALL"

Let the glory of this place swell and overflow,
As does the Tisza when it overruns its bank."[23]

ERNŐ SZÉP RECITING HIS POEM AT THE
INAUGURATION OF SZOLNOK NATIONAL THEATER
ON APRIL 20, 1912

---

22. "Ady Endre: Lédával a bálban," website of MEK (Magyar Elektronikus Könyvtár), http://mek.niif.hu/05500/05552/html/av0076.html.
23. Borus, *Szolnok Város Története*, 134–135.

An American Kremšnita

CREAM CAKES ARE UBIQUITOUS. VERSIONS OF NAPOLEON cream cakes are found in nearly every country. Hungarians call theirs *krémes*; Slovenians, *kremšnita*. Other countries have their own varieties. My preference falls to the Slovenian.

The father of the Slovenian cream cake kremšnita is Ištvan Lukačević from Senta, modern-day Serbia. Lukačević perfected Bled kremšnita while working at the bakery in the 1950s. Bled kremšnita continues to be made according to the original recipe in the Park Hotel.

I liked this cream cake so much that I worked with a chef to create an American cream cake inspired by all of the cream cakes of Europe, especially Slovenia, Hungary, and Austria.

This is a dessert that requires some love. It can take up to two days before it's fully assembled and ready to serve. It is a pastry and understanding how those are made will surely facilitate your creation.

An American Kremšnita

Number of servings: 12-15
Preparation Time: 3 hrs
Inactive Time: 12-24 hrs

To get started:
14x7-in cookie sheets (for baking the puff pastry)
13x9x2-in pan (*for assembling the Kremšnita)
2 sheets of puff pastry (found at supermarket; one sheet on the bottom and one on the top)
* *Using a larger size pan will yield a thinner layer of custard and more servings.*

Other items you will need:
Large pot
Three medium size bowls
Small bowl
Sharp knife
Measuring cups and spoons

Filling:
6 cups of milk
8 eggs (8 egg yolks, 8 egg whites)
1 1/2 cup granulated sugar
2/3 cup all-purpose flour
1/2 packet vanilla sugar* (found at international supermarkets or Whole Foods)
Juice one lemon
2 Tbsp dark rum (if you do not like rum, you can omit it)
2.5 packages of Knox unflavored gelatine (if using powdered gelatin use two and a half tablespoons)

*Don't substitute unless you have to. If you can't find vanilla *sugar, a good vanilla extract will work; however, the recipe will not taste as originally intended. Add a teaspoon of vanilla extract and one additional tablespoon of granulated sugar.*

Creme Chantilly layer:
1 1/2 quart whipping cream
1/2 cup confectioners sugar

Preheat oven to 400°. Lay out your puff pastry and prick the sheets with a fork to prevent them from rising. Place the puff pastry on a 14x17-inch cookie sheet, and bake for about 15 minutes or until golden brown.

When the pastry has cooled, cut the first sheet to the size of the pan in which you will be assembling the cake (this will be the bottom layer). Repeat with the other sheet.

Cut 1 puff pastry sheet into 12 rectangles. The best way to do this is to lay the pastry horizontally in front of you. Cut the sheet in half lengthwise. Now you will have two pieces of puff pastry. Make six vertical cuts to each half so that you have 12

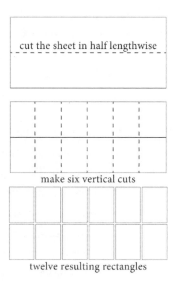

cut the sheet in half lengthwise

make six vertical cuts

twelve resulting rectangles

rectangles, these will be the top layer of the cake.

Now place them back onto the cookie sheet until ready to assemble. Pre-cutting the puff pastry is necessary because this dessert cannot be cut once the cream is spread between the puff pastry.

. . .

In a large pot, slowly bring the milk to a boil, and then turn the heat down to low. In a medium bowl, beat the egg yolks with 1 cup of sugar (reserve ½ cup of the sugar for later use). Whisk until the yolks have become light in color and fluffy. After you have achieved an airy consistency slowly start incorporating the flour into the egg mixture and whisk until smooth. Continue adding the flour a little at a time until it's all added in.

In a small bowl add vanilla sugar, lemon juice, and rum to the gelatin and set aside. This is the gelatin mixture to be used later. (Rum is optional).

Temper the egg mixture by pouring a little of the hot milk into the eggs while whisking vigorously (this will keep the eggs from curdling). When smooth, add some more hot milk and whisk. After it's well blended, add the mixture to the pot with the remaining milk. Turn the heat up to medium-low and continue to whisk (the high sugar content plus the flour should prevent the eggs from curdling if you whisk well and have tempered the eggs properly). Cook the custard until thick and the taste of flour has diminished, about 10 minutes.

Add the gelatin mixture and cook another 3 minutes.

In a large bowl add the 8 egg whites and the remaining sugar. Beat until the egg whites become glossy and fluffy and stiff peaks form. Gently fold the whites into the hot custard.

In a 13x9x2-inch pan, add the first layer of puff pastry, now spread all of the custard on the puff pastry. (You can use a larger pan but it will yield a thinner layer of custard and more servings.) Place in the refrigerator and let set for at least 4 hours. Overnight is preferable.

. . .

For the Crème Chantilly, add whipping cream to a medium-size bowl and whisk in the confectioners' sugar. Beat until firm. Spread the cream on top of the custard and assemble the puff pastry rectangles on top.

Dust with powdered sugar and keep cold until ready to serve.

. . .

Classic Puff Pastry (Pâte feuilletée)

For the dough a scale is recommended. Grams are the more accurate form of measurement for this recipe than ounces and teaspoons though we have provided them for your convenience.

Ingredients:

For the dough:
375g (13.5oz) all-purpose flour
7.5g (1 tsp) salt
75g (3oz) room-temperature butter
225g (7.5oz) cold water

For the butter block:
262.5g (9oz) cold butter

Sift the flour and salt onto the work surface. Make a well in the flour and run a finger through the center. Mix the butter into the dry ingredients either by rubbing it into the flour with the fingertips or using a metal pastry scraper. Work quickly to avoid melting the butter. When there are no particles of butter visible, add the cold water and make a paste using the fingertips of one hand. When the dough has formed, shape it into a square block. With a sharp knife, cut an X into the top—this helps cut the gluten strands so that they relax more quickly. Cover the dough with plastic wrap and refrigerate it for at least 30 minutes.

Take the cold butter out of the refrigerator and flatten it between sheets of plastic wrap, using a rolling pin. The butter should be pliable but should still be very cool. Form it into a square.

After the dough has chilled sufficiently, take it out of the refrigerator. At this point the dough and butter should be as close in consistency as possible. Sprinkle some flour on the work surface and roll out the dough, adding more flour if needed to prevent the dough from sticking. Make a square just large enough to enclose the butter.

Place the butter on top of the dough and fold the edges of the dough over the butter to enclose it, then pinch it to seal. With a rolling pin, press on the butter wrapped in the dough a couple of times along its length, or until it lengthens to 9 inches. Then, using flour to dust the work surface, roll it until it is about 22 inches long; do not roll its width. Keep the sides even and square while working.

Fold the dough into thirds. Roll the dough out again and fold into thirds. The pastry now has two turns. Wrap in plastic and refrigerate for 20 to 30 minutes.* Do two more turns by rolling and folding, which will make four turns. Refrigerate to rest. Make two more turns, refrigerate to rest, or freeze for future use. Refer to time and temperature found at the beginning of the recipe.

---

* Remember to refrigerate the dough between every two turns to rest it sufficiently. Regardless of the recipe you'll use this in, you may turn the pastry as many times as you'd like to give the pastry more layers of dough, which in turn will create a more flaky pastry.

ACKNOWLEDGMENTS

We gratefully acknowledge the following for permission to use previously published material:

Excerpt from "Belles of Budapest", Vogue by Bess Rattray
(Vogue magazine, 1999)
Reprinted by permission of CondeNast Licensing

Excerpt from *The Memoirs of Herbert Hoover Years of Adventure 1874–1920*
(New York: The Macmillan Company, 1952)
Reprinted by permission of Thomas F. Schwartz, PhD, Herbert Hoover Presidential Library-Museum

Excerpt from *Opatija – Abbazia A Stroll Through Space and Time* by Amir Muzur,
English translation by Slobodan Drenovac
(Rijeka: Adami d.o.o., 2007)
Reprinted by permission of Dragan Ogurlić, Adamić d.o.o.

Excerpt from *The Raven King Matthias Corvinus and the Fate of his Lost Library* by Marcus Tanner
(New Haven: Yale University Press, 2008)
Reprinted by permission of Donna Anstey, Yale University Press

Excerpt from *The Rebels* by Sándor Márai
(New York: Alfred A. Knopf, 2007)
Reprinted by permission of Alfred A. Knopf, a division of Random House, Inc.

Excerpt from *Vlad the Impaler: Dracula* by Ştefan Andreescu
English translation by Ioana Voia
(Bucharest: The Romanian Cultural Foundation Publishing House, 1999)
Reprinted by permission of Bogdan Popescu of the Romanian Cultural Institute

REFERENCES

Alden, Percy, ed. 1909. *Hungary of To-day by Members of the Hungarian Government, etc.* London: Eveleigh Nash.

Andreescu, Ștefan. 1999. *Vlad the Impaler: Dracula.* Translated by Ioana Voia. Bucharest: The Romanian Cultural Foundation Publishing House.

Ansted, David Thomas. 1862. *A Short Trip in Hungary and Transylvania in the Spring of 1862.* London: W.H. Allen & Co. Kessinger Publishing's Legacy Reprints.

Baedeker, Karl. 1900. *Austria, Including Hungary, Transylvania, Dalmatia, and Bosnia.* 9th revised ed. Leipsic: Karl Baedeker.

Boner, Charles. 1865. *Transylvania: Its Products and Its People.* London: Longmans, Green, Reader, and Dyer. Accessed at http://books.google.com/.

Borus, József, Gyula Kaposvári, László Selmeczi, Ilona Stanczik, Imre Szántó, László Szurmay, and Lajos Tiszai. 1975. *Szolnok Város Története.* Szolnok: Szolnok Megyei Lapkiadó Vállalat.

Bovill, Forster W. B. 1908. *Hungary and the Hungarians.* Illustrated by

William Pascoe. London: Methuen & Co.

Bowring, John. 1830. *Poetry of the Magyars, Preceded by a Sketch of the Language and Literature of Hungary and Transylvania*. London: Printed for the Author. Also available online at http://books.google.com/.

Browning, H. Ellen. 1897. *A Girl's Wanderings in Hungary*. 2nd ed. London: Longmans, Green, & Co. Also available online at http://books.google.com/.

Butler, E.D. 1877. *Hungarian Poems and Fables for English Readers* London: Trübner and Co.

Byrne, William Pitt. 1869. *Pictures of Hungarian Life*. Kessinger Publishing's Rare Reprint. London: William Ridgeway. Also available online at http://books.google.com/. This work was written by Julia Byrne, wife of William Pitt Byrne, and originally published anonymously. The book was re-printed erroneously under her husband's name.

De Burgh, Edward Morgan Alborough. 1899. *Elizabeth, Empress of Austria: A Memoir*. Kessinger Publishing's Legacy Reprint. London: Hutchinson & Co.

Eötvös, József. 1911. *A Karthauzi*. Magyar Klasszikusok Series. Budapest: Franklin-Társulat. Accessed at http://mek.oszk.hu/03100/03130/.

Felbermann, Louis. ca. 1892. *Hungary and Its People*. London: Griffith Farran & Co.

Fletcher, Margaret. 1892. *Sketches of Life and Character in Hungary*. Translations by Rose Le Quesme. London: Swan Sonnenschein & Co. Kessinger Publishing's Legacy Reprints. Also available online at http://books.google.com/.

Gerard, Jane Emily. 1888. *Land Beyond the Forest: Facts, Figures and Fancies from Transylvania*. New York: Harper & Brothers. Accessed at

http://books.google.com/.

Hoover, Herbert. 1952. *The Memoirs of Herbert Hoover: Years of Adventure 1874–1920*. New York: Macmillan Co.

Huszadik Század. 2014. *"Varsányi Gyula: Álarcos bálban."* Accessed at http://www.huszadikszazad.hu/1900-junius/kultura/varsanyi-gyula-alarcos-balban.

Katona, József. 1958. *Bánk Bán*. Budapest: Szépirodalmi Könyvkiadó.

Kohl, Johann Georg. 1843. *Austria, Prague, Hungary, Bohemia, and the Danube, Galicia, Styria, Moravia, Buckovina, and the Military Frontier*. Kessinger Publishing's Rare Reprints. London: Chapman and Hall. Also available online at http://books.google.com/.

Loew, William N. 1908. *Magyar Poetry: Selections from Hungarian Poets*. New York: Amerikai Magyar Népszava. Also available online at http://mek.oszk.hu/03900/03966/html/index.htm.

Loew, William N. 1926. *Modern Magyar Lyrics: Selected Gems from Alex Petőfi and Other Modern Hungarian Poets*. Budapest: Wodianer F. és Fiai R.T.

Loew, William N. 1914, 2003. *Selected Lyrics and Ballads by John Arany* Honolulu, Hawaii: University Press of the Pacific.

Magyar Elektronikus Könyvtár. 1914, 2003. *"Ady Endre: Lédával a bálban."* Website of MEK (Magyar Elektronikus Könyvtár), http://mek.niif.hu/05500/05552/html/av0076.html.

Márai, Sándor. 2007. *The Rebels*. Translated by George Szirtes. New York: Alfred A. Knopf.

Mazuchelli, Nina Elizabeth. 1881. *"Magyarland;" Being the Narrative of Our Travels Through the Highlands and Lowlands of Hungary*. 2 vols. London: Sampson Low, Marston, Searle, & Rivington. Vol. 1. Accessed at http://books.google.com/.

McArmor, Charles. 1879. *The New Handbook of Vienna: Including a Guide for the Danube, the Austrian Alps and Their Watering Places.* Vienna: Otto Maass.

Mindszenty, Gedeon. 1913. *Mindszenty Gedeon Költeményei.* Eger: Egri Egyházmegyei Irodalmi Egyesület.

Muzur, Amir. 2007. *Opatija – Abbazia A Stroll Through Space and Time.* Translated by Slobodan Drenovac. Rijeka: Adamić.

Paget, John. 1839. *Hungary and Transylvania with Remarks on Their Condition, Social, Political, and Economical.* Vols. 1 and 2. London: John Murray. Vol. 1, title page. Also available online at http://books.google.com/.

Paton, Andrew Archibald. 2005. *Researches on the Danube and the Adriatic; or, Contributions to the Modern History of Hungary and Transylvania, Dalmatia and Croatia, Servia and Bulgaria.* 2 vols. Elibron Classics Replica ed. Unabridged facsimile of the edition published in 1861 by F. A. Brockhaus. N.p.: Adamant Media Corporation, Vol. 2.

Pardoe, Miss. 1840. *The City of the Magyar, or Hungary and Her Institutions in 1839–40.* Vol. 1. London: George Virtue. Accessed at http://books.google.com/.

Quin, Michael J. 1839. *A Steam Voyage Down the Danube: With Sketches of Hungary, Wallachia, Servia, Turkey,* etc. 3rd ed. Paris: A. & W. Galignani & Co. Accessed at http://books.google.com/.

Rattray, Bess. August 1999. *Belles of Budapest,* Vogue.

Riedl, Frederick. 1906. *A History of Hungarian Literature.* New York: D. Appleton & Co. Also available online at http://books.google.com/.

Rudolf of Austria. 1889. *His Imperial and Royal Highness the Late Crown Prince. Notes on Sport and Ornithology.* Translated by C. G. Danford. London: Gurney and Jackson. Also available online at

http://books.google.com/.

Stokes, Adrian. 1909. *Hungary*. Painted by Adrian & Marianne Stokes. London: Adam and Charles Black. Also available online at http://books.google.com/.

Tanner, Marcus. 2008. *The Raven King: Matthias Corvinus and the Fate of his Lost Library*. New Haven: Yale University Press.

Tissot, Victor. 1881. *Unknown Hungary*. Translated from the 4th ed. by A. Oswald Brodie. Vol 1. BiblioBazaar Reproduction Series. London: Richard Bentley and Son.

Tschudi, Clara, and E. M. Cope. 1901. *Elizabeth: Empress of Austria and Queen of Hungary*. Kessinger Publishing's Legacy Reprint. London: Swan Sonnenschein & Co.

Twain, Mark. 1919. *What is Man? And Other Essays*. London: Chatto & Windus, Accessed at http://books.google.com/.

BIBLIOGRAPHY

Ardó, Zsuzsanna. *Culture Shock! A Survival Guide to Customs &*
Etiquette: Hungary. New York: Marshall Cavendish, 2008.

Baedeker, Karl. *Vienna*. Ostfildern: Baedeker, 2008.

Beattie, William. *The Danube, Its History, Scenery, and Topography*.
Illustrated by Abresch, W. Henry Bartlett et al. London: George
Virtue, 1844. Accessed at http://books.google.com/.

Beneš, Edward. "The Problem of the Small Nations after the World
War." *The Slavonic Review* 4, No. 11 (December, 1925): 257-277.

Berkovits, Ilona. *Illuminated Manuscripts from the Library of Matthias*
Corvinus. Translated by Susan Horn. Budapest: Corvina Press,
1964.

Beutler, Gigi. *The Imperial Vaults of the PP Capuchins in Vienna*
(Capuchin Crypt). 3rd revised ed. Vienna: Beutler-Heldenstern,
2007.

Bíró, Sándor. *The Nationalities Problems in Transylvania 1867–1940: A*
Social History of the Romanian Minority Under Hungarian Rule,
1867–1918 and of the Hungarian Minority under Romanian Rule,
1918–1940. Translated by Mario F. Fenyo. New York: Columbia
University Press, 1992.

Bogle, James, and Joanna Bogle. *A Heart for Europe: The Lives of*

Emperor Charles and Empress Zita of Austria-Hungary.
Leominster, UK: Gracewing Books, 1993.

Bödy, Paul. *Joseph Eötvös and the Modernization of Hungary, 1840-1870: A Study of Ideas of Individuality and Social Pluralism in Modern Politics.* New York: Columbia University Press, 1985.

Bödy, Pál, ed. *Hungarian Statesmen of Destiny, 1860-1960.* Distributed by Columbia University Press. Highland Lakes, NJ: Atlantic Research and Publications, 1989.

Bralić, Andrea. *Rijeka: Love at First Sight. Tourism and Heritage 48.* Zagreb: Turistička Naklada, 2007.

Burford, Tim and Norm Longley. *The Rough Guide to Romania.* 4th ed. New York: Rough Guides, 2004.

Can, Turhan. *Istanbul: Gate to the Orient.* Translated by Gaye Tinaztepe. 5th ed. Istanbul: Orient, 1990.

Carney, Peter, Steve Fallon, Kate Galbraith, Mark Honan, Patrick Horton, Keti Japaridze, Steve Kokker, et al. *Eastern Europe.* 6th ed. Melbourne: Lonely Planet Publications, 2001.

Converso, Claudia. *Budapest: Civilisation Art and History.* Budapest: Europe Unlimited Kft., n.d.

Crosse, Andrew F. *Round About The Carpathians.* Edinburgh: William Blackwood and Sons, 1878. Kessinger Publishing's Rare Reprints.

Csapodi, Csaba, and Klára Csapodi-Gárdonyi. *Bibliotheca Corviniana: The Library of King Matthias Corvinus of Hungary.* Budapest: Magyar Helikon, 1967.

Csomor, Lajos. *Magyarország Szent Koronája.* Vaja: Vay Ádám Múzeum Baráti Köre, 1988.

Csorba, Csaba. *Pécs.* Panoráma Magyar Városok Sorozat. Budapest: Panoráma, 1983.

Csorba, Csaba, János Estók, and Konrád Salamon. *The Illustrated History of Hungary.* Translated by Gabriella Baksa-Schön. Budapest: Magyar Könyvklub, 1999.

Curta, Florin, and Paul Stephenson. *Southeastern Europe in the Middle Ages, 500–1250.* Cambridge: Cambridge University Press,

2006.

Deak, Istvan. *The Lawful Revolution: Louis Kossuth and the Hungarians 1848-1849*. London: Phoenix Press, 2001. First published 1979 by Columbia University Press.

Deák, István. "Mindless Efficacy." *Hungarian Quarterly*. 49 (Winter 2008).

Deletant, Dennis. *Ceausescu and the Securitate: Coercion and Dissent in Romania, 1965-89*. London: Hurst & Co., 1995.

De Daruvar, Yves. *The Tragic Fate of Hungary: A Country Carved-up Alive at Trianon*. Munchen: "Nemzetör" e.V., 1974.

Dent, Bob. *Mesélő szobrok*. Budapest: Európa Könyvkiadó, 2009.

Eighty Club. *Hungary: Its People, Places, and Politics: The Visit of the Eighty Club in 1906*. London: T. Fisher Unwin, 1907. Also available online at http://books.google.com/.

Eötvös, József. *The Village Notary; A Romance of Hungarian Life*. Translated by Otto Wenckstern. London: Longman, Brown, Green, and Longmans, 1850.

Evans, David. *Teach Yourself: The First World War*. Teach Yourself. Chicago: McGraw-Hill Companies, 2004.

Fajfar, Janez. *Bled: Impressions Slovenia*. Photographed by Christian Prager. Germany: OrbiVision, 2006.

Florescu, Radu R., and Raymond T. McNally. *Dracula, Prince of Many Faces: His Life and His Times*. New York: Little, Brown and Co., 1989.

Frojimovics, Kinga, Géza Komoróczy, Viktória Pusztai, and Andrea Strbik. *Jewish Budapest: Monuments, Rites, History*. Budapest: CEU Press, 1999.

Grun, Bernard. *The Timetables of History A Horizontal Linkage of People and Events*. New York: Simon & Schuster, 2005.

H. Nagy, Peter. "Az Ady-líra értelmezhetőségének ezredvégi horizontjai." *Iskolakultúra*. 1998. 3. Accessed at http://www.epa.hu/00000/00011/00014/pdf/9803.pdf.

Halász, Zoltán, and George Lang. *Gundel 1894–1994*. Budapest: Helikon, 2001.

304

Hamann, Brigitte. *The Reluctant Empress.* Translated by Ruth Rein. Berlin: Ullstein, 1982.

Hamann, Brigitte. *Rudolf Trónörökös.* Budapest: Európa, 2008.

Hárs, Éva. *Zsolnay Ceramics Factory: Pécs.* Translated by Éva Moskovszky. Budapest: Helikon, 1997.

Held, Joseph, ed. *The Columbia History of Eastern Europe in the Twentieth Century.* New York: Columbia University Press, 1992.

Hubbell, Jay B., and John O. Beaty. *An Introduction to Poetry.* New York: Macmillan, 1922. Accessed at http://books.google.com/.

Egger, Klaus and Rudolf Riedinger. *Hundertwasser–Krawina House, Vienna.* Photographs by Gregor Semrad and Harald Böhm. Wien: Harald Böhm, 2007.

Hupchick, Dennis P., and Harold E. Cox. *A Concise Historical Atlas of Eastern Europe.* New York: St. Martin's Press, 1996.

Jellinek, George. *History Through the Opera Glass: From the Rise of Caesar to the Fall of Napoleon.* 2nd printing. White Plains, NY: Pro/Am Music Resources, 1994.

Johnston, William M. *The Austrian Mind: An Intellectual and Social History 1848–1938.* Berkeley and Los Angeles: University of California Press, 2000. First published 1972 by The Regents of the University of California.

Jones, D. Mervyn. *Five Hungarian Writers.* Oxford: Clarendon Press, 1966.

Kay, David. *Austria-Hungary.* London: Sampson Low, Marston, Searle, & Rivington, 1888.

Kirkconnell, Watson, M.A., ed. *The Magyar Muse: An Anthology of Hungarian Poetry 1400–1932.* Foreword by Francis Herczeg. Canada: Kanadai Magyar Ujság Press, 1933.

Kodály 1882-1967. Compiled by Mihály Ittzés. Edited by the Foundation for the Kodály Institute, Kecskemét, n.d.

Komroff, Manuel, ed. *Contemporaries of Marco Polo.* New York: Boni & Liveright, 1928.

Kovač, Mojca M. *Piran St. George.* Cultural and Natural Monuments of Slovenia: A Guidebooks Collection 211. Ljubljana: Institute for the Protection of Cultural Heritage of Slovenia, 2006.

Kőhegyi, Orsolya. *The Herend Porcelain*, Tájak Korok Múzeumok Kiskönyvtára 678A, n.p.: TKM Egyesület, 2001.

Lendvai, Paul. *The Hungarians: A Thousand Years of Victory in Defeat.* Translated by Ann Major. Princeton, New Jersey: Princeton University Press, 2003.

Letcher, Piers. *Croatia: The Bradt Travel Guide.* 3rd ed. UK: Bradt Travel Guides, 2007.

Lovag, Zsuzsa. *The Hungarian Crown and Other Regalia.* A Pamphlet of the Hungarian National Museum. Translated by Miklós Uszkay. Budapest: Széchenyi Publishing House Ltd., 1986.

Lukacs, John. B*udapest 1900: A Historical Portrait of a City & Its Culture.* New York: Grove Press, 1988.

MacMillian, Margaret. *Paris 1919: Six Months That Changed the World.* Foreword by Richard Holbrooke. New York: Random House, 2003. Originally published as Peacemakers. London: J. Murray, 2001.

Magaš, Branka. *Croatia Through History: The Making of a European State.* London: SAQI, 2007.

Magocsi, Paul Robert. *Historical Atlas of East Central Europe.* Vol. 1. Cartographic design by Geoffrey J. Matthews. Seattle: University of Washington Press, 1993.

May, Arthur J. "R.W. Seton-Watson and British Anti-Hapsburg Sentiment." *American Slavic and East European Review* 20, no.5 (February, 1961): 40–54. http://www.jstor.org/stable/3001244 (accessed June 10, 2008).

Mazsu, János. "The Intelligentsia in Hungary Prior to World War I." *Hungarian Studies Review* 24, Nos. 1-2 (Spring-Fall, 1997): 81–96.

Mazsu, János. *The Social History of the Hungarian Intelligentsia, 1825–1914.* Translated by Mario D. Fenyo. New York: Columbia University Press, 1997.

McLean, Brian. *Culture Smart! Hungary: A Quick Guide to Customs & Etiquette.* 2nd revised print. London: Kuperard, 2006.

McNally, Raymond T., and Radu R. Florescu. *In Search of Dracula: The History of Dracula and Vampires Completely Revised*. New York: Houghton Mifflin, 1994.

Milhench, Heike. *Flavors of Slovenia: Food and Wine from Central Europe's Hidden Gem*. New York: Hippocrene Books, 2007.

Millett, F. D. *The Danube: From the Black Forest to the Black Sea*. Illustrated by F. D. Millett and Alfred Parsons. New York: Harper & Brothers, 1892. Also available online at http://books.google.com/.

Molnár, Miklós. *A Concise History of Hungary*. Translated by Anna Magyar. Cambridge: Cambridge University Press, 2005. First published in 2001.

Morris, William. *A Dream of John Ball and a King's Lesson*. London: Longmans, Green, and Co., 1910. Accessed at http://books.google.com/.

Muzur, Amir. *Opatija – Abbazia Itinerary for Researchers and the Inquisitive*. Translated by Melita Sciucca (Italian), Lenemarie Lehmann (German), and Slobodan Drenovac (English). Opatija: Grafika Zambelli, 2001.

Nazor, Ante. *Croatia: History, Culture, Art, Natural Features, Tourism, Map*. Tourism and Heritage 14. Zagreb: Turistička Naklada, 2004.

Nemes, Janos and Verlag Ikon. *Baedeker's Hungary*. Basingstoke, Hampshire: The Automobile Association, 2000.

Niszkács, Miklós. *The Gerbeaud*. Budapest: Gerbeaud Gasztronómia Kft., 2008.

Oliver, Jeanne. *Croatia*. 4th ed. Australia: Lonely Planet Publications, 2007.

Paris, Matthew. *Matthew Paris's English History V1: From the Year 1235 to 1273*. Translated by J. A. Giles. London: George Bell & Sons, 1889.

Patai, Raphael. *The Jews of Hungary: History, Culture, Psychology*. Detroit: Wayne State University Press, 1996.

Patterson, Arthur J. *The Magyars: Their Country and Institutions*. 2 vols. London: Smith, Elder & Co., 1869. Also available online at

http://books.google.com/.

Phillimore, Lion. *In the Carpathians*. London: Constable & Co., 1912.

Plachy, Sylvia. *Self Portrait with Cows Going Home*. New York: Aperture Foundation, 2004.

Preveden, Francis R. *A History of the Croatian People*. Vol. 2. New York: Philosophical Library, 1962.

Radešček, Rado. *Slovenske Legende 2*. Idrija: Založba Bogataj, 1996.

Rapport, Mike. *1848: Year of Revolution*. New York: Basic Books, 2009.

Reid, Robert and Lief Pettersen. *Romania & Moldova*. 4th ed. Australia: Lonely Planet Publications, 2007.

Sági, Károly, and Zákonyi Ferenc. *Balaton*. Budapest: Panoráma, 1970.

Scarre, Chris. *Chronicle of the Roman Emperors: The Reign-by-Reign Record of the Rules of Imperial Rome*. London: Thames & Hudson, Ltd., 1995.

Seton-Watson, R. W. *Racial Problems in Hungary*. London: Constable & Co., 1908.

Seton-Watson, R. W. *Treaty Revision and the Hungarian Frontiers*. London: Eyre and Spottiswoode, 1934.

Sinor, Denis. *History of Hungary*. New York: Praeger, 1959. Reprint, Westport, CT: Greenwood Press, 1976.

Sugar, Peter F., Péter Hanák, and Tibor Frank, eds. *A History of Hungary*. Bloomington: Indiana University Press, 1994.

Szabó, István. *Városi Polgárok a Századelőn: Történelmi Állandó Kiállitás a Szolnoki Damjanich János Múzeumban*. Szolnok: dr. Kertész Róbert, 1999.

Tarda, Miklós. *Magyarország Uralkodói: Királyok, Kormányzók, Miniszterelnökök, Erdélyi Fejedelmek*. Veszprém: Tarlan, 2008.

Taylor, A. J. P. *The Habsburg Monarchy, 1809–1918: A History of the Austrian Empire and Austria-Hungary*. Chicago: University of Chicago Press, 1976. First published 1948 by Hamish Hamilton.

The Rough Guide to Slovenia. Written by Norm Longley. 2nd ed. New York: Rough Guides, 2007.

Tollas, Tibor, ed. *Gloria Victis 1848–49: Szabadságharcunk a*

Világirodalomban. München: Nemzetőr, 1973. [Selected literature on the Hungarian War of Liberation including works by Ralph Waldo Emerson, Abraham Lincoln, Daniel Webster, and Theodore Roosevelt in English as well as in Hungarian].

Ungváry, Krisztián. *Battle for Budapest: One Hundred Days in World War II*. New York: I.B. Tauris, 2007.

Wallis, Helen G., and Arthur H. Robinson. *Cartographical Innovations: An International Handbook of Mapping Terms to 1900*. N.p.: International Cartographic Association, 1987. First published in Great Britain by Map Collector Publications in 1982.

Walker, Mary Adelaid. *Untrodden Paths in Romania*. Illustrated by Author. London: Chapman and Hall, 1888.

Where? Ljubljana Tourist Guide. Ljubljana: Ljubljana Tourist Information Centre, 2006.

Whitman, Sidney. *The Realm of the Habsburgs*. Tauchnitz ed. Vol. 2910. Paris: Bernard Tauchnitz, 1915.

Williamson, Maya Bijvoet. *The Memoirs of Helene Kottanner (1439–1440): Translated from the German with Introduction, Interpretative Essay and Notes*. The Library of Medieval Women. Rochester, NY: Boydell & Brewer, 1998.

Zweig, Stefan. *The World of Yesterday: An Autobiography by Stefan Zweig*. Introduction by Harry Zohn. Lincoln: University of Nebraska Press, 1964. First published 1943 by Viking Press.

ENCYCLOPEDIAS, LEXICONS, AND RELATED SOURCES

CIA, *The World Factbook*, s.v. "Romania," http://cia.gov/library/publications/the-world-factbook/print/ro.html.

Czigány, Lóránt, *Oxford Dictionary of National Biography*, s.v. "Paget, John" (by), http://www.oxforddnb.com/view/article/21115.

Encyclopaedia Britannica, 9th ed., s.v. "Croatia and Slavonia," Accessed at http://books.google.com/.

Encyclopaedia Britannica, 11th ed., s.v. "Abbazia," "Croatia-Slavonia,"

"Dacia," "Damjanich, János," "Fiume," "Habsburg," "Hungary,"
"Jellachich, Josef," "Kisfaludy, Karoly," "Kolozsvár," "Laibach,"
"Matthias I.," Hunyadi," "Nagy-Várad," "Pécs," "Petofi, Alexander,"
"Pirano," "Pola," "Rumania," "Transylvania," "Zrinyi, Miklós,"
Accessed at http://books.google.com/.
Encyclopaedia Britannica, 12th ed., s.v. "Bosnia-Herzegovina,"
"Hungary," "Temesvár," Accessed at http://books.google.com/.
Encyclopaedia Britannica, New Werner ed., s.v. "Croatia and Slavonia,"
Accessed at http://books.google.com/.
Johnson's (Revised) Universal Cyclopaedia, 1886, s.v. "Bank-Ban,"
Accessed at http://books.google.com/.
Magyar Életrajzi Lexikon, s.v. "Varsányi, György," Accessed at http://
mek.oszk.hu/00300/00355/html/index.html.
Magyar Zsidó Lexikon, s.v. "Varsányi, Gyula," Accessed at
http://mek.niif.hu/04000/04093/html/0948.html.
Magyar Zsido Lexikon, s.v. "Varsányi Gyula," http://mek.niif.
hu/04000/04093/html/szocikk/15263.htm.
The World Almanac and Book of Facts 2007, s.v. "under the entry –
Military Affairs."
The World Almanac and Book of Facts 2008. 140th Anniversary ed.,
s.v. "United States History, 1907."

NEWSPAPERS AND ARTICLES

"A Romance of Hungarian Life," *The Times*, April 3, 1850, http://
archive.timesonline.co.uk.
"Az ománi szultán kincsei Zsolnayból," *Pécsi Napilap*, June 29, 2007,
http://www.pecsinapilap.hu/cikk/AZ_omani_szultan_kincsei_
Zsolnaybol/57718.
Blackwood's Magazine, "A Hungarian Alfold," *New York Times*, June
22, 1879, http://www.newyorktimes.com/.
Bodnar, Theodore, A. "Letters; Yorkville Recalled," *New York Times*,
July 3, 1983, http://www.newyorktimes.com/.
Cullen, Robert, "Report from Romania," *The New Yorker*, April 2,

1990, http://www.newyorker.com/.

"Divided We Sprawl," *Time Out New York*, August 23–29, 2007.

Halasz, George, "Kossuth," *The New Yorker*, March 17, 1928, 18–19, http://www.newyorker.com/.

"Hungarians Coming for Kossuth Fetes," *New York Times*, February 26, 1928, http://www.newyorktimes.com/.

Hunt, Kathleen, "Letter from Bucharest," *The New Yorker*, July 23, 1990, http://www.newyorker.com/.

Kimmelman, Michael, "A Writer Who Always Sees History in the Present Tense," *New York Times*, November 01, 2007, http://www.newyorktimes.com/.

Kovacs, Davis, "Péter Nádas," *Bomb*, no. 100 (Summer, 2007): 40–45.

Macra, Mieria, "A Fekete Sas Palota Története," *A Polgármesteri Hivatal Újságja Nagyvárad*, July 3, 2007.

Nicholas Kulish, "Kosovo's Actions Hearten a Hungarian Enclave," *New York Times*, April 7, 2008, http://www.newyorktimes.com/.

Paul Hond, "Look Homeward, Angel," *Columbia Magazine*, Spring 2006, Accessed at http://www.columbia.edu/cu/alumni/Magazine/Spring2006/kossuth.html.

Roger W. Babson, "'Watch Austria-Hungary' says Roger W. Babson," *New York Times*, January 19, 1913, http://www.newyorktimes.com/.

Sanders, Michael S. "An Old Breed of Hungarian Pig Is Back in Favor," *New York Times*, April 1, 2009, http://www.newyorktimes.com.

Schmemann, Serge, "Mayerling Journal; Lurid Truth and Lurid Legend: A Habsburg Tale," *New York Times*, March 10, 1989, http://www.newyorktimes.com/.

Special to The New York Times. "Hungary's Crown is 'In Trust' but U.S. Won't Indicate Where," *New York Times*, August 16, 1965, http://www.newyorktimes.com/.

Szulc, Tad, "Letter from Bucharest," *The New Yorker*, September 6, 1969. http://www.newyorker.com/.

"The Kossuth Dinner," *New York Times*, December 12, 1851, http://www.newyorktimes.com/.

Vames, Amy, Hungarian Art Mecca: Zimmerli Receives a World-Class Collection, *Rutgers Magazine*, Spring 2007.

Wechsberg, Joseph, "Profiles: City of the Baroque: II - Schwebezustand," *The New Yorker*, October 5, 1968, 58–92, http://www.newyorker.com/.

Wilkin, Walter, "The Budapest Exhibition," *The Times*, April 24, 1896, http://archive.timesonline.co.uk.

Wilson, Edmund, "Notes from a European Diary ~ 1963–64: III – Budapest," *The New Yorker*, June 4, 1966, http://www.newyorker.com/.

BROCHURES/BOOKLETS

Art Nouveau Ljubljana. Ljubljana Tourist Information Center's City Map and Brochure (Ljubljana: Ljubljana Tourist Board, 2004).

Baroque Ljubljana. Ljubljana Tourist Information Center's City Map and Brochure (Ljubljana: Ljubljana Tourist Board, 2004).

The Benedictine Abbey at Tihany. A Booklet (Tihany: Benedictine Abbey, 1997).

"Budapest: Keleti Pályaudvar." Tájak Korok Múzeumok Kiskönyvtára 421, 2nd ed. (n.p.: TKM Egyesület, 1996).

Berza, László, and Miklós Marót, "*Citadella*." A Brochure (Budapest: Fővárosi Idegenforgalmi Hivatal, n.d.).

The Cistercian Monastery Heiligenkreuz. Produced by the Monks of Heiligenkreuz. Baden: Meixner, 1985.

Gödöllő: The Royal Mansion, Tájak Korok Múzeumok Kiskönyvtára 510B, 3rd ed. (n.p.: TKM Egyesület, 2003).

"Have a Wash!—Hygiene in the 20th Century Village." Hungarian title: "Meg is Mosakodjál!—Higénia a 20. századi falun." Ethnographic Exhibition in the Skanzen Galéria of the Hungarian Open Air Museum in the Confines of the Series Domino Exhibitions 2006, 25 August–8 October.

Kőhegyi, Orsolya. "*Herend Porcelain*." A Booklet (Veszprém–Budapest: Magyar Képek, 2003).

312

Labyrinth of Buda Castle. A brochure. Printed by Diamond Digital
    Printing Ltd. Eger, n.d.

Lincoln Center. *Playbill.* February 2008.

Ljubljana in Antiquity. Ljubljana Tourist Information Center's City
    Map and Brochure (Ljubljana: Ljubljana Tourist Board, 2004).

Ljubljana Town Hall. Ljubljana Town Hall Brochure (Ljubljana:
    Ljubljana Tourist Board, 2007).

*The Magyar Imagination: Selection from the Salgo Trust Donation of
    Hungarian Art.* Jane Voorhees Zimmerli Art Museum, New
    Jersey. Exhibition from December 9, 2007 – March 16, 2008.

Mayerling: History and Art. Mayerling: Karmel St. Joseph, n.d.

Mayor's Office of Szolnok, "*Szolnok Megyei Jogú Város,*" A Brochure
    (Szolnok: Szalay Ferenc, n.d.).

Oradea, City Map and Brochure (Oradea: Doru Sicoe, 2005).

Plan of Paris with Street Index. Nouvelle ed. Paris: L'indispensable,
    n.d.

Plečnik's Ljubljana. Tourist Map and Brochure (Ljubljana: Ljubljana
    Tourism, 2011).

Roman Ljubljana. Tourist Map and Brochure (Ljubljana: Ljubljana
    Tourism, 2013).

Rudolf, the Desperate Admirer. Seasonal exhibition in the Royal Palace
    Museum of Gödöllő from 5 June 2008 to 28 September 2008.
    Gödöllő: Gödöllői Királyi Kastély Kht., 2008.

Szolnok. A Brochure Made on Behalf of Szolnok Town of County
    Rank. Edited by Ferenc Varga. Szolnok: Gravámen Studió, 2006.

"Transylvania Romania." A Brochure (Bucureşti: National Authority
    For Tourism, n.d.).

Varga Design. A Brochure. Further info: www.vargadesign.hu.

*Walk Around the Town and Surroundings, Škofja Loka, Ancient
    Beauty, Slovenija.* A Tourist Guide (Škofja Loka: The
    Munincipality of Škofja Loka, 2007).

Welcome to Romania, Transilvania, Guest Information. Guest Book
    from a Hotel in Transylvania (Romania: Crystal Publishing
    Group S.R.L., 2000).

313

WEBSITES

A Magyar Irodalom Története, "Petőfi Költő-Barátai," http://vmek.
niif.hu/02200/02228/html/03/462.html.

A Magyarság Története, "Orseolo Péter Magyar Király,"
http://magyartortenelem.lapunk.hu/?modul=oldal&tartalom=10621.

Babeş-Bolyai University, "The Multicultural Character,"
http://www.ubbcluj.ro/en/despre/multicultural.html.

Báró Eötvös József Szobra az Eötvös Téren,
http://www.budapest-photo.hu/Eotvos%20szobor_1.htm.

BBC News, "Prague Floods Surge to New Peaks," http://news.bbc.
co.uk/1/hi/world/europe/2189695.stm.

Bibliotheca Corviniana Digitalis, http://www.corvina.oszk.hu/.

Bled, Slovenia, "Legends and Folklore," http://bled-slovenia.com/bled-
slovenia-legends-folklore.html.

"Budapest Cafés," http://www.gotohungary.com/budapest/cafes.shtml
(Accessed May 13, 2007).

Budapest Tourist Guide, "Gerbeaud Café – Symbol of Budapest,"
http://www.budapest-tourist-guide.com/gerbeaud-cafe.html.

Budavári Labirintus, "The Labyrinth of Buda Castle," http://www.
labirintus.com/en.

"Ceausescu's Nemesis Rejects Romania's 'shop window ecumenism,"
Romania News Watch, September 12, 2007, http://www.
romanianewswatch.com/2007/09/ceausescus-nemesis-rejects-
romanians.html (Accessed September 24, 2008).

Cameron, Rob, and Jan Velinger, "Worst Flooding in Prague in More
Than a Hundred Years," *Current Affairs sec. Czech Radio 7, Radio
Prague.* August 08, 2002. http://www.radio.cz/print/en/31239.

City of New York Parks & Recreation, "Lajos Kossuth Monument
Riverside Park," plaque.

Dobó István Vármúzeum, http://www.egrivar.hu/magyar.html.

Gödöllői Királyi Kastély, http://www.kiralyikastely.hu/.

Grad Novska, http://www.novska.hr.

Grad Novska, "Povijest," http://www.novska.hr/hr/o_novskoj/

314

povijest/.

Gödöllő, "Guide to Gödöllő," http://www.godollo.hu.

Gurman.eu, "Blejske kremšnite," http://www.gurman.eu/recepti.
php?S=6&Article=2353.

Holocaust Victim Assets Litigation, "Certified Awards Rendered by
the Tribunal," http://www.crt-ii.org/_awards/awards_list_A.
phtm.

Hotel Scorilo, http://www.hotelscorilo.ro/en/index.php?op=hotel
(Accessed July 25, 2007).

Hrvatska Kulturna Baština, "Gjuro Szabo," http://www.kultura.hr/hr/
predstavljamo/osobe/gjuro_szabo.

Hungarian Central Statistical Office, "A Népesség Számának
Alakulása, Terület, Népsűrűség,"http://www.ksh.hu/
nepszamlalas/.

Hungarian Central Statistical Office, "A Népesség Vallás, Felekezet,
Nemek és Korcsoport Szerint," http://www.ksh.hu/nepszamlalas/.

Hungarian Human Rights Foundation, http://www.hhrf.org/hhrf/
index_en.php.

Hungarian Ministry of Education and Culture, "Hungary Travelogue
on Show in London," http://kultura.hu/main.php?folderID=1085
&articleID=278215&ctag=articlelist&iid=1.

"Mindszenty Gideon," in Magyar Költők Élete es Munkái by József
Szinnyei, http://mek.niif.hu/03600/03630/html/m/m16364.htm.

National Geographic, "Week in Photos: Croc Bites Off Hand, Easter
Fertility Ritual, Chinese Cherry Blossoms, More," http://news.
nationalgeographic.com/news/2007/04/photogalleries/wip-
week24/photo2.html.

New York City Department of Parks & Recreation, "Riverside Parks,"
http://www.nycgovparks.org/parks/riversidepark/
monuments/879.

Oradea City's Official Website, "Short History of Oradea City," http://
www.oradea.ro/index.php?option=com_content&view=article&i
d=171&Itemid=250.

Oradea Jewish Community, "Oradea–An Introduction to its Jewish

History," http://www.jewishgen.org/databases/holocaust/0109_ oradea.html (Accessed August 06, 2007).

Pécsi Egyházmegye, "A Pécsi Püspökség Rövid Története," http:// www.pecs.edgyhazmegye.hu/puspokseg_tortenete.html.

Petőfi Irodalmi Múzeum, "Sütő András Életrajz," http://www.pim.hu/ object.6B2035C0-08C5-446E-8681-C20FC829B6E5.ivy.

Quotes.net, "George-Louis Leclerc de Buffon Quotes," http://www. quotes.net/authors/George-Louis+Leclerc+de+Buffon.

Radnóczi László, "A Mangalica Fajta Kialakulása és Értékei," http:// www.agr.unideb.hu/kiadvany/bodo/Radnoczi.pdf.

Republic of Slovenia, "Path to Independence," http://www.ukom.gov. si/10years/path/.

"Romániai Népszámlási Adatok 2002," http://nepszamlalas.adatbank. transindex.ro/?pg=3&id=819.

Romanian Government Agency for Governmental Strategy, Romania, Bucureşti, Romania: NOI Media Print S.R.L. CD-ROM.

Statistical Office of the Republic of Slovenia, "Population of Slovenia 2006," http://www.stat.si/doc/pub/05-RR-007-0801.pdf.

Sylvia Plachy's official Website, http://www.sylviaplachy.com.

Szolnok Art, "Verebes György," http://www.szolnokart.hu.

Szolnok Városi Információk, "Szolnok Története 1850-től Megyeszékhellyé Válásáig," http://info.szolnok.hu/alap.php?mi=d sp&msid=48&mpid=1&hid=25&moduls=2_4_&arc=&kw.

Szolnoki Művészeti Egyesület, "Történet–A Művésztelep Története," http://www.szolnokimuvesztelep.com.

Szolnokvédő: Városvédők és Lokálpatrióták Honlapja, "Kossuth tér," http://szolnokvedo.hu/fotoa/index.htm#cf.

The Protestant Homepage, "Református Templom–Bánffyhunyad," http://www.lutheran.hu/z/honlapok/protestans/erdely/ banffyhunyad/pk_romania_banffyhunyad_reftemplom.

The Romanian Jewish Community, "Our Reality... of Oraeda," http:// www.romanianjewish.org/en/mosteniri_ale_culturii_ iudaice_03_11_17.html.

Varga Design, http://www.vargadesign.hu.

Vendégváró, "Szabadság-szobor, Budapest," http://vendegvaro.
utazom.com/szabadsag-szobor-budapest.

"What Is Stift Heiligenkreuz?" http://stift-heiligenkreuz.org/English.
kinder-und-jugendfuehrungen.0.html (Accessed February 19,
2008).

Welcome to Romania, "The Fortress of Oradea," http://www.
welcometoromania.ro/Oradea/Oradea_Cetate_e.htm.

YouTube, "Are You Smarter than a 5th Grader: Dumb Blonde
American," http://www.youtube.com/watch?v=zqi0DwNLJdM.

YouTube, "Gwen Stefani–Wind It Up," http://www.youtube.com/
watch?v=XjeP2GTHNuE.

YouTube, "Palya Bea–Transylvania," http://www.youtube.com/watch?
v=LrzlVrglDx4&feature=related.

YouTube, "The View 11/25/08 (1of 5)," http://www.youtube.com/
watch?v=FDmD5oL432k&NR=1.

E-MAILS

E-mail message to the author from the Tourist Information Office of
Opatija, May 15, 2009.

Gödöllői Királyi Kastély Múzeum, e-mail message to Richard Bogdán,
forwarded to author, May 10, 2009.

MISCELLANEOUS

World Heritage: Proof of Origin of a Zsolnay Roof Tile. A Certificate
from the Church of Our Lady in the Buda Castle from Budapest.

New York Café. A placemat with The History of New York Palace and
Café printed on.

FURTHER READING–ARTICLES

American Brides for Noble Foreigners. The Scrapbook: First Section.
Vol. 5. January-June. New York: The Frank A. Munsey Company,

1908, http://books.google.com/.

Associated Press. "Count Szechenyi, Ex-Envoy, Is Dead," *New York Times*, July 06, 1938, http://www.newyorktimes.com/.

"Long and Illustrious Record of Ancient Hungarian Family Into Which Miss Gladys Vanderbilt Will Be Married To-morrow," *New York Times*, January 26, 1908, http://www.newyorktimes. com/.

Special Cable to The New York Times. "Countess Szechenyi Ill With Smallpox," *New York Times*, March 9, 1915, http://www. newyorktimes.com/.

Special Cable to The New York Times. "Countess Szechenyi's Illness Confirmed," *New York Times*, March 10, 1915, http://www. newyorktimes.com/.

Special Cable to The New York Times. "May Be Szechenyi Divorce," *New York Times*, July 31, 1913, http://www.newyorktimes.com/.

"Szechenyi Company Uses His Invention," *New York Times*, August 28, 1912, http://www.newyorktimes.com/.

FURTHER READING–BOOKS

Allen, Armin Brand, curator. *The Cornelius Vanderbilts of the Breakers: A Family Retrospective*. Published in conjunction with the exhibition "The Cornelius Vanderbilts of the Breakers: A Family Retrospective" held at the Newport Art Museum, Newport, Rhode Island, May 27 – October 1, 1995. Rhode Island: The Preservation Society of Newport County, 1995.

Anonymous. *Louis Kossuth and the Lost Revolutions in Hungary and Transylvania: Containing a Detailed Biography of the Leader of the Magyar Movement*. Kessinger Publishing's Legacy Reprint. London: John Rodwell, 1850.

Anonymus. *The Martyrdom of an Empress: With Portraits from Photographs*. New York: Harper & Brothers Publisher, 1899.

Balogh, Sándor and Sándor Jakab. *The History of Hungary after the Second World War 1944–1980*. Budapest: Corvina, 1986.

318

Biro, Adam. *One Must Also Be Hungarian.* Translated by Catherine Tihanyi. Chicago: The University of Chicago Press, 2006.

Bowring, John. *Translations from Alexander Petöfi, the Magyar Poet.* London: Trübner & Co., 1866.

Crankshaw, Edward. *The Fall of the House of Hapsburg.* London: Sphere Books, 1974. First published 1963 by Longmans.

Creagh, James. *Over the Borders of Christendom and Eslamiah V2: A Journey Through Hungary, Slavonia, Servia, Bosnia, Bersegobina, Dalmatia, and Montenegro, to the North of Albania in the Summer of 1875.* Vol. 2. Kessinger Publishing's Legacy Reprint. London: Samuel Tinsley, 1876. Also available online at http://books. google.com/.

CroatiaChic. Text by Françoise Raymond Kuijper, Kerry O'Neill, Richard Nichols. Archipelago Press, 2007.

Cushing, G.F. *Hungarian Prose and Verse.* London: Athlone Press, 1956.

Edwards, Edward. *Memoirs of Libraries: Including a Handbook of Library Economy.* Vol. 2. London: Trüber & Co., 1859. Accessed at http://books.google.com/.

Faber, Erika Papp. *A Sampler of Hungarian Poetry.* Budapest: Romanika Kiadó, 2012.

Farkas, Zsuzsanna, Marianna Kaján, and Éva Marianna Kovács. *The Memory of Queen Elisabeth preserved in postcards.* Budapest: Kossuth Kiadó, 2007.

Fučić, Branko. *Saint Vitus: Cathedral, Rijeka–Croatia.* Photographs by Petar Trinajstić. Rijeka: Rijeka Cathedral, 1994.

Géza Gárdonyi. *Slave of the Huns.* Budapest: Corvina, 1969.

Gibbon, Edward. *The Decline and Fall of the Roman Empire.* Vol. 3. New edition with complete index of the whole work. New York: Peter Fenelon Collier, 1899. Accessed at http://books.google. com/.

Gilpin, William. *The Cosmopolitan Railway: Compacting and Fusing Together All the World's Continents.* San Francisco: The History Company, 1890. Accessed at http://books.google.com/.

Hanák, Péter. *The Garden and the Workshop: Essays on the Cultural History of Vienna and Budapest.* Princeton, NJ: Princeton University Press, 1998.

Helmreich, Ernest, ed., *Hungary: A Volume in the Mid-European Studies Center Series.* New York: Frederick A. Praeger Publishers, 1957.

Hotbauer, Renate. *Empress Elisabeth of Austria: The Fate of a Woman Under the Yoke of the Imperial Court.* Translation by JLQJ Translations. Austria Imperial ed. Vienna: Lindenau Productions GmbH, 1998.

Janos, Andrew C. *The Politics of Backwardness in Hungary 1825–1945.* Princeton, NJ: Princeton University Press, 1982.

Kahn, Robert, ed. *City Secrets: New York City.* New York: The Little Bookroom, 2002.

Kaiser, Reinhard. *Paper Kisses.* Translated by Anthea Bell. New York: Other Press, 2006.

Kalla-Bishop, P.M. *Hungarian Railroads.* Railroads Histories of the World. New York: Drake Publishers Inc., 1973.

Kennedy, Paul. *The Rise and Fall of the Great Powers: Economic Change and Military Conflict from 1500 to 2000.* New York: Vintage Books, 1989. First published 1987 by Random House.

Keresztes, László. *A Practical Hungarian Grammar.* 3rd ed. Debrecen: Debreceni Nyári Egyetem, 1999.

Király, Béla K., Pastor Peter, and Ivan Sanders. *War and Society in East Central Europe Vol. 6.: Essays on World War I: Total War and Peacemaking, a Case Study on Trianon.* New York: Columbia University Press, 1982.

Kirkconnell, Watson, trans. *The Hungarian Helikon: Epic and Other Poetry.* Canada: Széchenyi Society, 1985.

Konrád, George. *A Guest in My Own Country A Hungarian Life.* Translated by Jim Tucker, Edited by Michael Henry Heim. New York: Other Press, 2007.

Kovács, Imre. *Facts About Hungary: The Fight for Freedom.* Revised ed. New York: The Hungarian Committee, 1966.

Kramer, Alan. *Dynamic of Destruction: Culture and Mass Killing in the First World War*. New York: Oxford University Press, 2007.

Magaš, Branka, and Ivo Žanić. *The War In Croatia and Bosnia-Herzegovina 1991–1995*. Foreword by Noel Malcolm. London: Frank Cass, 2001.

Lukacs, John. *George Kennan: A Study of Character*. New Haven: Yale University Press, 2007.

Mackenzie, Georgina Mary Muir, and Irby Paulina. *Across the Carpathians*. Cambridge: Macmillan and Co., 1862. Accessed at http://books.google.com/.

Magocsi, Paul Robert, and Ivan Pop. *Encyclopedia of Rusyn History and Culture*, rev. & expanded ed. Toronto: University of Toronto Press, 2000.

Makkai, Adam. I*n Quest of the Miracle Stag: The Poetry of Hungary: An Anthology of Hungary Poetry from the 13th Century to the Present in English Translation*, Vol. 1. Foreword by Dr. Árpád Göncz. Chicago: Atlantis-Centaur, 1996.

Maney, Henry. *Memories over the Water: Stray Thoughts on a Long Stroll*. Introduction by Edwin H. Ewing. Nashville: Toon, Nelson, & Co., 1854. Also available online at http://books.google.com/.

Marton, Kati. *The Great Escape: Nine Jews Who Fled Hitler and Changed the World*. New York: Simon & Schuster, 2006.

Márai, Sándor. *Embers*. Translated by Carol Brown Janeway. New York: Vintage, 2002.

Márai, Sándor. *Esther's Inheritance*. Translated by George Szirtes. New York: Alfred A. Knopf, 2008.

Morton, Frederic. *A Nervous Splendor: Vienna 1888/1889*. New York: Penguin Books. Reprint, London: Little, Brown, 1979.

Nádas, Péter. *Fire and Knowledge: Fiction and Essays*. Translated by Imre Goldstein. New York: Farrar, Straus and Giroux, 2007.

Nicholas, Lynn H. *The Rape of Europe: The Fate of Europe's Treasures in the Third Reich and the Second World War*. New York: Vintage Books, 1995. Originally published in New York: Alfred A. Knopf, 1994.

Palmer, Alan. *Twilight of the Habsburgs: The Life and Times of Emperor Francis Joseph.* New York: Atlantic Monthly Press, 1994. First published in Great Britain in 1994 by Weidenfeld & Nicolson.

Petőfi, Alexander. *Sixty Poems by Alexander Petőfi (1823–1849).* Translated by Eugénie Bayard Pierce and Emil Delmár. 1948. Reprint, New York: Kraus Reprint Co., 1976.

Prodan, D. *Supplex Libellus Valachorum, or The Political Struggle of the Romanians in Transylvania During the 18th Century.* Translated by Mary Lăzărescu. Bucharest: Publishing House o f the Academy of the Socialist Republic of Romania, 1971.

Pryce-Jones, David. *The Hungarian Revolution.* New York: Horizon Press, 1970.

Rab, Gusztav. *Sabaria.* 1963. Translated by Florence Ignotus and Anthony Rhodes. New York: W.W. Norton & Company, Inc., 1964.

Redlich, Joseph. *Emperor Francis Joseph of Austria: A Biography.* New York: Macmillan Co., 1929.

Reich, Emil. *Hungarian Literature: An Historical and Critical Survey.* New York: Benjamin Blom, 1972. First published in London, 1898.

Reményi, Joseph. *Hungarian Writers and Literature: Modern Novelists, Critics, and Poets.* Edited by August J. Molnar. New Brunswick, NJ: Rutgers University Press, 1964.

Rubruck, William of. *The Journey of William of Rubruck to the Eastern Parts of the World, 1253-55, as Narrated by Himself, with Two Accounts of the Earlier Journey of John of Pian de Carpine.* Translation and introduction by William Woodville Rockhill. London: Hakluyt Society, 1900. Also available online at http://books.google.com/.

Salue, Béatrix, and Daniel Meyer, eds. *Versailles: Visitor's Guides.* Versailles: Éditions Art Lys, 2006.

Seton-Watson, R. W. *Absolutism in Croatia.* London: Constable & Co., 1912.

322

Seton-Watson, R. W. *Roumania and the Great War*. London: Constable & Co., 1915.

Singer, Ignatius. *Simplified Grammar of the Hungarian Language*. London: Trübner & Co., 1882.

Stillman, Edmund, and William Pfaff. *Power and Impotence: The Failure of America's Foreign Policy*. New York: Random House, 1966.

Strachan, Hew. *The First World War*. New York: Penguin Books, 2003.

Swatridge, Colin. *A Country Full of Aliens: A Briton in Hungary*. Budapest: Corvina, 2005.

Szabó, Magda. *The Door*. Translated by Len Rix. London: Harvill Secker, 2005.

Szabó, Magda. *The Fawn*. Translated by Kathleen Szasz. New York: Alfred A. Knopf, 1963.

'The Tisza Valley: The Cradle of Our Race': A Millennium in the Tisza Region. Responsible editor: Sári Zsolt. Szolnok: Jász-Nagykun-Szolnok Megyei Múzeumok Igazgatósága, 2000.

Török, András. *Budapest: A Critical Guide*. Illustrated by András Felvidéki. Translated by Peter Doherty and Ágnes Enyedi. Hungary: Park Publishing Ltd., 2007.

Travirka, Antun. *Istria: History, Culture, Art Heritage*. Zadar, Slovenia: Forum, 2006.

Vambéry, Arminius. *Arminius Vambery: His Life and Adventures*. Kessinger Publishing's Rare Reprints. London: T. Fisher Unwin, 1886. Also available online at http://books.google.com/.

Vehse, E., Dr. *Memoirs of the Court, Aristocracy, and Diplomacy of Austria*. Translated by Franz Demmler. Vol. 1 & 2. London: Longman, Brown, Green, and Longmans, 1856. Accessed at http://books.google.com/.

Völgyes, Iván, ed. *Hungary in Revolution 1918-19: Nine Essays*. Lincoln, Nebraska: University of Nebraska Press, 1971.

Zarek, Otto. *The History of Hungary*. Translated by H.S.H. Prince Peter P. Wolkonsky. London: Selwyn & Blount Ltd., Paternoster House, 1939.

Zeman, Z. A. B. *Twilight of the Habsburgs: The Collapse of the Austro-Hungarian Empire*. Edited by John Roberts. New York: American Heritage Press, 1971.

PHOTO CREDITS

TITLE PAGE

Fischer, Linda. *Crown of St. Stephen*. Photograph. Private Collection. 2011.

Mr. and Mrs. Adrian Stokes. "Sketch Map of Hungary." Map. *Hungary*. 1909.

PREFACE

Fischer, Linda. *Fisherman's Bastion*. Photograph. Private Collection. 2014.

Csurla, *Tombstone of John Paget*, Uploaded May 29, 2010, via http://commons.wikimedia.org/wiki/File:Paget_Bf_Gyogy1.jpg, Creative Commons License CC-BY-SA-3.0.

PART I

Fischer, Linda. *The Memory Book*. Photograph. Private Collection. 2011.

Anonymous, *Prince Vlad the Impaler*, Uploaded August 25, 2008, via http://commons.wikimedia.org/wiki/File:Vlad_Tepes_001.jpg, Public Domain.

326

PART II

Fischer, Philip. *The Black Eagle*. Photograph. Private Collection. 2007.

Bain Collection, *Elizabeth of Austria*. ca 1910-1915. Library of Congress. LC-B2- 3128-3 [P&P].

Fototeca online a comunismului românesc, photo #BA231, 1/1978 (accessed 23:37, 16 September 2010 (UTC)), *Nicolae Ceaușescu*, via http://commons.wikimedia.org/wiki/File:Ceausescu_Anul_Nou.jpg.

PART III

Fischer, Philip. *Rose*. Photograph. Private Collection. 2009.

League of Nations Archives, *Béla Bartók*, Uploaded February 28, 2014, via http://commons.wikimedia.org/wiki/File:B%C3%A9la_Bart%C3%B3k_WDL11594.png, Public Domain.

PART IV

Fischer, Philip. *World War I Statue in Szolnok*. Photograph. Private Collection. 2008.

Bain Collection, *Crown Prince Rudolf*. ca 1910-1915. Library of Congress. LC-B2-2639-5 [P&P].

Bain Collection, *Marie Vetsera*. January 9, 1913. Library of Congress. LC-B2- 2638-7 [P&P].

Fischer, Linda. *Cake*. Photograph. Private Collection. 2014.

Fischer, Philip. *King St. Stephen*. Photograph. Private Collection. 2009.